High Score
iBT TOEFL READING For Junior

2nd Edition

Intermediate

DARAKWON

Dear Teachers and Parents,

Welcome to Darakwon's *High Score iBT TOEFL Reading for Junior* series.

When people study English, they often focus on learning the same topics that appear in all English textbooks. So while they learn how to have basic conversations with people, that is about all that they can do. The *High Score iBT TOEFL Reading for Junior* series hopes to change the way that students study English. This series focuses on teaching students English by introducing them to a wide number of topics. By learning about new and different subjects, students will not only become more interested in learning English but will also be able to greatly expand their English vocabulary and their knowledge base in general.

The *High Score iBT TOEFL Reading for Junior* series is written as a junior iBT TOEFL textbook. The books in this series cover topics that appear on the actual iBT TOEFL test. The questions in the books are also phrased just like those that students will find on the iBT TOEFL test. This should help familiarize students with the iBT TOEFL test and prepare them for when they take it in the future. By learning as much as they can about the iBT TOEFL test prior to taking it, the students will ensure that they will have some knowledge of many of the topics on the test and will be comfortable with the style of the test and the questions on it. All of these factors should lead to higher scores for the students.

It is my hope that students will use this series first to improve their knowledge of English. They will find the passages have been written at a level that they will be able to understand, and the students should find the passages themselves to be fun to read and full of interesting facts and information. Or course, as a junior iBT TOEFL book, a major emphasis of the series is to familiarize the students with the iBT TOEFL test. Most of all, I hope that this series will instill a love of English in students and inspire them to continue and to advance their studies of the English language.

Michael A. Putlack

Table of CONTENTS

About the TOEFL 4

How to Use This Book 8

Chapter 1 Chemistry (Chronological Order) 13

Chapter 2 Biology (Classification) 35

Chapter 3 Culture (Comparison and Contrast) 57

Chapter 4 Music (Cause and Effect) 79

Chapter 5 Anthropology (Guessing Unknown Words) 101

Chapter 6 Weather (Mapping) 119

Chapter 7 Geology (Identifying Cohesive Devices) 141

Chapter 8 Medicine (Outlining) 163

Actual Test 189

About the TOEFL

The TOEFL iBT

TOEFL is the Test of English as a Foreign Language. It measures the test taker's ability in English. Foreign students often need to take the TOEFL to get into an American college or university. For that reason, the TOEFL exam is very important.

The TOEFL iBT is an Internet-based test (iBT). Students take the TOEFL iBT on a computer at one of the test centers.

The TOEFL iBT tests four language skills. These skills are reading, listening, speaking, and writing. There are many different kinds of passages, lectures, conversations, and questions. Many sections combine two or more of these skills. So students must be capable in several English skills to get high scores on the exam.

The Format of the TOEFL iBT

There are four sections on the TOEFL iBT. These sections are Reading, Listening, Speaking, and Writing.

The Reading section has two passages. These passages are around 700 words long with 10 questions per passage. The Reading section of the test takes 35 minutes.

The Listening section has two types of passages. They are lectures and conversations. Each Listening section has 3 lectures. The lectures are 3-5 minutes each with 6 questions per lecture. Each listening section has 2 conversations. The conversations are 3 minutes each with 5 questions per conversation. The Listening section of the test takes 36 minutes.

The Speaking section has two types of questions. They are independent and integrated questions. There is 1 independent question. The independent question asks about your own ideas, opinions, and experiences. There are 3 integrated questions. The integrated questions consist of conversations, reading passages, lectures, or combinations of them—just as you would see in or out of a classroom. They ask questions based on the reading and listening passages. The Speaking section of the test takes 16 minutes.

The Writing section has two types of questions: 1 integrated task and 1 academic discussion task. The integrated task combines a short reading passage and a short lecture. The test taker must then write an essay about these two. The academic discussion task asks a question about a personal experience or opinion. The test taker must then write an essay about this question. The Writing section of the test takes 29 minutes.

The Test Format

Test Section	Number of Questions	Timing	Score
Reading	• 2 passages, 10 questions each	35 minutes	30
Listening	• 3 lectures, 6 questions each • 2 conversations, 5 questions each	36 minutes	30
Speaking	• 1 independent task • 3 integrated tasks	16 minutes	30
Writing	• 1 integrated task • 1 academic discussion task	29 minutes	30

The Reading Section

There are 10 different kinds of questions in the Reading section. Each question appears a different number of times.

The different kinds of questions are:

1 Factual Information Questions
   These ask about the facts in the passage.
   There are 1-3 of these questions in each passage.

2 Negative Factual Questions
   These ask about information that is NOT in the passage or which is NOT true.
   There are 0-2 of these questions in each passage.

3 Rhetorical Purpose Questions
   These ask about the reason why the author includes some information in the passage.
   There are 0-2 of these questions in each passage.

4 Inference Questions
   These ask about information the test taker must infer from the passage.
   There are 0-2 of these questions in each passage.

5 Vocabulary Questions
   These ask about the definitions of words or phrases in the passage.
   There are 1-3 of these questions in each passage.

6 Reference Questions
   These ask which word or words in the passage refers to.
   There are 0-1 of these questions in each passage.

About the TOEFL

7 Sentence Simplification Questions
These take one long sentence from the passage and ask the test taker to find a simplified version of that sentence. There are 0-1 of these questions in each passage.

8 Insert Text Questions
These show the test taker a new sentence and ask the test taker to determine where the sentence would fit best in the passage. There are 0-1 of these questions in each passage.

9 Prose Summary Questions
These provide a summary of the passage and then ask the test taker to choose 3 of 6 sentences that best relate to the summary. There are 0-1 of these questions in each passage.

10 Fill in a Table Questions
These ask the test taker to categorize various facts and information that appear in the passage. There are 0-1 of these questions in each passage.

How to Use This Book

Question Types
This section describes the question or questions covered in the chapter. It provides an explanation of each question and how to try to answer it.

Example Questions
This section shows the different ways that the questions appear on the TOEFL test. Students can learn how to recognize the different types of question in this section.

Useful Tips for Your Success
This section provides various tips on how to answer questions properly. It also provides hints on right and wrong approaches to answering each question.

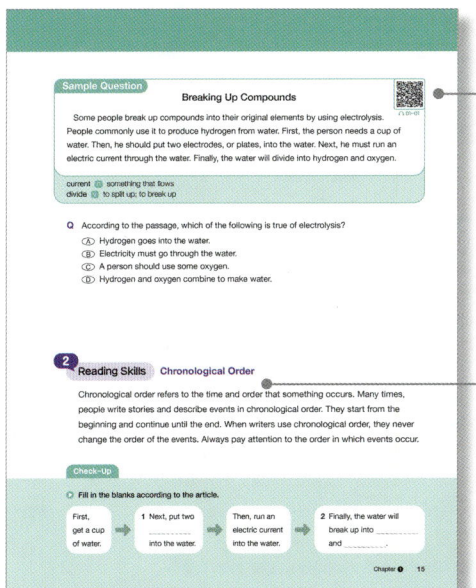

Sample Question
This is a short 60-word passage on one of the topics in the unit. It has one TOEFL question and one reading skills question.

Reading Skills
This is an explanation of the reading skill that the chapter covers.

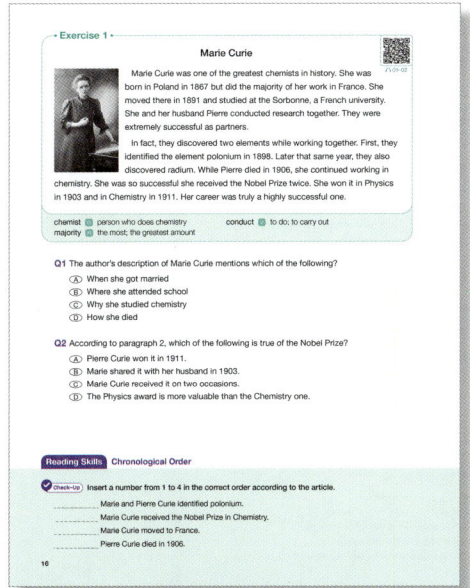

Medium Passages
There are four medium-length passages with 80-120 words each. Each passage is on a topic that concerns the subject of the unit and has two TOEFL questions and one reading skills question.

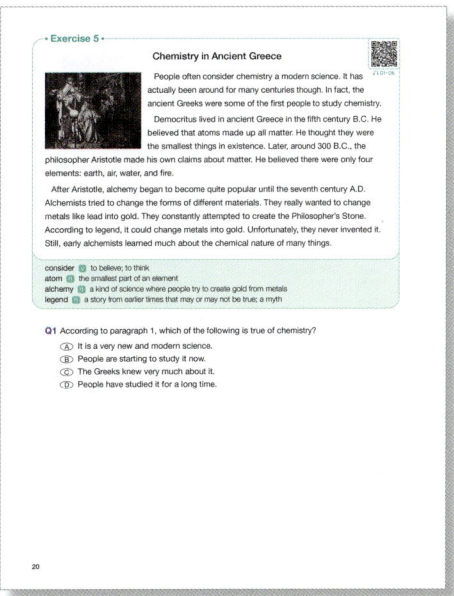

Long Passages
There are four long passages with 120-160 words each. Each passage is on a topic that concerns the subject of the unit and has three TOEFL questions and one reading skills question.

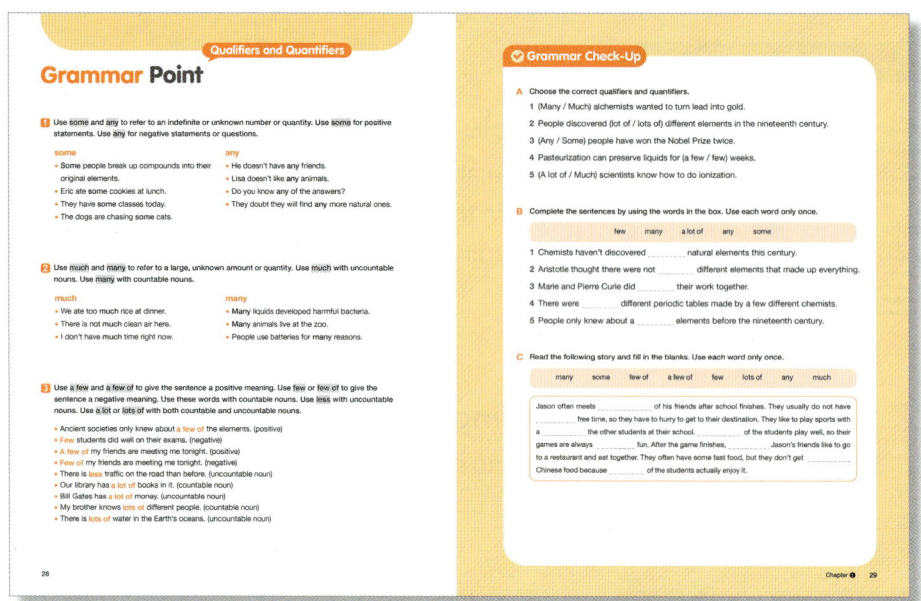

Grammar Point

This section explains a certain part of speech. It has one page of explanations and one page of various exercises for students to answer.

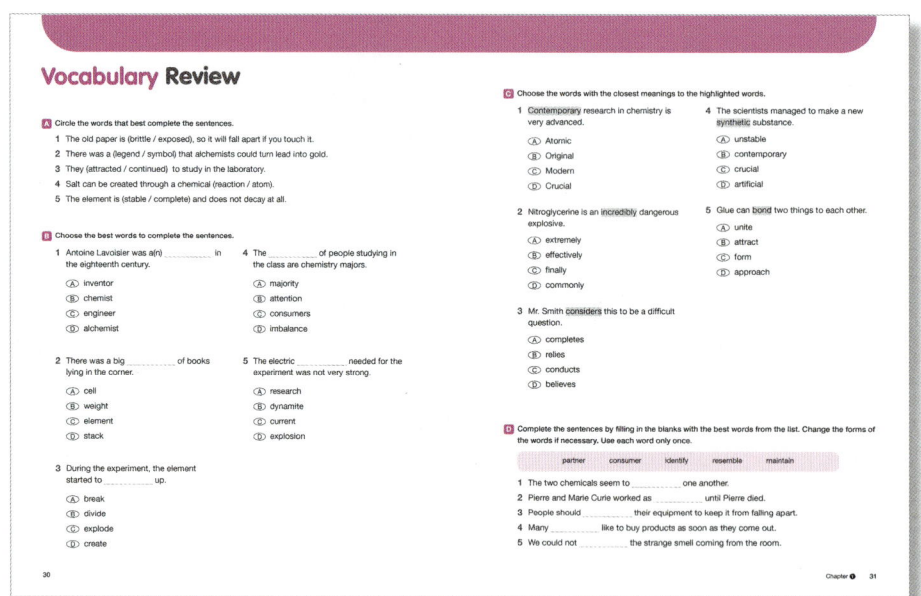

Vocabulary Review

This section provides a comprehensive review of the vocabulary found in the various passages in the unit. Each unit has twenty vocabulary review questions, and all of the answer choices are words that appear in the passages in the unit.

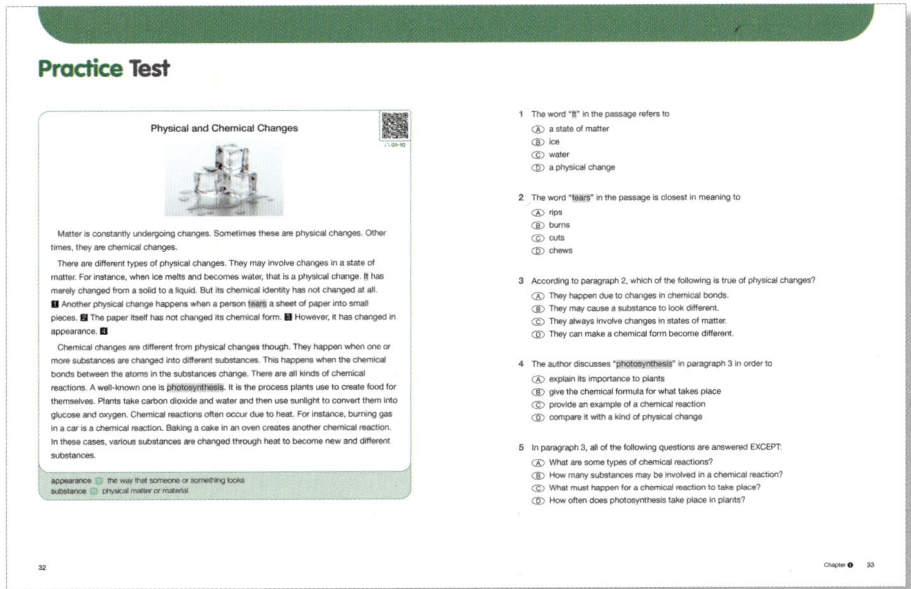

Practice Test

There is one passage with 160-220 words. The passage is on a topic that concerns the subject of the unit and has eight TOEFL questions.

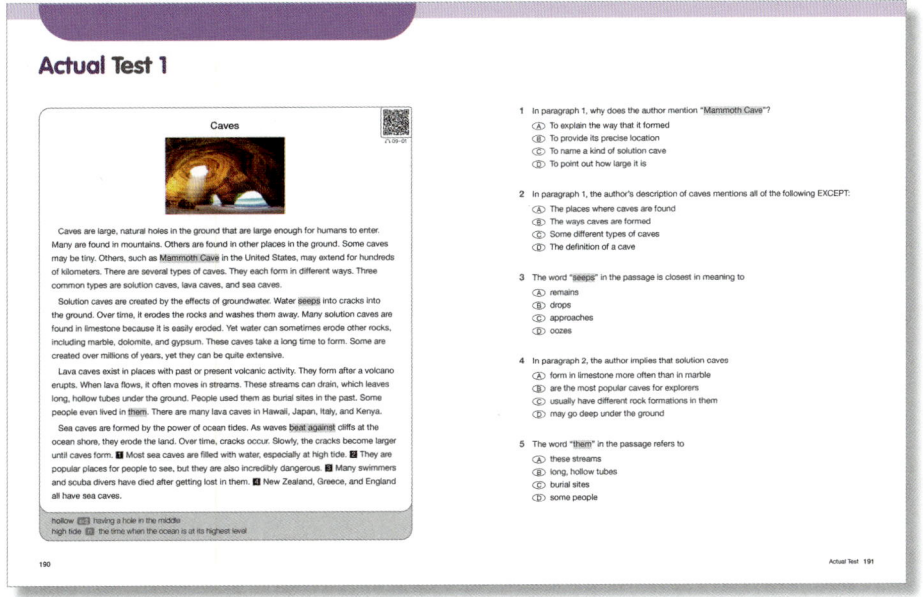

Actual Test

This section includes 3 passages with 220-300 words with 10 questions each. Every passage has different kinds of questions. There are questions from all 10 types found in the Reading section. Additionally, all of the passages are from topics that appear in the book. These passages and questions are shorter versions of a typical TOEFL iBT Reading section.

CHAPTER 01

Chemistry
(Chronological Order)

1. Marie Curie
2. Rust
3. Pasteurization
4. The Battery
5. Chemistry in Ancient Greece
6. The Discovery of Elements
7. Alfred Nobel
8. The Periodic Table of the Elements

CHAPTER 1 **Chemistry** (Chronological Order)

Understanding TOEFL Question Types & Reading Skills

1 Question Types   **Factual Information Questions**

Factual Information questions ask about the facts, details, definitions, or other information in the passage. They ask you to identify names, dates, places, or reasons why something happened. Read the facts in the passage carefully, and then you can answer the questions easily.

- **Example Factual Information Questions**
    - According to paragraph 1, what is true of X?
    - The author's description of X mentions which of the following?
    - According to the paragraph, X did Y because ~

- **Useful Tips for Your Success**

    - Pay attention to → any places the passage mentions.
        - → the names the passage gives.
        - → any dates in the passage.

    - Always → try to find the details in the passage.
        - → pay attention to the facts in the passage.

Sample Question

Breaking Up Compounds

Some people break up compounds into their original elements by using electrolysis. People commonly use it to produce hydrogen from water. First, the person needs a cup of water. Then, he should put two electrodes, or plates, into the water. Next, he must run an electric current through the water. Finally, the water will divide into hydrogen and oxygen.

current n something that flows
divide v to split up; to break up

Q According to the passage, which of the following is true of electrolysis?
  Ⓐ Hydrogen goes into the water.
  Ⓑ Electricity must go through the water.
  Ⓒ A person should use some oxygen.
  Ⓓ Hydrogen and oxygen combine to make water.

2 Reading Skills Chronological Order

Chronological order refers to the time and order that something occurs. Many times, people write stories and describe events in chronological order. They start from the beginning and continue until the end. When writers use chronological order, they never change the order of the events. Always pay attention to the order in which events occur.

Check-Up

▶ Fill in the blanks according to the article.

| First, get a cup of water. | ➡ | **1** Next, put two _____ into the water. | ➡ | Then, run an electric current into the water. | ➡ | **2** Finally, the water will break up into _____ and _____ . |

• Exercise 1 •

Marie Curie

Marie Curie was one of the greatest chemists in history. She was born in Poland in 1867 but did the majority of her work in France. She moved there in 1891 and studied at the Sorbonne, a French university. She and her husband Pierre conducted research together. They were extremely successful as partners.

In fact, they discovered two elements while working together. First, they identified the element polonium in 1898. Later that same year, they also discovered radium. While Pierre died in 1906, she continued working in chemistry. She was so successful she received the Nobel Prize twice. She won it in Physics in 1903 and in Chemistry in 1911. Her career was truly a highly successful one.

chemist [n] a person who does chemistry
majority [n] the most; the greatest amount
conduct [v] to do; to carry out

Q1 The author's description of Marie Curie mentions which of the following?
- Ⓐ When she got married
- Ⓑ Where she attended school
- Ⓒ Why she studied chemistry
- Ⓓ How she died

Q2 According to paragraph 2, which of the following is true of the Nobel Prize?
- Ⓐ Pierre Curie won it in 1911.
- Ⓑ Marie shared it with her husband in 1903.
- Ⓒ Marie Curie received it on two occasions.
- Ⓓ The Physics award is more valuable than the Chemistry one.

Reading Skills | Chronological Order

Check-Up Insert a number from 1 to 4 in the correct order according to the article.

_____ Marie and Pierre Curie identified polonium.
_____ Marie Curie received the Nobel Prize in Chemistry.
_____ Marie Curie moved to France.
_____ Pierre Curie died in 1906.

• **Exercise 2** •

Rust

Many buildings and structures are made with iron and steel. It is important for people to maintain them properly because both iron and steel can rust. Rust is a red or orange coating that can appear on metal.

Rust forms due to a chemical reaction. It happens when iron or steel is exposed to hydrogen and oxygen atoms. Usually, this occurs when metal is exposed to water. The reason is that water is composed of hydrogen and oxygen atoms. When water is added to the metal, the two begin to bond. This starts a chemical reaction called oxidation. Over time, the metal changes colors and becomes orange or red. As it rusts, the metal becomes brittle and can break apart.

coating n a layer of something spread over another thing
be exposed to phr to be opened to; to lay open to harm, danger, etc.
bond v to unite; to join together

Q1 According to paragraph 1, rust is
- Ⓐ a strong form of iron
- Ⓑ metal that has been painted red or orange
- Ⓒ a new way to manufacture steel
- Ⓓ a coating that forms on some metals

Q2 In paragraph 2, the author's description of rust mentions which of the following?
- Ⓐ The best methods for avoiding it
- Ⓑ The way in which it is created
- Ⓒ The amount of time it takes to form
- Ⓓ The elements that make it up

Reading Skills Chronological Order

✓ **Check-Up** Fill in the blanks according to the article.

| Expose iron or steel to moisture. | → | 1 Water bonds with the metal, and _____ occurs. | → | The metal changes colors and becomes red or orange. | → | 2 The metal becomes _____ and breaks apart. |

• Exercise 3 •

Pasteurization

In the past, people could not preserve liquids like milk for long periods of time. After a while, many liquids developed harmful bacteria or even viruses. If people drank them, they would become very sick. However, in 1862, Louis Pasteur developed a process to make liquids safe. He called this pasteurization.

Pasteurization relied upon heating liquids past their boiling point. This would eliminate most viruses, germs, bacteria, and other harmful microbes. This let people preserve various liquids for longer periods of time. In 1886, milk was first pasteurized. If a person refrigerates it, pasteurized milk can remain good for two to three weeks. Later, someone developed ultra-pasteurization. This can preserve milk for up to three months.

bacteria [n] kinds of one-celled organisms   refrigerate [v] to cool; to make something cold
eliminate [v] to kill; to destroy

Q1 According to paragraph 1, people became sick from drinking milk because

Ⓐ they pasteurized it
Ⓑ they boiled it for too long
Ⓒ the milk had bacteria or viruses
Ⓓ the milk was pasteurized for a long time

Q2 According to paragraph 2, which of the following is true of pasteurization?

Ⓐ Louis Pasteur pasteurized milk in 1886.
Ⓑ It can kill many dangerous organisms.
Ⓒ It works by boiling a liquid for several hours.
Ⓓ It is only effective for two or three weeks.

Reading Skills Chronological Order

Check-Up Insert a number from 1 to 4 in the correct order according to the article.

_____ People often became sick from drinking unpreserved milk.
_____ Someone pasteurized milk for the first time.
_____ Someone discovered the process of ultra-pasteurization.
_____ Louis Pasteur learned to pasteurize liquids.

• **Exercise 4** •

The Battery

Nowadays, people use batteries for many reasons. They effectively store energy for long periods of time. However, batteries are a fairly recent invention. They have also undergone many changes since their inventing.

In 1798, Alessandro Volta invented the first battery. It contained stacks of zinc, cardboard, and copper. It was not very effective. For one, it corroded too easily. So John Daniell improved Volta's batteries. In 1836, he developed batteries that did not corrode.

There were several more developments in the nineteenth century. However, a crucial one happened in 1888. That year, Carl Gassner, a German, invented the dry cell battery. This resembled the copper-zinc batteries people use today. Finally, in 1896, companies began selling batteries to consumers.

fairly adv somewhat
stack n a pile
corrode v to rot

Q1 In paragraph 2, the author's description of Alessandro Volta mentions which of the following?
  Ⓐ When he was born
  Ⓑ What he invented
  Ⓒ How people used his battery
  Ⓓ Whose idea he copied

Q2 According to paragraph 3, which of the following is true of Carl Gassner?
  Ⓐ He developed the first copper-zinc battery.
  Ⓑ He began selling batteries in 1896.
  Ⓒ He first made the dry cell battery.
  Ⓓ He improved Volta's battery in 1888.

 **Reading Skills** | **Chronological Order**

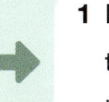 **Check-Up** Fill in the blanks according to the article.

| Alessandro Volta invented the first battery in 1798. | **1** Daniell improved these batteries in _____. | **2** _____ invented dry cell batteries in 1888. | Companies started selling batteries to consumers in 1896. |

Chapter ❶ 19

Exercise 5

Chemistry in Ancient Greece

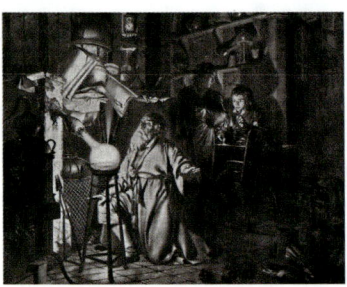

People often consider chemistry a modern science. It has actually been around for many centuries though. In fact, the ancient Greeks were some of the first people to study chemistry.

Democritus lived in ancient Greece in the fifth century B.C. He believed that atoms made up all matter. He thought they were the smallest things in existence. Later, around 300 B.C., the philosopher Aristotle made his own claims about matter. He believed there were only four elements: earth, air, water, and fire.

After Aristotle, alchemy began to become quite popular until the seventh century A.D. Alchemists tried to change the forms of different materials. They really wanted to change metals like lead into gold. They constantly attempted to create the Philosopher's Stone. According to legend, it could change metals into gold. Unfortunately, they never invented it. Still, early alchemists learned much about the chemical nature of many things.

consider [v] to believe; to think
atom [n] the smallest part of an element
alchemy [n] a kind of science where people try to create gold from metals
legend [n] a story from earlier times that may or may not be true; a myth

Q1 According to paragraph 1, which of the following is true of chemistry?
 Ⓐ It is a very new and modern science.
 Ⓑ People are starting to study it now.
 Ⓒ The Greeks knew very much about it.
 Ⓓ People have studied it for a long time.

Q2 In paragraph 2, the author's description of Aristotle mentions which of the following?

- Ⓐ Where in Greece he lived
- Ⓑ What elements he thought there were
- Ⓒ How he felt about the work of Democritus
- Ⓓ What the title of one of his book was

Q3 According to paragraph 3, why did alchemists try to make the Philosopher's Stone?

- Ⓐ It would teach them more about alchemy.
- Ⓑ It could help them create more lead.
- Ⓒ It would turn some metals into gold.
- Ⓓ They could learn about the nature of elements.

Reading Skills | Chronological Order

Check-Up Insert a number from 1 to 4 in the correct order according to the article.

_____ Alchemists tried to create the Philosopher's Stone.

_____ Democritus thought atoms made up all matter.

_____ Aristotle said the four elements were earth, air, water, and fire.

_____ Alchemists learned much about the chemical nature of things.

• Exercise 6 •

The Discovery of Elements

There are ninety-two naturally occurring elements on the Earth. However, it took centuries for people to discover them. In fact, chemists identified the last natural element in the twentieth century. They have also created many synthetic elements, even in the twenty-first century.

Ancient societies only knew about a few of the elements. These included gold, silver, copper, iron, and carbon. People discovered these elements thousands of years ago.

However, no one recognized the next element until 1250. This was arsenic. Albertus Magnus discovered it. After that, people slowly began finding more and more elements. In 1766, Henry Cavendish discovered hydrogen, and a few years later, in 1774, Joseph Priestley discovered oxygen. These are two of the most important of all the elements.

Later, in both the nineteenth and twentieth centuries, thanks to modern and better equipment, chemists started to find numerous elements. They doubt they will find any more natural ones. But they may be able to create some new artificial ones.

naturally adv by nature
synthetic adj artificial; manmade
recognize v to identify
doubt v not to be certain about

Q1 In paragraph 1, the author's description of naturally occurring elements mentions which of the following?

Ⓐ Which were discovered in the twenty-first century
Ⓑ How many of them there are
Ⓒ The names of the most common ones
Ⓓ Which century most of them were found in

Q2 According to paragraph 3, which of the following is true of the elements?
- Ⓐ Oxygen and hydrogen are two important ones.
- Ⓑ Albertus Magnus was the first to discover one.
- Ⓒ Henry Cavendish discovered oxygen in 1766.
- Ⓓ Joseph Priestley and Henry Cavendish worked together to find elements.

Q3 According to paragraph 4, why did chemists find more elements in the nineteenth century?
- Ⓐ They were able to manufacture some.
- Ⓑ They studied chemistry more closely.
- Ⓒ They updated all of their information.
- Ⓓ The equipment they used got better.

Reading Skills | Chronological Order

Check-Up Fill in the blanks according to the article.

| Ancient societies knew about some elements such as gold and silver. | 1 _____ discovered arsenic in 1250. | 2 _____ discovered oxygen in 1774. | 3 Chemists identified many elements in the _____ and _____ centuries. |

• Exercise 7 •

Alfred Nobel

In the nineteenth century, the construction and mining industries were very dangerous occupations. Many people died while working in them, and it took a long time to accomplish great feats of engineering. Then one man changed all of this. His name was Alfred Nobel.

Alfred Nobel was born in 1833. His father was an engineer, so that field naturally attracted his attention. In 1846, an Italian scientist invented nitroglycerine. This was an extremely powerful, yet very unstable, explosive. In 1849, Nobel met its inventor, and he began to experiment with it. He wanted to make it more stable.

Sadly, in 1864, Nobel's brother Emil died when some nitroglycerine exploded during an experiment. This made Nobel work even harder. In 1867, he managed to make nitroglycerine, a liquid, into a solid form. He called it dynamite. It was much more stable. The invention of dynamite helped the construction and mining industries worldwide. Because so many people used it, dynamite also made Nobel an incredibly rich and successful man.

feat [n] a deed; an accomplishment
inventor [n] a person who makes new things
stable [adj] secure; safe
incredibly [adv] very

Q1 According to paragraph 1, what is true of the nineteenth-century mining industry?

Ⓐ It was not particularly safe.
Ⓑ Alfred Nobel was involved in it.
Ⓒ It was more dangerous than engineering.
Ⓓ It took a long time to dig a mine.

Q2 According to paragraph 2, Alfred Nobel worked with nitroglycerine because

- Ⓐ he wanted to make it more powerful
- Ⓑ his father needed it for his company
- Ⓒ he was trying to make it safer
- Ⓓ he wanted to work with its inventor

Q3 In paragraph 3, the author's description of Emil Nobel mentions which of the following?

- Ⓐ The work he did with his brother
- Ⓑ The year that he was born
- Ⓒ The reason that he died
- Ⓓ The invention he created

Reading Skills Chronological Order

Check-Up Insert a number from 1 to 4 in the correct order according to the article.

_____ Emil Nobel died during an experiment.
_____ Alfred Nobel began experimenting with nitroglycerine.
_____ Alfred Nobel managed to create dynamite.
_____ Alfred Nobel was born in 1833.

• **Exercise 8** •

The Periodic Table of the Elements

01-09

Nowadays, most high school students study the periodic table of the elements. However, it has changed numerous times over the years. Now, most chemists consider it complete. But this was not always the case.

Antoine Lavoisier made the first periodic table in 1789. His table contained just thirty-three elements, and he only divided them into metals and nonmetals. Jons Jakob Burzelius made the next contribution. He gave the elements letters to serve as their symbols and determined the atomic weights of some elements. In 1864, John Newlands arranged the sixty or so known elements according to their atomic weights.

But Dmitri Mendeleev, in 1869, became the real father of the periodic table of the elements. His table arranged the elements according to their atomic weights. However, he left gaps for where he believed other elements should be. People later discovered them. He also arranged the elements according to their characteristics. His table is the one contemporary students study.

periodic adj occurring at regular intervals
contribution n an addition
arrange v to order
gap n an empty space

Q1 According to paragraph 2, which of the following is true of Antoine Lavoisier?

Ⓐ Most students study his periodic table.
Ⓑ His periodic table was incomplete.
Ⓒ He improved upon Berzelius's table.
Ⓓ His periodic table had thirty-three metals.

Q2 In paragraph 2, the author's description of John Newlands mentions which of the following?

- Ⓐ Which elements he discovered
- Ⓑ Who he worked together with
- Ⓒ Why he assigned letters for the elements
- Ⓓ What he included on his periodic table

Q3 According to paragraph 3, Dmitri Mendeleev lefts gaps in his periodic table because

- Ⓐ he did not know the elements' atomic weights
- Ⓑ he thought unknown elements belonged there
- Ⓒ he wanted to arrange the elements by their characteristics
- Ⓓ he was not able to assign symbols to every element

Reading Skills — Chronological Order

Check-Up Fill in the blanks according to the article.

1		2		3
1 _____ _____ made the first periodic table in 1789.	➡	Jons Jakob Burzelius gave elements letters as their symbols.	➡	2 _____ _____ arranged the elements by their atomic weights.	➡	3 Dmitri Mendeleev created the modern periodic table in _____.

Grammar Point

Qualifiers and Quantifiers

1 Use **some** and **any** to refer to an indefinite or unknown number or quantity. Use **some** for positive statements. Use **any** for negative statements or questions.

some
- **Some** people break up compounds into their original elements.
- Eric ate **some** cookies at lunch.
- They have **some** classes today.
- The dogs are chasing **some** cats.

any
- He does not have **any** friends.
- Lisa does not like **any** animals.
- Do you know **any** of the answers?
- They doubt they will find **any** more natural ones.

2 Use **much** and **many** to refer to a large, unknown amount or quantity. Use **much** with uncountable nouns. Use **many** with countable nouns.

much
- We ate too **much** rice at dinner.
- There is not **much** clean air here.
- I don't have **much** time right now.

many
- **Many** liquids developed harmful bacteria.
- **Many** animals live at the zoo.
- People use batteries for **many** reasons.

3 Use **a few** and **a few of** to give the sentence a positive meaning. Use **few** or **few of** to give the sentence a negative meaning. Use these words with countable nouns. Use **less** with uncountable nouns. Use **a lot** or **lots of** with both countable and uncountable nouns.

- Ancient societies only knew about *a few of* the elements. (positive)
- *Few* students did well on their exams. (negative)
- *A few of* my friends are meeting me tonight. (positive)
- *Few of* my friends are meeting me tonight. (negative)
- There is *less* traffic on the road than before. (uncountable noun)
- Our library has *a lot of* books in it. (countable noun)
- Bill Gates has *a lot of* money. (uncountable noun)
- My brother knows *lots of* different people. (countable noun)
- There is *lots of* water in the Earth's oceans. (uncountable noun)

Grammar Check-Up

A Choose the correct qualifiers and quantifiers.

1 (Many / Much) alchemists wanted to turn lead into gold.
2 People discovered (lot of / lots of) different elements in the nineteenth century.
3 (Any / Some) people have won the Nobel Prize twice.
4 Pasteurization can preserve liquids for (a few / few) weeks.
5 (A lot of / Much) scientists know how to do oxidation.

B Complete the sentences by using the words in the box. Use each word only once.

| few | many | a lot of | any | some |

1 Chemists have not discovered _____ natural elements this century.
2 Aristotle thought there were not _____ different elements that made up everything.
3 Marie and Pierre Curie did _____ their work together.
4 There were _____ different periodic tables made by a few different chemists.
5 People only knew about a _____ elements before the nineteenth century.

C Read the following story and fill in the blanks. Use each word only once.

| many | some | few of | a few of | few | lots of | any | much |

Jason often meets _____ of his friends after school finishes. They usually do not have _____ free time, so they have to hurry to get to their destination. They like to play sports with a _____ the other students at their school. _____ of the students play well, so their games are always _____ fun. After the game finishes, _____ Jason's friends like to go to a restaurant and eat together. They often have some fast food, but they do not get _____ Chinese food because _____ of the students actually enjoy it.

Vocabulary Review

A Circle the words that best complete the sentences.

1 The old paper is (brittle / exposed), so it will fall apart if you touch it.
2 There was a (legend / symbol) that alchemists could turn lead into gold.
3 They (attracted / continued) to study in the laboratory.
4 Salt can be created through a chemical (reaction / atom).
5 The element is (stable / complete) and does not decay at all.

B Choose the best words to complete the sentences.

1 Antoine Lavoisier was a(n) _____ in the eighteenth century.
   - Ⓐ inventor
   - Ⓑ chemist
   - Ⓒ engineer
   - Ⓓ alchemist

2 There was a big _____ of books lying in the corner.
   - Ⓐ cell
   - Ⓑ weight
   - Ⓒ element
   - Ⓓ stack

3 During the experiment, the element started to _____ up.
   - Ⓐ break
   - Ⓑ divide
   - Ⓒ explode
   - Ⓓ create

4 The _____ of people studying in the class are chemistry majors.
   - Ⓐ majority
   - Ⓑ attention
   - Ⓒ consumers
   - Ⓓ imbalance

5 The electric _____ needed for the experiment was not very strong.
   - Ⓐ research
   - Ⓑ dynamite
   - Ⓒ current
   - Ⓓ explosion

C Choose the words with the closest meanings to the highlighted words.

1 Contemporary research in chemistry is very advanced.
   - Ⓐ Atomic
   - Ⓑ Original
   - Ⓒ Modern
   - Ⓓ Crucial

2 Nitroglycerine is an incredibly dangerous explosive.
   - Ⓐ extremely
   - Ⓑ effectively
   - Ⓒ finally
   - Ⓓ commonly

3 Mr. Smith considers this to be a difficult question.
   - Ⓐ completes
   - Ⓑ relies
   - Ⓒ conducts
   - Ⓓ believes

4 The scientists managed to make a new synthetic substance.
   - Ⓐ unstable
   - Ⓑ contemporary
   - Ⓒ crucial
   - Ⓓ artificial

5 Glue can bond two things to each other.
   - Ⓐ unite
   - Ⓑ attract
   - Ⓒ form
   - Ⓓ approach

D Complete the sentences by filling in the blanks with the best words from the list. Change the forms of the words if necessary. Use each word only once.

| partner | consumer | identify | resemble | maintain |

1 The two chemicals seem to _____ one another.
2 Pierre and Marie Curie worked as _____ until Pierre died.
3 People should _____ their equipment to keep it from falling apart.
4 Many _____ like to buy products as soon as they come out.
5 We could not _____ the strange smell coming from the room.

Practice Test

Physical and Chemical Changes

Matter is constantly undergoing changes. Sometimes these are physical changes. Other times, they are chemical changes.

There are different types of physical changes. They may involve changes in a state of matter. For instance, when ice melts and becomes water, that is a physical change. It has merely changed from a solid to a liquid. But its chemical identity has not changed at all. **1** Another physical change happens when a person tears a sheet of paper into small pieces. **2** The paper itself has not changed its chemical form. **3** However, it has changed in appearance. **4**

Chemical changes are different from physical changes though. They happen when one or more substances are changed into different substances. This happens when the chemical bonds between the atoms in the substances change. There are all kinds of chemical reactions. A well-known one is photosynthesis. It is the process plants use to create food for themselves. Plants take carbon dioxide and water and then use sunlight to convert them into glucose and oxygen. Chemical reactions often occur due to heat. For instance, burning gas in a car is a chemical reaction. Baking a cake in an oven creates another chemical reaction. In these cases, various substances are changed through heat to become new and different substances.

appearance n the way that someone or something looks
substance n physical matter or material

1. The word "It" in the passage refers to
   A. a state of matter
   B. ice
   C. water
   D. a physical change

2. The word "tears" in the passage is closest in meaning to
   A. rips
   B. burns
   C. cuts
   D. chews

3. According to paragraph 2, which of the following is true of physical changes?
   A. They happen due to changes in chemical bonds.
   B. They may cause a substance to look different.
   C. They always involve changes in states of matter.
   D. They can make a chemical form become different.

4. The author discusses "photosynthesis" in paragraph 3 in order to
   A. explain its importance to plants
   B. give the chemical formula for what takes place
   C. provide an example of a chemical reaction
   D. compare it with a kind of physical change

5. In paragraph 3, all of the following questions are answered EXCEPT:
   A. What are some types of chemical reactions?
   B. How many substances may be involved in a chemical reaction?
   C. What must happen for a chemical reaction to take place?
   D. How often does photosynthesis take place in plants?

6 In paragraph 3, the author implies that chemical reactions

    Ⓐ can happen almost instantly

    Ⓑ happen much more often than physical changes do

    Ⓒ only take place in living things

    Ⓓ may require an outside force for them to occur

7 Look at the four squares [■] that indicate where the following sentence could be added to the passage.

It is still composed of two hydrogen atoms and one atom of oxygen.

Where would the sentence best fit?

Click on a square [■] to add the sentence to the passage.

8 *Directions:* Complete the table below to summarize information about changes discussed in the passage. Match the appropriate statements to the changes with which they are associated. *This question is worth 3 points.*

CHANGES	STATEMENTS
Physical Changes	Select 2 • •
Chemical Reactions	Select 3 • • •

Statements

1. The chemical bonds between the atoms in substances change.
2. Baking something such as cake may cause them.
3. They tend to take a very long time to occur.
4. They may happen when a substance's state of matter changes.
5. They happen more commonly than the other one.
6. One example is a piece of paper being ripped apart.
7. Heat may be responsible for them occurring.

CHAPTER 02

Biology
(Classification)

1. Genetically Modified Foods
2. Coral Reefs
3. Marsupials
4. Microorganisms
5. Microscopes
6. Photosynthesis
7. Biofuel
8. The History of Botany

CHAPTER 2 **Biology** (Classification)

Understanding TOEFL Question Types & Reading Skills

1 Question Types — **Negative Factual Questions**

Negative Factual questions ask you to confirm correct information in the passage and then to find the information that is NOT true. One of the answer choices will have incorrect information. This is the correct answer. Pay attention to the facts in the passage. Make sure you can find the answer choice that is incorrect.

- **Example Negative Factual Questions**
    - According to the passage, which of the following is NOT true of X?
    - The author's description of X mentions all of the following EXCEPT:
    - In paragraph 2, all of the following questions are answered EXCEPT:

- **Useful Tips for Your Success**

    - Pay attention to → the facts in the entire passage.
      → answer choices with information not in the passage.

    - Don't → choose an answer choice with information not from the passage.
      → choose any answers mentioned in the passage.

Sample Question

Ecosystems

An ecosystem is an area with plants and animals living together. There are many different types of ecosystems. Some, like desert ecosystems, are difficult places for animals to survive. They have little rain, and few animals live there. However, marine ecosystems are rich in life. A wide variety of animal species live there, and they are full of food for animals to eat.

survive v to live
marine adj aquatic; relating to the sea

Q According to the passage, which of the following is NOT true of ecosystems?

- Ⓐ Some ecosystems have very little life.
- Ⓑ Animals and plants live together in them.
- Ⓒ Almost all ecosystems are full of food.
- Ⓓ There are several kinds of ecosystems.

2 Reading Skills — Classification

Classification is organizing similar things or ideas into groups. People use classification to understand how two or more things or ideas relate to each other. When a writer uses classification, you should be able to notice the similarities in different things.

Check-Up

▶ The following are classified according to the article. Choose one characteristic to fill in the blank below.

Desert Ecosystems	Marine Ecosystems
Are hard places for animals to survive Do not have not much rain there _____	Have many animals there Have many species of animals Have much food for animals to eat

- Ⓐ Have many animal species
- Ⓑ Have few animals
- Ⓒ Have no animals
- Ⓓ Are rich in life

• Exercise 1 •

Genetically Modified Foods

02-02

In some parts of the world, crops grow poorly. Perhaps there is not enough rain, or the soil is very poor. Additionally, diseases and pests occasionally kill plants. Because of these problems, biologists are working to change plants' genetic structures to develop genetically modified (GM) crops.

Scientists have made many kinds of GM corn. It is often able to resist diseases. Sometimes it can make the plants stronger and healthier. Other GM corn can produce more grain than regular corn plants.

Soybeans are another popular GM food. GM soybeans often have a high nutritional value. Others can grow well in poor soil. Farmers also like them since they can reduce the amount of pesticides they need to use.

structure n makeup; organization   pesticide n a poison used to kill insects; an insecticide

Q1 In paragraph 1, all of the following questions are answered EXCEPT:
- Ⓐ In which countries do plants grow poorly?
- Ⓑ What does GM stand for?
- Ⓒ Who is trying to change the structures of plants?
- Ⓓ What can make plants not grow well?

Q2 According to paragraphs 2 and 3, which of the following is NOT true of GM crops?
- Ⓐ They can produce more food than regular plants.
- Ⓑ They cost more money to purchase from farmers.
- Ⓒ They can grow well even when the soil is bad.
- Ⓓ Farmers can use fewer pesticides because of them.

Reading Skills   Classification

 **Check-Up** The following are classified according to the article. Choose one benefit to fill in the blank below.

GM Corn	GM Soybeans
Can resist disease Can make plants stronger and healthier Can produce more grain than regular corn	_____ Can grow well in poor soil Require fewer pesticides

- Ⓐ Are high in nutrition
- Ⓑ Taste much better
- Ⓒ Can grow faster
- Ⓓ Cost much less

• **Exercise 2** •

Coral Reefs

Coral is a fossilized substance and looks like a hard, underwater plant. Coral reefs are great masses of coral growing together. Two kinds of coral reefs are fringing reefs and barrier reefs.

Fringing reefs are the most common kind. They exist right next to the coast and tend to extend away from the shore. They live in shallow waters like those off the Florida coast.

Barrier reefs are another type of reef. They are known to grow along continental shelves, so the ocean separates them from the mainland. They are not usually connected but are instead just groups of coral located near one another. The Great Barrier Reef in Australia is the best example of these reefs.

mass n a large amount
tend v to be likely

shallow adj low; not deep

Q1 In paragraph 2, the author's description of fringing reefs mentions all of the following EXCEPT:
- Ⓐ The places where they appear
- Ⓑ The depth of the water they are in
- Ⓒ The types of sea creatures that live in them
- Ⓓ The direction in which they extend

Q2 According to paragraph 3, which of the following is NOT true of barrier reefs?
- Ⓐ They can be far away from the coast.
- Ⓑ They are not one continuous reef.
- Ⓒ People can find them on continental shelves.
- Ⓓ They are larger than any other kind of reef.

Reading Skills Classification

Check-Up The following are classified according to the article. Choose one characteristic to fill in the blank below.

Fringing Reefs	Barrier Reefs
Are the most common	Are often far from the shore
_____	Are groups located near one another
Are some off the Florida coast	Is one near Australia

- Ⓐ Are located near islands
- Ⓑ Are separated from the mainland
- Ⓒ Are fossilized substances
- Ⓓ Are found near the shore

• Exercise 3 •

Marsupials

There are more than 300 species of marsupials. These include animals such as kangaroos, koalas, wombats, and possums. Marsupials are mammals, but they do not share all of the characteristics of mammals. In fact, marsupials have a few differences.

The main difference is that unlike mammals, marsupial babies are born undeveloped. These small animals climb into a pouch in their mother's stomach after being born. There, they drink milk and continue to develop. Marsupial babies are also born with no ears and back legs. They are blind, too. Marsupials have lower body temperatures than mammals. They are also found in fewer places. Mammals are found all around the world. Marsupials are found mainly in Australia and the Americas.

undeveloped **adj** not complete; immature   blind **adj** unable to see

Q1 According to paragraph 1, which of the following is NOT true of marsupials?
- Ⓐ They have some differences with mammals.
- Ⓑ Kangaroos and possums are marsupials.
- Ⓒ They are not considered types of mammals.
- Ⓓ There are hundreds of species of them.

Q2 In paragraph 2, the author's description of marsupials mentions all of the following EXCEPT:
- Ⓐ Where most of them live
- Ⓑ What they do after they are born
- Ⓒ What their body temperatures are
- Ⓓ How they look when they are born

Reading Skills   **Classification**

✓ Check-Up   The following are classified according to the article. Choose one description to fill in the blank above.

Mammals	Marsupials
Are born developed Have higher body temperatures than marsupials Are found all around the world	Are more than 300 species of them .... Have no ears and back legs at birth

- Ⓐ Are larger than mammals
- Ⓑ Are undeveloped when born
- Ⓒ Live in a pouch in their fathers
- Ⓓ Can see well at birth

• Exercise 4 •

Microorganisms

02-05

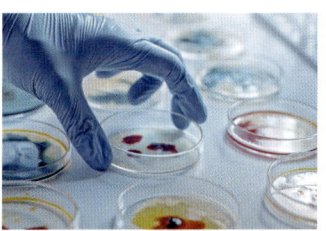
There are many very small animals on the Earth. In fact, sometimes people cannot even see these creatures without the help of a microscope. Biologists call these animals microorganisms. There are several different kinds of microorganisms, including bacteria and fungi.

Bacteria are usually one-celled organisms. Next to viruses, they are the smallest creatures on the Earth. They can live anywhere, including the air, but they require water to survive. They can also multiply incredibly fast.

Fungi are often one celled as well. They mostly live in soil and dead matter. They are important to the ecosystem though because they decompose waste to get rid of unwanted or unneeded products. So while people might not like bacteria and fungi, they are still important.

microscope n an instrument used to make small things appear bigger
multiply v to reproduce
decompose v to rot; to break down

Q1 In paragraph 2, the author's description of bacteria mentions all of the following EXCEPT:

Ⓐ The number of cells they usually have
Ⓑ The speed that they can reproduce
Ⓒ The harm they cause to people
Ⓓ The places where they live

Q2 According to paragraph 3, which of the following is NOT true of fungi?

Ⓐ They live in the ground.
Ⓑ They often have one cell.
Ⓒ They can eat waste material.
Ⓓ They are more important than bacteria.

Reading Skills   Classification

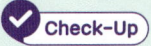 **Check-Up** The following are classified according to the article. Choose one characteristic to fill in the blank below.

Bacteria	Fungi
Often have one cell Can survive anywhere Can multiply incredibly fast	Often have one cell Live in soil and dead matter ....

Ⓐ Are mostly unneeded by people
Ⓑ Are as important as bacteria
Ⓒ Do not help the ecosystem
Ⓓ Break down unwanted waste

Exercise 5

Microscopes

For centuries, men observed plants and animals in the wild. They longed to learn more about them; however, it was difficult to study them closely. Scientists needed a tool to make the objects they were observing seem larger.

This need caused people to invent microscopes. The most common type is the compound microscope. It is also the cheapest. It uses light to produce a two-dimensional image. Compound microscopes can magnify images very much, but they are not always clear.

Dissection microscopes are another kind. They also rely on light, but they are able to show objects in three dimensions. Biologists use them to help see dissected animals. Unfortunately, they cannot show single cells since their magnification levels are low.

Electron microscopes are highly advanced models. They are extremely expensive to buy. They can give two-dimensional or three-dimensional images and can magnify images with great clarity. However, they only show images in black and white, not in color.

---

observe [v] to see; to look at; to study
invent [v] to develop; to create
magnify [v] to enlarge; to increase
dissection [n] an analysis; the act of cutting up animals and studying them

---

Q1 In paragraph 2, the author's description of compound microscopes mentions all of the following EXCEPT:

Ⓐ How common they are
Ⓑ The types of images they produce
Ⓒ A problem with these microscopes
Ⓓ The average price of them

Q2 According to paragraph 3, which of the following is NOT true of dissection microscopes?

- Ⓐ They can show images of individual cells.
- Ⓑ They show their images in three dimensions.
- Ⓒ They cannot show objects at high magnification.
- Ⓓ They use light to show their images.

Q3 In paragraph 4, all of the following questions are answered EXCEPT:

- Ⓐ What colors are the images from electron microscopes?
- Ⓑ What kinds of images can electron microscopes produce?
- Ⓒ What types of people use electron microscopes?
- Ⓓ How clear are the images electron microscopes produce?

Reading Skills | Classification

 **Check-Up** The following are classified according to the article. Choose two characteristics to fill in the blanks below.

Compound Microscope
Is most common and cheapest type
Uses light to make 2-dimensional images
Can magnify images very much
Does not always show clear images

Dissection Microscope
①
Can show objects in three dimensions
Is unable to show single cells
Cannot magnify images very much

Electron Microscope
②
Can show 2-D or 3-D images
Can present very clear pictures
Only shows objects in black and white

- Ⓐ Relies on electrons to show images – Is not available to many people
- Ⓑ Costs more than compound microscopes – Is used mostly by scientists
- Ⓒ Uses light to show pictures – Is very advanced and expensive
- Ⓓ Shows objects with good clarity – Cannot show pictures in color

Exercise 6

Photosynthesis

Photosynthesis is how plants take sunlight and convert it into the energy they use to survive. The process works identically in all plants. In this chemical reaction, plants need carbon dioxide, water, and the sun's light energy. Then, through photosynthesis, plants change them into glucose—a kind of sugar—water, and oxygen. These three products are all important.

First, plants create glucose for themselves. This is essentially their food. Without glucose, they would die. The glucose goes to various parts of the plant to provide it with energy.

The next product is water. Plants produce it as a byproduct of photosynthesis. Of course, water is important to all life on the Earth. Without it, every creature would perish. The plants either reuse the water, or it evaporates or disappears some other way.

Finally, plants also give off oxygen. This is important since humans need oxygen to survive. So do most other animals. Therefore, without photosynthesis, most life on the Earth would die.

---

convert [v] to change
glucose [n] a sugar
byproduct [n] a side-effect; a secondary product
perish [v] to die

Q1 In paragraph 1, the author's description of photosynthesis mentions all of the following EXCEPT:

A. The type of reaction it is
B. How plants use it
C. How much light plants need to do it
D. What plants create with it

Q2 In paragraph 3, all of the following questions are answered EXCEPT:

Ⓐ What happens to the water plants produce?
Ⓑ What byproduct is produced during photosynthesis?
Ⓒ How much water are plants able to produce?
Ⓓ What would happen to life on the Earth without water?

Q3 According to paragraph 4, which of the following is NOT true of oxygen?

Ⓐ Humans cannot live without it.
Ⓑ It is more common than carbon dioxide.
Ⓒ Plants help to create it through photosynthesis.
Ⓓ Animals need oxygen in order to live.

Reading Skills **Classification**

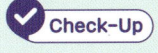 The following are classified according to the article. Choose two characteristics to fill in the blanks below.

Glucose	Water
Created by plants themselves ① Plants cannot live without it Provides energy to plants	Is a byproduct of photosynthesis ② Plants might reuse it May evaporate or disappear

Oxygen
Given off by plants Needed by humans Needed by animals All life would die without it

Ⓐ Is a kind of sugar – People need to reuse it
Ⓑ Is food for plants – Is important to all life on the Earth
Ⓒ Is most important to plants – Is necessary for photosynthesis
Ⓓ Is a chemical reaction – Plants only use it once

Exercise 7

Biofuel

People use many different types of energy. One common kind is biofuel. Biofuel comes from biomass; this is anything living or recently dead. There are several different ways to produce biofuel.

The first method is to burn various kinds of biomasses. Wood is the most popular biomass used, but people might also burn any other agricultural products, such as corn, sugarcane, and soybeans. They can also use industrial and agricultural waste to make energy.

Another way to get more biofuel is to raise fast-growing trees for their wood. Poplar and willow trees can grow incredibly high in just a few years. Switchgrass is another fast-growing plant, so people might be able to grow it quickly to use for biofuel.

Finally, people have produced biogas from rotting wet waste. Scientists can do this with animal dung and sewage. They can also capture gas created at landfills from rotting garbage. Altogether, biofuels promise to help reduce people's reliance on fossil fuels.

waste [n] refuse; garbage
rotting [adj] decomposing
dung [n] manure
landfill [n] a place where people throw their garbage; a garbage dump

Q1 In paragraph 2, all of the following questions are answered EXCEPT:

Ⓐ What is the most popular biomass used for fuel?
Ⓑ How much energy is created by burning biomass?
Ⓒ What are some types of biomass?
Ⓓ What types of things can be burned to make energy?

Q2 According to paragraph 3, which of the following is NOT true of fast-growing trees?

- Ⓐ Poplars take several months to grow very high.
- Ⓑ Switchgrass is a fast-growing plant.
- Ⓒ People can raise them for their wood to burn.
- Ⓓ Willow trees grow quickly in a few years.

Q3 In paragraph 4, the author's description of biogas mentions all of the following EXCEPT:

- Ⓐ Who can produce it
- Ⓑ Where it comes from
- Ⓒ How it is produced at landfills
- Ⓓ How common it is today

Reading Skills Classification

 The following are classified according to the article. Choose two biomasses to fill in the blanks below.

Burning Biomass	Fast-Growing Trees
Wood ① Industrial and agricultural waste	Poplar trees Willow trees Switchgrass

Biogas
Rotting wet waste Animal dung and sewage ②

- Ⓐ Corn, sugarcane, and soybeans – Gas from landfills
- Ⓑ Sugarcane, dung, and switchgrass – Manure
- Ⓒ Poplar and willow trees – Human waste products
- Ⓓ Dung and sewage – Industrial waste products

• **Exercise 8** •

The History of Botany

Biology is the study of life. There are many different fields of biology. One popular field is botany. A botanist studies plants and plant life. Over the years, botanists have used different methods to study plants.

In the past, people relied upon trial and error. They learned to avoid poisonous plants and to eat the healthy, safe plants. They passed on their knowledge to other generations through tribal lore. Their tribal elders became knowledgeable botanists and even managed to use plants as medicines or remedies for illnesses.

Modern botanists, however, utilize different methods to study their field. They do their research in laboratories and use high-tech equipment to conduct their studies of plants. They rely upon the scientific method to study plants. Many botanists have even studied the genetic structures of plants, so some can alter a plant's cellular structure. While modern botanists are different from tribal elders, both of them are interested in the same thing: learning about plants.

field n an area of study	**lore** n teachings; wisdom
rely upon phr to depend on	**alter** v to change

Q1 According to paragraph 1, which of the following is NOT true of biology?
- Ⓐ It can look at plants.
- Ⓑ It has many different areas of study.
- Ⓒ It examines life.
- Ⓓ It is a field of botany.

Q2 In paragraph 2, the author's description of tribal lore mentions all of the following EXCEPT:

Ⓐ Which people in tribes learned it
Ⓑ How it was taught to others
Ⓒ What people learned from it
Ⓓ What sicknesses it could cure

Q3 In paragraph 3, all of the following questions are answered EXCEPT:

Ⓐ What is the scientific method that botanists use?
Ⓑ What can some botanists do to plants' cellular structures?
Ⓒ What are modern botanists interested in learning?
Ⓓ Where do modern botanists conduct their research?

Reading Skills Classification

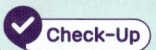 **Check-Up** The following are classified according to the article. Choose two characteristics to fill in the blank below.

Tribal Elders	Modern Botanists
Relied on trial and error Knew about good and bad plants Passed on knowledge to others ①	Work in laboratories ② Rely on the scientific method Study genetic structures of plants

Ⓐ Sometimes died from poison – Learn from tribal elders
Ⓑ Trained younger people in lore – Use trial and error
Ⓒ Used plants as medicines and remedies – Use high-tech equipment
Ⓓ Taught modern botanists their skills – Know about healthy, safe plants

Grammar Point

Infinitives

1 Uses of Infinitives

Functions	Example Sentences
Subject	• To read books is to gain knowledge. • To err is human. • To spend time at home made him happy.
Object	• We are allowed to stay out until eleven. • John began to think of some other ideas. • They longed to learn more about them.
Complement	• Our goal is to help as many people as possible. • Her idea was to wake up early in the morning. • Sumi's plan is to study hard during winter vacation.
Adjective	• David needs some food to eat. • He went to the library to find a book to read. • She has a gold necklace to wear to the party.
Adverb	• He thought animals evolved to live better in their environment. • She went outside to throw away the garbage. • Greg canceled his plans to stay home and study.

2 Using Infinitives with "It is"

Sometimes it may look awkward or strange to begin a sentence with an infinitive. In this case, you can change infinitives used as subjects to sentences using "It is." The meaning remains the same, and the sentence looks a little more normal.

- To eat three times a day is healthy. = It is healthy to eat three times a day.
- To call your parents every day is considerate. = It is considerate to call your parents every day.
- To practice a language often is best. = It is best to practice a language often.
- To ignore people is very rude. = It is very rude to ignore people.

Grammar Check-Up

A Choose the correct words for the blanks.

1 You should remember _____ for your test tomorrow.
   ⓐ to learn　　ⓑ to study　　ⓒ to understand　　ⓓ to write

2 Many people visit coral reefs _____ around them.
   ⓐ to study　　ⓑ to drive　　ⓒ to scuba-dive　　ⓓ to hunt

3 Electron microscopes are very expensive _____.
   ⓐ to purchase　　ⓑ to use　　ⓒ to make　　ⓓ to research

4 It is difficult for lots of animals _____ in desert ecosystems.
   ⓐ to sleep　　ⓑ to drink　　ⓒ to run　　ⓓ to live

B Complete the sentences by using the words in the box.

> eat　　alter　　decompose　　create　　live

1 Fungi can help to _____ lots of unwanted waste.
2 Thanks to evolution, animals change to _____ better in their environment.
3 Botanists have learned how to _____ the genetic structures of plants.
4 Some ecosystems have very much food for animals to _____.
5 Plants use photosynthesis to _____ their own food.

C Choose the sentences that are NOT grammatically correct.

1 ⓐ To study hard is good.
   ⓑ To read many books is important.
   ⓒ Exercise every day makes healthy.
   ⓓ To wake up early is diligent.

2 ⓐ The workers wanted to go home soon.
   ⓑ We all prefer to take the train.
   ⓒ David loves to talk to his friends.
   ⓓ Mr. Lee enjoys to works with his computer.

3 ⓐ She called to asked about his health.
   ⓑ To read many books is important.
   ⓒ The farmer planted the crops to raise them.
   ⓓ They drank water to make themselves healthier.

Vocabulary Review

A Circle the words that best complete the sentences.

1 (Microscopes / **Microorganisms**) are tiny creatures that people cannot see.
2 Farmers are now planting many genetically (changed / **modified**) crops in their fields.
3 The young child will (**develop** / development) at a fast rate.
4 Many animals cannot live in a (**desert** / marine) ecosystem because there is little food.
5 A coral (ecosystem / **reef**) can be near the coast or far away from it.

B Choose the best words to complete the sentences.

1 Oxygen is an important _____ plants make from photosynthesis.
   A structure
   B byproduct
   C evolution
   D glucose

2 _____ are smaller than every creature on the Earth except for viruses.
   A Creatures
   B Corals
   C Bacteria
   D Fungi

3 The doctor gave the patient a(n) _____ for his back pain.
   A oxygen
   B food
   C sugar
   D remedy

4 People can use _____ like sewage to create biogas.
   A waste
   B dung
   C landfill
   D biofuel

5 Many farmers must use _____ to kill all of the insects in their fields.
   A glucose
   B pesticides
   C coral
   D remedies

C Choose the words with the closest meanings to the highlighted words.

1. Plants use glucose made from photosynthesis to feed themselves.
   - Ⓐ lore
   - Ⓑ sugar
   - Ⓒ dung
   - Ⓓ biomass

2. The baby is still undeveloped and cannot be born yet.
   - Ⓐ young
   - Ⓑ blind
   - Ⓒ unaware
   - Ⓓ immature

3. Plants have the ability to change light energy into food for them to consume.
   - Ⓐ survive
   - Ⓑ pass on
   - Ⓒ burn
   - Ⓓ convert

4. You must carefully observe the organism to understand it fully.
   - Ⓐ study
   - Ⓑ capture
   - Ⓒ reduce
   - Ⓓ resist

5. Some animals on the Earth are beginning to perish because of industrialization.
   - Ⓐ reduce
   - Ⓑ die
   - Ⓒ exist
   - Ⓓ separate

D Complete the sentences by filling in the blanks with the best words from the list. Change the forms of the words if necessary. Use each word only once.

| fringing | invent | decompose | share | resist |

1. When people _____ new tools, they can help science to advance.
2. The scientists learned how the plant could _____ the disease so well.
3. The children are expected to _____ their snacks with one another.
4. A(n) _____ reef has a large amount of sea life in it.
5. The garbage began to _____ when the fungi started eating it.

Practice Test

Tree Diseases

It is possible for plants to suffer from diseases just like humans do. They can get both infectious diseases and noninfectious diseases.

Infectious diseases can go from one plant to another. They can be caused by viruses as well as other things, including bacteria, fungi, and worms. They often spread to other plants because of the wind, insects, or even farm machinery. These diseases can make leaves change colors. They can also make plants grow in strange shapes. Some of them even kill plants. In many cases, they can spread far, killing large numbers of plants. For example, a fungus killed many potato crops in Ireland in the 1800s. This was the direct cause of the Irish Potato Famine.

Noninfectious plant diseases do not go from one plant to another. However, they can still make plants very sick. Environmental conditions frequently cause them. For instance, a lack of nutrients in the soil can make plants sick. ■1 Too much or too little water can cause problems as well. ■2 Air pollution as well as chemicals such as pesticides can cause some noninfectious diseases. ■3 Acid rain is another problem that makes plants sick. ■4 In many cases, plants die due to problems caused by noninfectious diseases.

noninfectious adj not able to go from one organism to another
famine n a time when food is scarce or unavailable

1. In paragraph 2, the author uses "bacteria, fungi, and worms" as examples of
   - (A) the most common infectious diseases
   - (B) symptoms caused by infectious diseases
   - (C) things that can cause infectious diseases
   - (D) the name of certain infectious diseases

2. The phrase "spread to" in the passage is closest in meaning to
   - (A) move to
   - (B) grow with
   - (C) sicken
   - (D) appear as

3. Which of the following can be inferred from paragraph 2 about infectious diseases?
   - (A) They can affect plants in many different ways.
   - (B) They are common in places with hot weather.
   - (C) They usually happen during the spring months.
   - (D) They can be caused by the actions of humans.

4. According to paragraph 2, which of the following is true of the Irish Potato Famine?
   - (A) It killed many people in the county.
   - (B) It was caused by a fungus.
   - (C) It happened in several countries.
   - (D) It happened due to a noninfectious plant disease.

5. The word "them" in the passage refers to
   - (A) noninfectious plant diseases
   - (B) plants
   - (C) environmental conditions
   - (D) nutrients

6 In paragraph 3, the author's description of noninfectious plant diseases mentions all of the following EXCEPT:

- Ⓐ Some causes of them
- Ⓑ How they spread
- Ⓒ What can happen to plants with them
- Ⓓ The names of some of them

7 Look at the four squares [■] that indicate where the following sentence could be added to the passage.

When it falls, the harmful substances in it can make plants very sick.

Where would the sentence best fit?

Click on a square [■] to add the sentence to the passage.

8 *Directions:* Complete the table below to summarize information about plant diseases discussed in the passage. Match the appropriate statements to the plant diseases with which they are associated. *This question is worth 3 points.*

PLANT DISEASES	STATEMENTS
Infectious Diseases	Select 2 • •
Noninfectious Diseases	Select 3 • • •

Statements

1. Happen most often to trees and flowers
2. Can spread from one plant to another
3. Can be caused by few nutrients in the soil
4. Do not move from one plant to another
5. Can make plants become sick very fast
6. Are sometimes caused by pesticides
7. Are able to kill large numbers of plants

CHAPTER 03

Culture
(Comparison and Contrast)

① Monoculturalism and Multiculturalism
② Changes in Marriage
③ The Cowboy
④ Confucianism and Buddhism
⑤ Urban and Rural Environments
⑥ Folk Culture
⑦ Hollywood and Bollywood Movies
⑧ Spreading Culture through Colonization

CHAPTER 3 Culture (Comparison and Contrast)

Understanding TOEFL Question Types & Reading Skills

1 Question Types — Rhetorical Purpose Questions

Rhetorical Purpose questions ask the reason why the author mentions certain information in the passage. These questions ask you to understand the function of a word or phrase. Try to understand the logic in why the author mentions various facts or incidents.

- **Example Rhetorical Purpose Questions**
  - The author discusses "X" in paragraph 2 in order to ~
  - Why does the author mention "X"?
  - The author uses "X" as an example of ~

- **Useful Tips for Your Success**

  - Learn to
    → recognize important words and phrases.
    → understand the meanings of these words and phrases.

  - Think about
    → the connections between sentences.
    → the connections between paragraphs.

Sample Question

The Globalization of Cultures

Thanks to globalization, cultures are spreading everywhere. It often has positive effects. People watch exciting foreign movies or read books in other languages. They also visit other countries and live in fascinating new lands. But globalization has some negative effects, too. Some people feel their cultures are disappearing. And people from different nations are losing their differences. Everyone is becoming similar.

globalization n the process of becoming global; the act of spreading worldwide
fascinating adj attractive; amazing

Q The author mentions "foreign movies" in the passage in order to

Ⓐ prove that people are becoming similar
Ⓑ show a positive effect of globalization
Ⓒ emphasize how culture is disappearing
Ⓓ stress their negative effect on people

2 Reading Skills — Comparison and Contrast

Comparing two or more things shows their similarities. Contrasting two or more things shows their differences. By using comparison and contrast, writers can show relationships between two or more things. Writers often use words such as *more*, *less*, *as ... as*, and *the same as* to make comparisons and contrasts.

Check-Up

▶ **Which comparison between the positive and negative effects of globalization is accurate?**

Ⓐ Globalization has both positive effects and negative effects.
Ⓑ Globalization has a few more negative effects than positive ones.
Ⓒ Globalization has as many negative effects as positive ones.
Ⓓ Globalization has many more negative effects than positive ones.

• **Exercise 1** •

Monoculturalism and Multiculturalism

Some countries have people from only one ethnic group. Sociologists refer to this as monoculturalism. For example, countries such as Japan, Korea, and Cambodia are monocultures. They have a high amount of cultural unity. The great majority of the people in these countries speak the same language. Most of the natives follow certain binding cultural standards, too.

There are also multicultural countries. These countries have people from many different ethnic groups living in them. Countries such as Canada, England, and Australia are multicultural. They typically celebrate the diversity of the people living inside their borders. The countries follow certain cultural standards, but they encourage people from different places to maintain their cultures. This makes their cultures more diverse.

ethnic [adj] related to a certain group of people   binding [adj] uniting; unifying
unity [n] togetherness

Q1 In paragraph 1, the author uses "Cambodia" as an example of

Ⓐ a place with low cultural unity
Ⓑ a country with a monoculture
Ⓒ a country with many ethnic groups
Ⓓ a place near Korea and Japan

Q2 The author discusses "multicultural countries" in paragraph 2 in order to

Ⓐ compare them with monocultural countries
Ⓑ argue they are weaker than monocultures
Ⓒ state that Canada and England are different
Ⓓ mention they are not common countries

Reading Skills Comparison and Contrast

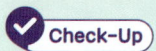 Write "D" for difference or "S" for similarity in the blanks for each sentence.

1. _____ England is a multicultural country, but Japan is a monocultural country.
2. _____ Multicultural and monocultural countries both follow certain cultural standards.
3. _____ Australia is a multicultural country, and so is England.
4. _____ Multicultural countries are more diverse than monocultural ones.

• **Exercise 2** •

Changes in Marriage

Virtually all cultures have some tradition of marriage. Over the years, however, marriage has changed very much.

Traditionally, in most of the world's cultures, husbands dominated marriages. Husbands made the major binding decisions. Often, only husbands worked. Wives usually raised their children and took care of their households. Essentially, women were like second-class citizens.

Nowadays, thanks to feminism, many modern marriages are equal partnerships. Both husband and wives normally have jobs. Sometimes wives have high-paying jobs while their husbands have low-paying ones. In addition, both the husband and the wife make decisions in their families. Neither one of them dominates; they both work together as partners in marriage.

virtually adv practically; almost
second-class adj lower-rated

feminism n the concept that women are equal to men

Q1 The author discusses "Wives" in paragraph 2 in order to
- Ⓐ describe the kinds of jobs they worked
- Ⓑ show they were lower than husbands in marriage
- Ⓒ prove they made the major binding decisions
- Ⓓ discuss their lives as child raisers

Q2 In paragraph 3, why does the author mention "feminism"?
- Ⓐ To blame it for lowering the status of the husband
- Ⓑ To claim it has not really helped women very much
- Ⓒ To explain why most modern wives now have jobs
- Ⓓ To explain why marriages are now equal partnerships

Reading Skills | Comparison and Contrast

 Which comparison between traditional and modern marriages is accurate?

- Ⓐ Women are less equal in modern marriages.
- Ⓑ Husbands dominate modern marriages more than traditional ones.
- Ⓒ Women work more now than they did in traditional marriages.
- Ⓓ Wives dominated traditional marriages more than modern marriages.

• **Exercise 3** •

The Cowboy

In the nineteenth century, cowboys became an important part of American culture. They lived in the west and mostly worked on ranches. Many stories told about cowboys are true; however, there are countless exaggerated myths about them.

Cowboys tended horses and cattle for ranchers. They typically worked long, grueling hours with few breaks. They were quite individualistic and learned to depend upon themselves for everything.

However, thanks to movies, there are numerous false stories about cowboys. Many people believe cowboys were bloodthirsty killers or gunslingers. Actually, they rarely fought or killed others. Nor did they attack and kill Native Americans like movies show them doing. And cowboys' lives were not particularly glamorous; they usually led simple lives instead.

ranch n a large farm that typically has cattle or sheep   bloodthirsty adj ferocious; cruel
exaggerated adj overstated

Q1 In paragraph 1, why does the author mention "myths"?
- Ⓐ To argue that cowboy myths are not true
- Ⓑ To state that most of them are true
- Ⓒ To admit to knowing some good ones about cowboys
- Ⓓ To describe a couple of true cowboy myths

Q2 The author discusses "Native Americans" in paragraph 3 in order to
- Ⓐ name them as cowboys' enemies
- Ⓑ claim they were bloodthirsty killers
- Ⓒ state that cowboys did not kill them
- Ⓓ compare them with gunslingers

Reading Skills Comparison and Contrast

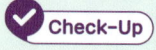 **Check-Up** Write "D" for difference or "S" for similarity in the blanks for each sentence.

1 _____ Movie cowboys fought very often, but real cowboys did not.
2 _____ Real cowboys had simple lives, but movie cowboys had glamorous ones.
3 _____ Both movie cowboys and real cowboys lived in the American west.
4 _____ Real cowboys often worked on ranches, and so did movie cowboys.

• **Exercise 4** •

Confucianism and Buddhism

Religions and philosophies often greatly affect countries and their cultures. Two examples are Confucianism and Buddhism. These are both very strong in many Asian countries.

Confucianism stresses relationships between people. It has many rituals for people to follow while also emphasizing devotion to others. It spread from China to many other countries. Japan, Korea, and Taiwan are countries influenced by it. Because of Confucianism, their cultures have changed very much.

Buddhism, on the other hand, emphasizes peace, kindness, and wisdom. According to Buddhism, all people are equal, and everyone can find happiness and live a good life. Buddhism originated in India but has spread to China, Korea, Japan, and Vietnam, influencing the people and the cultures in these countries.

stress v to emphasize
devotion n loyalty
originate v to begin; to start

Q1 In paragraph 2, why does the author mention "Taiwan"?

Ⓐ To say that Confucianism began there
Ⓑ To describe it as a leader in Confucianism
Ⓒ To compare it with Korean Confucianism
Ⓓ To say that Confucianism has influenced it

Q2 The author discusses "Buddhism" in paragraph 3 in order to

Ⓐ recommend that people study it
Ⓑ give a description of it
Ⓒ show how it has improved several countries
Ⓓ say how many people practice it

Reading Skills **Comparison and Contrast**

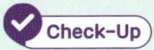 **Check-Up** Which comparison between Confucianism and Buddhism is accurate?

Ⓐ Both Confucianism and Buddhism started in China.
Ⓑ Confucianism stresses peace more than Buddhism.
Ⓒ Buddhism has been more successful than Confucianism.
Ⓓ Buddhism began in India while Confucianism began in China.

• Exercise 5 •

Urban and Rural Environments

Ever since civilization began, most people have lived in urban or rural environments. Urban environments are cities. Rural environments are places in the countryside. These two places have many differences.

The most obvious one is population. Urban areas have large populations. Today, cities have millions of residents. The largest, such as Tokyo, Cairo, and Shanghai, may have twenty million people living around them. Rural areas are much less populated. So people live far from one another. They typically dwell in houses. In cities, most people live in apartments. A single apartment building may have hundreds or thousands of people living in it.

Rural places tend to be quiet. They also have much less air pollution, too. People in rural areas often have personal vehicles. However, many people in cities rely on public transportation. They take buses, subways, and trains to reach their destinations. Cities can also be quite dangerous. They have much higher crime rates than rural areas.

---

civilization n an advanced state of human society
population n the number of people living in a certain place
resident n a person who lives in a certain place
destination n the place a person is going

Q1 In paragraph 2, the author uses "Tokyo, Cairo, and Shanghai" as examples of

Ⓐ famous cities in the world
Ⓑ the world's safest cities
Ⓒ cities with huge populations
Ⓓ cities that have many apartment buildings

Q2 The author discusses "public transportation" in paragraph 3 in order to

  Ⓐ state that people in cities often use it
  Ⓑ claim it does not exist in rural areas
  Ⓒ point out how useful it is in many places
  Ⓓ argue that it costs too much in some cities

Q3 In paragraph 3, why does the author mention "crime rates"?

  Ⓐ To note that they are getting lower in places around the world
  Ⓑ To point out that cities are more dangerous than rural areas
  Ⓒ To describe the types of crimes that are common in urban areas
  Ⓓ To name an advantage of living in a large city

Reading Skills Comparison and Contrast

Check-Up Write "D" for difference or "S" for similarity in the blanks for each sentence.

1. _____ People have lived in cities and rural areas ever since civilization began.
2. _____ Rural areas have small populations, but urban areas can have large populations.
3. _____ People in the countryside have their own vehicles while people in urban areas use public transportation.
4. _____ Cities are dangerous and have higher crime rates than rural areas.

• Exercise 6 •

Folk Culture

Many people from ethnic groups or geographical regions maintain certain traditions. Even though the world is changing, they keep their traditions from generation to generation. People call this folk culture. Folk culture can appear in many different ways.

One very common way is with music. In America, some groups in the Appalachian Mountains area pass on bluegrass music to later generations. People from the Hawaiian Islands also have their own folk music based on instruments like the ukulele. And Australian aborigines pass on the music of the didgeridoo, a traditional instrument.

Another kind of folk culture is in arts and crafts. The Inuit in Canada and other countries in the Arctic make carved figurines from bones, stone, and ivory. Many Americans in the Midwest region sew their own quilts. Even origami from Japan is a kind of folk culture. Origami is the folding of paper into different designs.

maintain v to keep; to retain
pass on phr to convey; to teach
aborigine n one of the original natives of a country or region
figurine n a small statue; a statuette

Q1 The author discusses "Folk culture" in paragraph 1 in order to

Ⓐ describe it
Ⓑ praise it
Ⓒ compare it with traditions
Ⓓ explain its origins

Q2 In paragraph 2, why does the author mention "the didgeridoo"?

- Ⓐ To compare it with the ukulele
- Ⓑ To say bluegrass music often uses it
- Ⓒ To describe a folk music instrument
- Ⓓ To explain how to play it

Q3 In paragraph 3, the author uses "origami" as an example of

- Ⓐ a type of folk culture
- Ⓑ a common Japanese activity
- Ⓒ a figurine-making method
- Ⓓ the ideal kind of folk culture

Reading Skills **Comparison and Contrast**

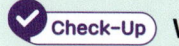 Which comparison between music and arts and crafts is accurate?

- Ⓐ Both music and arts and crafts are kinds of folk culture.
- Ⓑ Music is much more popular than arts and crafts.
- Ⓒ Arts and crafts are more common in America than music.
- Ⓓ Music is less popular in Asia than arts and crafts are.

• Exercise 7 •

Hollywood and Bollywood Movies

When most people think of movies, Hollywood comes to mind. Hollywood is a city in California, and people film many movies near there. There is also Bollywood in India. Bollywood too makes lots of movies.

Most people have positive images of Hollywood movies. The actors and the actresses are very glamorous and striking, and the special effects in the action movies are amazing. The movies are always in English though, so some international audiences can become confused. And sometimes Hollywood movies are too violent and have lots of bad language.

Bollywood movies are from the area around Mumbai, India. However, Bollywood is not a real place. Bollywood produces over 1,000 movies every year. The movies are in Hindi, Urdu, and English. Most Bollywood movies are musicals with lots of singing and dancing. They are not as popular as Hollywood movies. But many people still enjoy them.

---

come to mind `phr` to occur
film `v` to make a movie; to record
striking `adj` impressive
audience `n` viewers; spectators

Q1 In paragraph 2, the author uses "The actors and the actresses" as examples of

- Ⓐ a positive image of Hollywood movies
- Ⓑ a reason Hollywood movies are in English
- Ⓒ a negative factor in Hollywood movies
- Ⓓ the excessive violence in Hollywood movies

Q2 The author discusses "Bollywood movies" in paragraph 3 in order to

- Ⓐ argue they are not as good as Hollywood movies
- Ⓑ describe some of their characteristics
- Ⓒ explain their incredible popularity
- Ⓓ note there are more than 1,000 every year

Q3 In paragraph 3, why does the author mention "Urdu"?

- Ⓐ To name a language Bollywood films use
- Ⓑ To give the place Bollywood makes its film
- Ⓒ To note where Bollywood films are popular
- Ⓓ To say it is close to Mumbai, India

Reading Skills — Comparison and Contrast

Check-Up Write "D" for difference or "S" for similarity in the blanks for each sentence.

1. _____ Hollywood is a real place, but Bollywood is not.
2. _____ Hollywood movies are in English, and sometimes Bollywood movies are, too.
3. _____ Both Bollywood and Hollywood movies are popular with people.
4. _____ Bollywood movies have lots of singing and dancing while Hollywood movies can be very violent.

Exercise 8

Spreading Culture through Colonization

Throughout history, nations have always colonized one another. They have often done this by winning wars against their opponents. This has enabled nations to spread their cultures to other places.

Most people have a negative view of colonization. Yet some people argue that it can have a few positive effects on colonized places. Sometimes the colonizers bring new technology with them. So the colonized country can become more developed. In addition, the conquering nation sometimes builds up the other country's infrastructure. It might construct roads and railroads, for example. The colonizers might also improve the education and political systems in the colonized country.

Of course, there are many reasons people dislike colonization. For one, the defeated country loses its independence. It is now a colony and no longer independent. Many colonies begin to lose their own cultures, too. They also might not want to change their own systems. Many prefer to keep their own traditions and methods instead of adopting new ones.

---

colonize v to make an area into a colony
conquering adj winning; successful
infrastructure n the network of roads, bridges, and railways in an area
independence n freedom

Q1 In paragraph 1, why does the author mention "wars"?

- Ⓐ To compare wars' effects with colonization
- Ⓑ To note how colonies are formed
- Ⓒ To say all losers in them become colonies
- Ⓓ To argue that war is the only reason colonies get formed

Q2 In paragraph 2, the author uses "infrastructure" as an example of

- Ⓐ a benefit of improved education in a colony
- Ⓑ a positive effect of colonization
- Ⓒ a reason people like being in colonies
- Ⓓ something all conquerors must improve in colonies

Q3 In paragraph 3, why does the author mention "traditions"?

- Ⓐ To say that they improve under colonization
- Ⓑ To argue that many people want them to change
- Ⓒ To state a negative effect of colonization
- Ⓓ To compare them with the loss of independence

Reading Skills   Comparison and Contrast

Check-Up Which comparison between the positive and negative effects of colonization is accurate?

- Ⓐ There are more positive than negative effects of colonization.
- Ⓑ The negative effects of colonization are not as severe as the positive effects.
- Ⓒ Colonization can have both good and bad effects on the colonized people.
- Ⓓ More traditions are lost than infrastructure improved under colonization.

Grammar Point — Participles

1 Present Participles

1. Form present participles by adding *-ing* to the end of the verb. If the verb finishes with the letter "e," then take off the "e" and add *-ing*.

   - go → going
   - disappear → disappearing
   - work → working
   - run → running
   - swim → swimming
   - become → becoming

2. Use present participles like adjectives to describe a present action or state.

   - Some people feel their cultures are disappearing.
   - The athletes are running in the race now.
   - Everyone is becoming similar.

2 Past Participles

1. Form the past participles of regular verbs by adding *-ed* to the end of the verb. Form the past participles of irregular verbs in many different ways. There are no patterns. You must memorize irregular verbs' past participle forms.

   - confuse → confused
   - go → gone
   - clean → cleaned
   - find → found
   - brush → brushed
   - please → pleased
   - learn → learned
   - influence → influenced

2. Use past participles like adjectives to describe a past or completed action.

   - Kevin was confused by her actions.
   - We were pleased with the decision.
   - Korea and Taiwan are countries influenced by it.

3 Present vs Past Participles

Present participles have an active use. Past participles have both active and passive uses.

Active
- We are learning a foreign language.
- The cow has eaten grass.
- This movie is really fascinating.
- Doing math can be very boring.

Passive
- The foreign language was learned by us.
- The cow was eaten.
- I was fascinated by the movie.
- David was bored by his math homework.

Grammar Check-Up

A Choose the correct participles.

1 Many people think that sports are very (excited / **exciting**).

2 I was (**amazed** / amazing) by the discovery.

3 Many immigrants celebrate (respected / **respecting**) American holidays.

4 The world is becoming more and more (**globalized** / globalizing) every year.

5 Hollywood actors and actresses are often very (struck / **striking**).

B Choose the sentences that do NOT use a participle.

1 ⓐ The colonized country finally became independent.
   ⓑ We all enjoy watching Hollywood movies.
   ⓒ Many Inuit make carved figurines to sell to tourists.
   ⓓ The husband and the wife both have high-paying jobs.

2 ⓐ Changing traditions are confusing people in many countries.
   ⓑ Singing songs is very common in musicals.
   ⓒ I am surprised by your attitude.
   ⓓ We were pleased by the movie's ending.

3 ⓐ A multicultural society can be interesting to live in.
   ⓑ The researchers looked at the written papers.
   ⓒ We are influenced very much by popular culture.
   ⓓ Many believe cowboys did not mind shooting people.

C Read the following story and fill in the blanks with the participles in the box. Use each word only once.

> interested   published   exhausting   influenced   written   interesting

Allen was _____ in learning about culture, so he took a class in it. However, his teacher assigned _____ homework every night, so Allen thought it was a bit _____. But he learned many fascinating things about culture, so this made the class rather _____ to him. He was _____ by the class to read more _____ books about culture. After some time, he learned much more about culture and how people lived around the world.

Vocabulary Review

A Circle the words that best complete the sentences.

1 The country needs more (railroads / roads) for its trains to run on.
2 People against colonization are its (generations / opponents).
3 In many traditional households, the husband (raised / dominated) the marriage.
4 A (monocultural / multicultural) country has just one ethnic group in it.
5 Because of (globalization / colonization), people are learning more about the world.

B Choose the best words to complete the sentences.

1 Some movies have excellent _____ effects.
   A amazing
   B glamorous
   C special
   D fascinating

2 Immigrants usually _____ the holidays in their new countries.
   A celebrate
   B defeat
   C lose
   D disappear

3 The Inuit often make _____ figurines to sell to tourists.
   A confused
   B carved
   C exaggerated
   D negative

4 Jason made a _____ impression on his new teacher.
   A various
   B positive
   C reserved
   D traditional

5 Husbands and wives are now _____ in their marriages.
   A ranchers
   B partners
   C residents
   D audience

C Choose the words with the closest meanings to the highlighted words.

1. In most cultures, men typically had higher positions than women.
   - Ⓐ merely
   - Ⓑ naturally
   - Ⓒ virtually
   - Ⓓ normally

2. Christianity has deeply influenced many Western countries and their cultures.
   - Ⓐ colonized
   - Ⓑ affected
   - Ⓒ enabled
   - Ⓓ maintained

3. Many families are moving to rural environments to enjoy life in them.
   - Ⓐ city
   - Ⓑ suburban
   - Ⓒ busy
   - Ⓓ country

4. Many people live in urban environments because of their jobs.
   - Ⓐ small
   - Ⓑ city
   - Ⓒ unique
   - Ⓓ country

5. The professor emphasized that his students must understand this important tradition.
   - Ⓐ stressed
   - Ⓑ produced
   - Ⓒ referred
   - Ⓓ respected

D Complete the sentences by filling in the blanks with the best words from the list. Change the forms of the words if necessary. Use each word only once.

| infrastructure | feminism | dwell | cowboy | produce |

1. _____ has helped men and women to become more equal in society.
2. Film studios _____ a large number of films each year.
3. Because of the war, the country's _____ suffered a lot of damage.
4. There were several _____ working on the ranch.
5. The family hopes to _____ in a large house in the countryside soon.

Practice Test

The Cultural Legacy of the Roman Empire

In the second century A.D., the Roman Empire was at its greatest extent. It covered most of Western Europe, including modern-day Italy, France, Spain, and Portugal, parts of England and Germany, some of North Africa, and much of Eastern Europe and the Middle East. It was one of the greatest empires in history. However, by the end of the fifth century, the Roman Empire in Europe was gone, and only the Byzantine Empire in the east remained. Nevertheless, Rome has had an important effect on European culture in several ways. Two are language and the introduction of Christianity.

In the Roman Empire, the citizens spoke Latin. While now a dead language, all cultured people once spoke Latin. And many modern languages have evolved from it. The romance languages, such as Italian, French, and Spanish, are all very similar to Latin. In fact, they came directly from Latin. They only developed once the Roman Empire fell and there was less contact between the people in these different lands. Even English, while not coming directly from Latin, has a large number of words that it has stolen from Latin.

Christianity was perhaps one of the most important legacies of the Roman Empire. **1** While early Roman emperors, like Nero, had Christians executed, Constantine the Great became the first Christian emperor in the 330s. **2** After him, virtually every Roman emperor was Christian. **3** Christianity then spread rapidly all throughout the enormous empire, and the countries in Europe today remain mostly Christian. **4** The introduction of Christianity had a civilizing effect on the people living in these areas, and it was Christian monks who would preserve culture and knowledge during the Dark Ages after Rome fell.

While Rome had many influences, language and Christianity were among the most important. Without them, the world would look like a very different place.

---

legacy (n) a remnant; an inheritance   **extent** (n) a reach; a degree

1. In paragraph 1, the author uses "the Middle East" as an example of
   - Ⓐ a land that once resisted the Roman Empire
   - Ⓑ a land that is bigger than the Roman Empire
   - Ⓒ a land that was once part of the Roman Empire
   - Ⓓ a land that neighbored the Roman Empire

2. Which of the following can be inferred from paragraph 1 about the Roman Empire?
   - Ⓐ It still exists in some small parts of Europe.
   - Ⓑ It never got bigger than it was in the second century.
   - Ⓒ Its citizens were proud to be members of it.
   - Ⓓ The Byzantine Empire conquered it in the fifth century.

3. The word "evolved" in the passage is closest in meaning to
   - Ⓐ changed
   - Ⓑ developed
   - Ⓒ created
   - Ⓓ altered

4. Which of the following best expresses the essential information in the highlighted sentence? *Incorrect* answer choices change the meaning in important ways or leave out essential information.
   - Ⓐ When the Roman Empire ended and people met one another less, the languages developed.
   - Ⓑ During the Roman Empire, people talked to each other less, so the language developed.
   - Ⓒ People lost contact after the Roman Empire, so they tried to develop a new language.
   - Ⓓ Without the development of new languages, the Roman Empire would not have fallen.

5. The word "him" in the passage refers to
   - Ⓐ Nero
   - Ⓑ Constantine the Great
   - Ⓒ Roman emperor
   - Ⓓ Christian

6 According to paragraph 3, which of the following is true of Christianity in the Roman Empire?

- Ⓐ Nero made it illegal for Romans to be Christians.
- Ⓑ Some emperors killed every Christian in Rome.
- Ⓒ Christian monks were very important in Rome.
- Ⓓ Constantine became a Christian in the fourth century.

7 Look at the four squares [■] that indicate where the following sentence could be added to the passage.

He was baptized right before he died, but he had been a Christian for many years before.

Where would the sentence best fit?

Click on a square [■] to add the sentence to the passage.

8 *Directions:* An introductory sentence for a brief summary of the passage is provided below. Complete the summary by selecting the THREE answer choices that express the most important ideas in the passage. *This question is worth 2 points.*

The Roman Empire had many cultural legacies, but language and Christianity were two of the most important.

- •
- •
- •

Answer Choices

1. French, Spanish, and Italian are all romance languages.
2. Countries in Europe have strong Christian influences today.
3. Constantine the Great became the first Christian emperor.
4. Latin led to the development of other European languages.
5. English is one language that does not come directly from Latin.
6. Christian monks preserved knowledge during the Dark Ages.

CHAPTER

04

Music
(Cause and Effect)

1. Epic Poems and Music
2. Wind Instruments
3. John Williams
4. Wolfgang Amadeus Mozart
5. The Grammy Awards
6. The Development of the Saxophone
7. Rock and Roll
8. Changes in Classical Music

CHAPTER 4 Music (Cause and Effect)

Understanding TOEFL Question Types & Reading Skills

1 Question Types — Inference Questions

Inference questions ask about arguments or ideas that the passage does not mention. The author implies these things but does not actually include them in the passage. Pay attention to the causes and effects of different arguments or ideas. Think about why something happened or why something will happen in the future.

- **Example Inference Questions**
  - Which of the following can be inferred about X?
  - The author of the passage implies that X ~
  - Which of the following can be inferred from paragraph 1 about X?

- **Useful Tips for Your Success**
  - Pay attention to → causes and effects.
    → suggestions and results.
  - Don't → pick answers that contradict the main idea.
    → choose answers just because they look right.

Sample Question

Troubadours

In the Middle Ages, music was very popular. People especially loved singing. So troubadours began traveling from city to city to sing for people. Writing songs and singing them were troubadours' specialties. They often sang about chivalry and the great deeds of knights and lords. Nobles usually loved their songs; therefore, troubadours often played their music in castles and palaces.

troubadour n a wandering singer; a minstrel
chivalry n courtesy; politeness

Q Which of the following can be inferred about troubadours?

Ⓐ They did not stay in one place for a long time.
Ⓑ They often made a lot of money from singing.
Ⓒ They sometimes went out fighting with knights.
Ⓓ They only played songs in castles and palaces.

2 Reading Skills — Cause and Effect

The cause is the reason something happened. The effect is the result of that action. By using cause and effect, writers can show how one action caused another. Writers often use words and phrases like *so*, *because*, *therefore*, *due to*, and *thanks to* to connect a cause and its effect.

Check-Up

▶ For the pair of sentences below, mark "C" for cause and "E" for effect.

_____ Nobles usually loved their songs.
_____ Troubadours often played their music in castles and palaces.

• Exercise 1 •

Epic Poems and Music

🎧 04-02

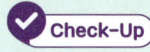

Many cultures have collections of long poems, called epics. These poems are about relating stories of great feats by heroes. Some of the more famous epic poems are the *Iliad* and the *Odyssey* of ancient Greece, the Mesopotamian *Gilgamesh*, and the Anglo-Saxon *Beowulf*. However, most of these epic poems were thousands of lines long. Therefore reading them was difficult because most people were illiterate.

People had to think of other better ways to remember these poems, so some decided to sing them. Singing the poems made them easier to remember. Listening to epic poems therefore became an early form of entertainment. After eating, people would listen to a person sing stories of great deeds.

collection [n] a set; a compilation **deed** [n] an accomplishment; a feat
illiterate [adj] unable to read; uneducated

Q1 In paragraph 1, the author implies that epic poems
- Ⓐ are sometimes very short
- Ⓑ only come from Europe
- Ⓒ are usually written in English
- Ⓓ do not appear in every culture

Q2 Which of the following can be inferred from paragraph 2 about epic poems?
- Ⓐ Only reading them made them hard to remember.
- Ⓑ Only people with good voices could sing them.
- Ⓒ They were most people's favorite kind of entertainment.
- Ⓓ People always listened to them after finishing a meal.

Reading Skills | Cause and Effect

✓ **Check-Up** For each pair of sentences below, mark "C" for cause and "E" for effect.

1 _____ Reading them was difficult because most people were illiterate.
  _____ Most of these epic poems were thousands of lines long.
2 _____ Some decided to sing them.
  _____ People had to think of other better ways to remember these poems.

• **Exercise 2** •

Wind Instruments

Among the oldest musical instruments in the world are wind instruments. Archaeologists have found bone flutes created by prehistoric people thousands of years ago. Wind instruments rely on air to produce sound. The air comes from the mouth of a person. There are several types of wind instruments.

There are several woodwinds. They include the flute, the clarinet, and the saxophone. Brass instruments are also considered wind instruments. Some of them are the trumpet, the trombone, and the tuba. Brass instruments are usually made of brass. Woodwinds are made of wood or metal. These two types of instruments produce different sounds. However, the way people play them is fairly similar. Musicians blow air into the instruments. Then, the instruments create music.

prehistoric adj relating to the time before recorded history   **brass** n a metal made of copper and zinc
produce v to create; to make

Q1 In paragraph 1, the author implies that flutes
- Ⓐ are always made from bones
- Ⓑ can produce sound in a variety of ways
- Ⓒ are preferred over other instruments by most musicians
- Ⓓ have been played by people for thousands of years

Q2 Which of the following can be inferred from paragraph 2 about brass instruments?
- Ⓐ They take a short time to learn to play.
- Ⓑ They sound different from woodwinds.
- Ⓒ They can be difficult for people to play.
- Ⓓ They are some of the oldest musical instruments.

Reading Skills Cause and Effect

Check-Up For each pair of sentences below, mark "C" for cause and "E" for effect.

1. _____ The air comes from the mouth of a person.
   _____ Wind instruments rely on air to produce sound.
2. _____ Musicians blow air into the instruments.
   _____ The instruments create music.

• Exercise 3 •

John Williams

Early films were silent movies. However, technology rapidly improved. So this allowed directors to add sound to their films. They often not only added sound but also included soundtracks to their films. Soundtracks are musical compositions accompanying the film. Over the years, soundtracks have often become associated with various movies.

John Williams has composed some of the world's most famous soundtracks. Some are simple, such as his theme from the movie *Jaws*. Others are more inspiring, like his introduction to the movie *Star Wars*. Many of the movies Williams wrote soundtracks for became blockbusters. This, in turn, made him famous. Today, his albums have sold millions of copies.

silent adj soundless; having no sound
accompany v to go together with
inspiring adj uplifting; heartening; moving

Q1 Which of the following can be inferred from paragraph 1 about silent movies?
- Ⓐ They are very uncommon nowadays.
- Ⓑ They were more interesting than films with sound.
- Ⓒ They were sometimes filmed in color.
- Ⓓ They always had a live soundtrack.

Q2 In paragraph 2, the author implies that John Williams
- Ⓐ is the only famous composer of soundtracks
- Ⓑ gets his inspiration from blockbuster movies
- Ⓒ became famous because of the soundtrack for *Jaws*
- Ⓓ can compose many different kinds of music

Reading Skills Cause and Effect

Check-Up For each pair of sentences below, mark "C" for cause and "E" for effect.

1. _____ This allowed directors to add sound to their films.
   _____ Technology rapidly improved.

2. _____ Many of the movies Williams wrote soundtracks for became blockbusters.
   _____ This, in turn, made him famous.

• Exercise 4 •

Wolfgang Amadeus Mozart

One of the most brilliant musicians ever was Wolfgang Amadeus Mozart. Born in 1756, Mozart was a child prodigy. Learning to play the piano at age three, he began writing his own music at the age of five. Because of his brilliance, he played for Bavarian royalty when he was only six.

Throughout his short life, Mozart composed over 600 pieces of music. He was a musical genius, creating symphonies, operas, masses, and other kinds of music. During his life, people widely acknowledged him as one of the greatest of all composers. His works showed a clarity and balance that virtually no one has ever matched. For this reason, Mozart's works have remained popular up to current times.

prodigy n a child genius
brilliance n intelligence; ability
acknowledge v to recognize; to admit

Q1 Which of the following can be inferred from paragraph 1 about Mozart?
- Ⓐ His father helped him very much.
- Ⓑ He was a very unusual child.
- Ⓒ He excelled in all subjects.
- Ⓓ He became a member of the royalty.

Q2 In paragraph 2, the author implies that Mozart's music
- Ⓐ is the most popular even today
- Ⓑ should often be listened to
- Ⓒ was in a large number of genres
- Ⓓ often used trumpets and pianos

Reading Skills Cause and Effect

Check-Up For each pair of sentences below, mark "C" for cause and "E" for effect.

1 _____ Learning to play the piano at age three, he began writing his own music at the age of five.
  _____ Because of his brilliance, he played for Bavarian royalty when he was only six.

2 _____ Mozart's works have remained popular up to current times.
  _____ His works showed a clarity and balance that virtually no one has ever matched.

• **Exercise 5** •

The Grammy Awards

In the 1950s, music was becoming a big part of the American consciousness. Many exciting bands were forming. Listening to them on the radio or watching them on television became common. People wanted to reward the best bands by recognizing them with awards. So the National Academy of Recording Arts and Sciences created the Gramophone Awards. Later, they changed the name to the Grammy Awards.

The academy holds these awards yearly. It nominates artists for awards in many categories. Winning an award has become prestigious, so artists try their best to receive one. A Grammy-winning artist can also expect to see sales of his or her records increase after winning.

Nowadays, the Grammy Awards are televised globally; therefore, millions watch them each year. The awards for record, song, and album of the year and best new artist are the most desired. So competition for these prizes is fierce. Every year, new winners receive fame and fortune following their victories.

consciousness n awareness
nominate v to put forward; to suggest
prestigious adj esteemed; important
fierce adj severe

Q1 In paragraph 1, the author implies that the 1950s
  Ⓐ was the most exciting decade for music in America
  Ⓑ was the decade with the first Gramophone Awards
  Ⓒ was the first decade people had radios in their homes
  Ⓓ had only a few popular bands and musicians

Q2 Which of the following can be inferred from paragraph 2 about a Grammy-winning artist?

    (A) The artist will earn more money.
    (B) The artist will retire soon afterward.
    (C) The artist will create better music.
    (D) The artist will appreciate the award.

Q3 Which of the following can be inferred from paragraph 3 about the Grammy Awards?

    (A) There are only three separate awards given.
    (B) An artist never repeats as an award winner.
    (C) Some artists win awards in the three main categories.
    (D) The winning artists are very pleased with their awards.

Reading Skills — Cause and Effect

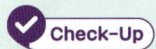 **Check-Up** Which sentence group below does NOT show cause and effect?

(A) Winning an award has become prestigious. So artists try their best to receive one.
(B) The academy holds these awards yearly. It nominates artists for awards in many categories.
(C) People wanted to reward the best bands by recognizing them with awards. So the National Academy of Recording Arts and Sciences created the Gramophone Awards.
(D) Nowadays, the Grammy Awards are televised globally. Therefore, millions watch them each year.

Exercise 6

The Development of the Saxophone

There are many different musical instruments. However, people know very few of the inventors of these instruments. This is the case for the saxophone. Adolphe Sax, a Belgian, invented it in the 1840s. Sax was the son of an instrument designer. Because of this, he developed his own interest in musical instruments.

In the 1840s, Sax wanted a new instrument for military bands and orchestras. Therefore, he set out to design the saxophone. He was looking to combine a woodwind, like the clarinet, with a brass instrument, like the trumpet. The result of his work was the saxophone.

Designing instruments came easily to Sax, so he created several versions of the saxophone. However, it did not immediately become popular. Instead, only a few bands used it at first. Later, however, more individuals began experimenting with making saxophones. This helped to increase its popularity. Nowadays, the saxophone is incredibly popular, and people use it in many genres of music.

case n a situation
orchestra n an ensemble; a group of musicians
version n a type; a kind
experiment v to practice; to try

Q1 In paragraph 1, the author implies that Adolphe Sax
- Ⓐ could play many musical instruments
- Ⓑ learned to make instruments at college
- Ⓒ grew up in a musical household
- Ⓓ was not a good musician

Q2 Which of the following can be inferred from paragraph 2 about the saxophone?

Ⓐ It sounds very different from the clarinet.
Ⓑ Adolphe Sax designed it for a particular reason.
Ⓒ It took Adolphe Sax several years to design.
Ⓓ It is a member of the brass family of instruments.

Q3 In paragraph 3, the author implies that modern saxophones

Ⓐ are better than clarinets
Ⓑ are less popular than the piano
Ⓒ only appear in orchestras
Ⓓ have many different makers

Reading Skills Cause and Effect

Check-Up Which sentence group below does NOT show cause and effect?

Ⓐ Sax was the son of an instrument designer. Because of this, he developed his own interest in musical instruments.
Ⓑ Instead, only a few bands used it at first. Later, however, more individuals began experimenting with making saxophones.
Ⓒ Designing instruments came easily to Sax. So he created several versions of the saxophone.
Ⓓ In the 1840s, Sax wanted a new instrument for military bands and orchestras. Therefore, he set out to design the saxophone.

Exercise 7

Rock and Roll

People all over the world listen to rock music. However, it is a relatively new genre of music. It only developed in the 1940s and 1950s in America. Prior to this, Americans listened to different kinds of music like big band, country, and jazz. However, many people wanted a new sound. So people began combining different forms of music. Experimenting with music, especially jazz and the blues, became common. The result was rock and roll.

In 1954, Bill Haley's song *Rock Around the Clock* hit number one on the music charts. This led to an explosion in the popularity of rock music. This helped increase the popularity of other early rock musicians like Chuck Berry and Big Joe Turner. Finally, Elvis Presley started gaining popularity. This made rock music one of the most popular genres of music not only in America but also throughout the world.

prior to phr before
hit v to reach; to attain
explosion n an increase
gain v to build up; to improve

Q1 Which of the following can be inferred from paragraph 1 about rock music?

Ⓐ A large number of people dislike it.
Ⓑ It is newer than country music.
Ⓒ It had no other musical influences.
Ⓓ Only Americans listen to it.

Q2 In paragraph 2, the author implies that Bill Haley

- Ⓐ was an early leader in rock music
- Ⓑ had only one famous song
- Ⓒ performed together with a band
- Ⓓ sometimes toured with Chuck Berry

Q3 Which of the following can be inferred from paragraph 2 about Big Joe Turner?

- Ⓐ He had several number one hits.
- Ⓑ He came after Elvis Presley.
- Ⓒ He went on a couple of world tours.
- Ⓓ He became popular thanks to Bill Haley.

Reading Skills Cause and Effect

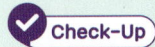 **Check-Up** Which sentence group below does NOT show cause and effect?

- Ⓐ It only developed in the 1940s and 1950s in America. Prior to this, Americans listened to different kinds of music like big band, country, and jazz.
- Ⓑ Experimenting with music, especially jazz and the blues, became common. The result was rock and roll.
- Ⓒ However, many people wanted a new sound. So people began combining different forms of music.
- Ⓓ Finally, Elvis Presley started gaining popularity. This made rock music one of the most popular genres of music not only in America but also throughout the world.

Exercise 8

Changes in Classical Music

Classical music is one of the most misunderstood forms of music. Many believe it has never changed over the years. Therefore, they hear it once, dislike it, and then refuse to listen to it again. In actuality, classical music has changed often during its 700-year-long history.

Classical music began as church chants in the Middle Ages. However, the coming of the Renaissance led to an alteration in classical music. As society became more secular, so did classical music. In addition, while chants were fairly simple, Baroque music became much more complex. Harmonizing all of the instruments became crucial during this period.

During and after the Baroque Period, classical music became quite varied. Countless individuals began composing their own music. Because of this, several types of classical music formed. For example, Bach, Beethoven, and Mozart are three of classical music's biggest names. However, after hearing their music, one will realize how unlike their styles were despite them being contemporaries of one another.

misunderstood adj misinterpreted
alteration n a change
complex adj complicated
compose v to write

Q1 Which of the following can be inferred from paragraph 1 about classical music?

Ⓐ Lots of people are unaware of the truth about it.
Ⓑ The majority of people never listen to it.
Ⓒ It is always undergoing periods of change.
Ⓓ It is difficult for people to understand its meaning.

Q2 In paragraph 2, the author implies that the Middle Ages

- Ⓐ had only one type of classical music
- Ⓑ came after the Renaissance
- Ⓒ saw the development of complicated music
- Ⓓ combined secular and church music

Q3 Which of the following can be inferred from paragraph 3 about the Baroque Period?

- Ⓐ No other period of classical music is better than it.
- Ⓑ It is one of several periods of classical music.
- Ⓒ There were three main composers in this period.
- Ⓓ It lasted for over one hundred years.

Reading Skills Cause and Effect

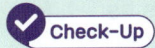 **Check-Up** Which sentence group below does NOT show cause and effect?

- Ⓐ Many believe it has never changed over the years. Therefore, they hear it once, dislike it, and then refuse to listen to it again.
- Ⓑ Countless individuals began composing their own music. Because of this, several types of classical music formed.
- Ⓒ Classical music began as church chants in the Middle Ages. However, the coming of the Renaissance led to an alteration in classical music.
- Ⓓ Society became more secular. So did classical music.

Chapter ❹   93

Grammar Point

Gerunds

1 Form gerunds by adding *-ing* to the end of verbs. Gerunds act like nouns in sentences.

- sing → singing
- show → showing
- play → playing
- travel → traveling
- walk → walking
- chase → chasing

2 Uses of Gerunds

Functions	Example Sentences
Subject	• **Composing** songs and **singing** them were troubadours' specialties. • **Collecting** stamps is his hobby. • **Jogging** is a great way to get some exercise.
Complement	• The best part of the song is **listening** to the ending. • Your chore is **cleaning** your room every day. • Allen's hobby is **playing** the trumpet.
Object	• So troubadours began **traveling** from city to city to sing for people. • Elvis Presley started **gaining** popularity. • I remember **meeting** you last year. • The dog loves **chasing** the cat around the house. • Do not stop **working** as hard as you can.

3 Gerunds vs Present Participles

Gerunds and present participles look the same. But use gerunds as nouns and use participles as adjectives.

Gerund

- **Working** at the factory is his job.
- We like **going** out to that restaurant.
- **Harmonizing** all of the instruments became crucial.

Participle

- Many **exciting** bands were forming.
- What a **frightening** ghost!
- The **dancing** bear made everyone laugh.

Grammar Check-Up

A Choose the correct gerunds.

1 (Listening / Writing) to classical music can be very relaxing.
2 Adolphe Sax was very good at (varying / designing) musical instruments.
3 (Nominating / Receiving) an award at the Grammy's is very prestigious.
4 Rock and roll began (increasing / losing) in popularity in the 1950s.
5 Troubadours preferred (traveling / staying) around to different towns and cities.

B Choose the sentences that do NOT use a gerund.

1 ⓐ Elvis Presley was an exciting new musician in the 1950s.
  ⓑ Composing music was one of Mozart's specialties.
  ⓒ John Williams excels at creating soundtracks for movies.
  ⓓ Singing poems was a common form of entertainment in the past.

2 ⓐ Recording music is easy nowadays because of computers.
  ⓑ Jason prefers listening to music to watching movies.
  ⓒ This CD has a lot of very inspiring songs.
  ⓓ Going to concerts is one of his favorite activities.

3 ⓐ His hobby is playing the piano.
  ⓑ They enjoyed hearing that song performed.
  ⓒ The musician is a very caring person.
  ⓓ Attending an opera is something he does every month.

C Read the following story and fill in the blanks with the gerunds in the box. Use each word only once.

| watching | paying | playing | going | doing | putting | staying |

Peter loves _____ to different concerts every month. In his city, many musicians enjoy _____ at the local theater. They say _____ on a concert there is a wonderful experience for them. Peter's family often attends the concerts even though _____ for the tickets can sometimes be expensive. For his family, _____ a concert is much better than _____ home and _____ nothing. This month, Peter is going to two different concerts. He is hoping to have a good time.

Vocabulary Review

A Circle the words that best complete the sentences.

1. The song he sang about his difficult life was very (inspiring / secular).
2. You must (increase / combine) the two sounds to make them harmonious.
3. There are several different (categories / albums) for musicians to win awards in.
4. Kevin could not read the book because he was (illiterate / misunderstood).
5. The child (designer / prodigy) could do feats few other people could.

B Choose the best words to complete the sentences.

1. I would like for you to _____ a brand-new product for me.
   - A increase
   - B decide
   - C experiment
   - D design

2. John was good at many things, so he had a lot of _____.
   - A designs
   - B specialties
   - C compositions
   - D blockbusters

3. The noble returned to spend the night in his _____.
   - A castle
   - B troubadour
   - C epic
   - D genre

4. The _____ trumpet makes a loud sound that many people enjoy.
   - A brass
   - B instrument
   - C wind
   - D sound

5. He has a large _____ of coins from ancient Rome and Greece.
   - A rejection
   - B attitude
   - C collection
   - D explosion

C Choose the words with the closest meanings to the highlighted words.

1 The composer made an alteration to the music she was writing.
   - A a contemporary
   - B an attitude
   - C a change
   - D a specialty

2 Many people recognize Johnny Cash as a great American country singer.
   - A dislike
   - B reward
   - C acknowledge
   - D nominate

3 Sometimes singers experience a tremendous explosion in their popularity.
   - A increase
   - B royalty
   - C form
   - D consciousness

4 In the song, one of the hero's great feats was killing a dragon.
   - A chants
   - B victims
   - C blockbusters
   - D deeds

5 Many modern musicians do not write their own songs.
   - A sing
   - B compose
   - C remember
   - D chant

D Complete the sentences by filling in the blanks with the best words from the list. Change the forms of the words if necessary. Use each word only once.

| result | version | chivalry | countless | televise |

1 The station is planning to _____ the event starting at seven o'clock.
2 Do you know the _____ of the vote for the best singer of the year?
3 The troubadour sang about _____ and knights in shining armor.
4 I believe that there are two different _____ of that song.
5 _____ musicians are trying to become famous with through their songs.

Practice Test

Renaissance Music

04-10

    The Renaissance began in Europe around 1400. It lasted for around 200 years. It came after the Middle Ages. These two periods were very different from each other. Some of the differences were in the music of the Renaissance.

    During the Middle Ages, most music was religious. ■1 People mostly listened to it in churches and cathedrals. ■2 But this changed in the Renaissance. ■3 There was still very much religious music. ■4 But there was a lot of secular music, too. In fact, music became a very important form of entertainment for people. The types of music people played expanded as well.

    Choir music became popular during the Renaissance. Choirs were formed of many people singing together. Madrigals were another popular type of music. There were usually three to six singers for them. Musicians sang emotional songs that were romantic poems.

    Many new musical instruments were introduced during the Renaissance. One of them was the violin. It was created in the 1500s. It became one of the most popular musical instruments in the world over time. Finally, people began to write down music during this period. This allowed music to spread widely.

---

secular *adj* relating to the world and not to religion
form *n* a type; a kind

1 According to paragraph 1, which of the following is NOT true of the Renaissance?
   Ⓐ It was the period after the Middle Ages.
   Ⓑ It lasted longer than the Middle Ages.
   Ⓒ It was different from the Middle Ages.
   Ⓓ It took place in Europe.

2 The word "expanded" in the passage is closest in meaning to
   Ⓐ improved
   Ⓑ appeared
   Ⓒ grew
   Ⓓ started

3 In paragraph 2, the author implies that secular music
   Ⓐ was more common in the Renaissance than in the Middle Ages
   Ⓑ was much harder to play than religious music
   Ⓒ was not entertaining to most people in the Renaissance
   Ⓓ was created by some famous Renaissance composers

4 The word "them" in the passage refers to
   Ⓐ choirs
   Ⓑ madrigals
   Ⓒ three to six singers
   Ⓓ musicians

5 In paragraph 4, the author uses "the violin" as an example of
   Ⓐ an instrument that was used for madrigals
   Ⓑ the first stringed instrument to be made
   Ⓒ a popular instrument in the Middle Ages
   Ⓓ a new musical instrument in the Renaissance

6 According to paragraph 4, music spread in the Renaissance because

- (A) people started writing music down
- (B) more musicians traveled from place to place
- (C) people started learning to play instruments
- (D) more new instruments were made then

7 Look at the four squares [■] that indicate where the following sentence could be added to the passage.

They also listened to and played music at various religious festivals.

Where would the sentence best fit?

Click on a square [■] to add the sentence to the passage.

8 *Directions:* An introductory sentence for a brief summary of the passage is provided below. Complete the summary by selecting the THREE answer choices that express the most important ideas in the passage. *This question is worth 2 points.*

Music in the Renaissance was popular and had many differences from the Middle Ages.

-
-
-

Answer Choices

1. Both choirs and madrigals were common in the Renaissance.
2. In the Renaissance, new instruments such as the violin were made.
3. People enjoyed listening to music in churches and cathedrals.
4. The Renaissance lasted for 200 years after the Middle Ages.
5. The Middle Ages did not have many popular composers of music.
6. Secular music was commonly played in the Renaissance.

CHAPTER 05

Anthropology
(Guessing Unknown Words)

1. Lucy
2. The Stone Age
3. Neanderthals
4. Early Tool Making
5. Margaret Meade
6. The Bering Strait Land Bridge
7. Homo Erectus
8. Hunter-Gatherers

CHAPTER 5 Anthropology (Guessing Unknown Words)

Understanding TOEFL Question Types & Reading Skills

1 Question Types — Vocabulary Questions

Vocabulary questions ask you to determine the meanings of words or phrases in the passage. Many times, a word may have several meanings. The meaning depends upon how the writer uses the word in the passage. Try to recognize how the writer is using a word or phrase. Then you will be able to answer the question correctly.

- **Example Vocabulary Questions**
  - The word "X" in the passage is closest in meaning to ~
  - In stating "X", the author means that ~

- **Useful Tips for Your Success**
  - Remember that → one word may have many meanings.
    → you should be able to substitute the new word into the passage.
  - Don't → simply choose a word's most common meaning.
    → choose an answer just because it looks right.

Sample Question

Folklore

🎧 05-01

Anthropologists study aspects of past human cultures. One way to do this is to inspect a culture's folklore. Folklore can combine many factors. It may include stories, legends, culture, and beliefs. Many contemporary people still pass on folklore to their children today. By learning about some of these traditions and customs, anthropologists can know very much about the past.

aspect [n] a situation; a quality
pass on [phr] to transmit

Q The word "inspect" in the passage is closest in meaning to
Ⓐ relieve
Ⓑ examine
Ⓒ understand
Ⓓ portray

2 Reading Skills — Guessing Unknown Words

Guessing unknown words is determining the meaning of a word from the context of the passage. Many times, you can guess the meaning of a word by looking at the other words in the same sentence or a sentence next to it. Look at these words carefully, and you should be able to guess the unknown word's meaning.

Check-Up

▶ Guess the meaning of the underlined word.

Many <u>contemporary</u> people still pass on folklore to their children today.

Ⓐ modern
Ⓑ wise
Ⓒ elderly
Ⓓ popular

• **Exercise 1** •

Lucy

05-02

One school of thought in anthropology states that humans have evolved from primates. These advancements, of course, must have taken millions of years. Unfortunately, anthropologists were never able to find any proof to back up their claims. This changed in 1974, though, when a team of scientists found Lucy.

Lucy was a humanoid. She was not quite human but something similar. Scientists have put her in the genus *Australopithecus*. Lucy was about one meter high and was a biped, so she could walk erect. More importantly, she was 3.5 million years old. Since then, anthropologists have determined that Lucy was one of the ancient ancestors of modern man. Some believe she is the missing link between apes and humans.

proof [n] evidence   link [n] a connection
biped [n] an animal that can walk on two feet

Q1 The word "evolved" in the passage is closest in meaning to
- Ⓐ changed
- Ⓑ remained
- Ⓒ moved away
- Ⓓ disappeared

Q2 The word "ancestors" in the passage is closest in meaning to
- Ⓐ descendants
- Ⓑ cousins
- Ⓒ relations
- Ⓓ forebears

Reading Skills Guessing Unknown Words

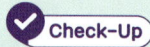 Guess the meaning of the underlined word.

Lucy was about one meter high and was a biped, so she could walk <u>erect</u>.
- Ⓐ sideways
- Ⓑ backward
- Ⓒ upright
- Ⓓ forward

• **Exercise 2** •

The Stone Age

The Stone Age encompassed an incredibly long period of time. It would begin around one million years ago and would end around 3500 B.C. During this time, human culture made a large number of advances.

The most important advance people made was in the use of tools. As the name states, people utilized stone tools during the Stone Age. This was not, however, the only progress people made. Humans had learned about agriculture, so they were able to begin farming the land and raising various crops. Additionally, they domesticated animals, most notably the dog, during this time. They also invented pottery and began to settle in large groups as they had abandoned their hunter-gatherer ways.

utilize v to use
agriculture n farming

pottery n ceramics; containers made of clay or other similar material

Q1 The word "encompassed" in the passage is closest in meaning to
- Ⓐ described
- Ⓑ covered
- Ⓒ revealed
- Ⓓ began

Q2 In stating that humans had "abandoned" their hunter-gatherer ways, the author means that humans
- Ⓐ wanted to change
- Ⓑ stopped
- Ⓒ reconsidered
- Ⓓ tried something different

Reading Skills   Guessing Unknown Words

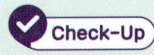 Guess the meaning of the underlined word.

Additionally, they domesticated animals, most notably the dog, during this time.
- Ⓐ learned
- Ⓑ fed
- Ⓒ tamed
- Ⓓ killed

• Exercise 3 •

Neanderthals

05-04

Neanderthals were close relatives of modern humans. They lived around 400,000 years ago. But they died out about 40,000 years ago. They lived mostly in Europe, Asia Minor, and some places in Central Asia.

Neanderthals stood up to around 168 centimeters high. They were much stronger than modern humans. Their brains were also bigger than those of modern humans. Experts believe they were intelligent. They were also capable of speech.

However, when Neanderthals encountered modern humans, they could not compete. Around 5,000 years after modern humans went to Europe, all of the Neanderthals were gone. There might have been wars. The climate undergoing alterations might have affected the Neanderthals, too. Nobody knows exactly why they went extinct.

Asia Minor [n] modern-day Turkey and the land around it   compete [v] to try to win against or to outdo
capable [adj] able to do something

Q1 The word "intelligent" in the passage is closest in meaning to
- Ⓐ smart
- Ⓑ hardworking
- Ⓒ diligent
- Ⓓ impressive

Q2 The word "encountered" in the passage is closest in meaning to
- Ⓐ fought
- Ⓑ introduced
- Ⓒ appeared
- Ⓓ met

Reading Skills   Guessing Unknown Words

 Guess the meaning of the underlined word.

The climate undergoing <u>alterations</u> might have affected the Neanderthals, too.
- Ⓐ changes
- Ⓑ droughts
- Ⓒ warmth
- Ⓓ severeness

• **Exercise 4** •

Early Tool Making

Men have long used tools; however, the nature of these tools has varied over thousands of years. When man first began to make tools, they were with the bones of animals and were not particularly effective.

When the Stone Age began a million years ago, humans could construct tools of stone. These were relatively simple as people would simply slowly chip stones into the shapes they desired. The most common tools were weapons, including tips for weapons like spears or arrows.

Not until the Copper Age did people start making metal tools. This period began around 4000 B.C. The Bronze and Iron ages rapidly followed as humans learned newer, better, and more efficient methods of making tools.

effective adj useful
construct v to make; to manufacture
tip n the sharp end of a weapon

Q1 The word "nature" in the passage is closest in meaning to
Ⓐ description
Ⓑ universe
Ⓒ style
Ⓓ effectiveness

Q2 The word "chip" in the passage is closest in meaning to
Ⓐ melt
Ⓑ tear
Ⓒ cut
Ⓓ repair

Reading Skills Guessing Unknown Words

 Guess the meaning of the underlined word.

These were relatively simple as people would simply slowly chip stones into the <u>shapes</u> they desired.
Ⓐ tools
Ⓑ forms
Ⓒ sizes
Ⓓ angles

• **Exercise 5** •

Margaret Meade

There have been many famous anthropologists over the course of time. One of the most famous was Margaret Meade. Born in 1901 and dying in 1978, Meade helped to bring the study of anthropology into the limelight. Without her, many anthropologists would still be working in anonymity.

Meade wrote a number of books, but her most influential was her first book, called *Coming of Age in Samoa*. This was actually the first of three books in a series about the South Pacific. In the book, she had explored gender roles. She believed culture, not biology, could determine the different roles of men and women.

During her life, Meade's findings were very controversial. Many people strongly supported her work while others were vehemently opposed to it. Since her death, that has not changed. Nevertheless, she remains an important figure in modern anthropology.

anonymity [n] obscurity
influential [adj] significant; powerful
figure [n] a person; a character

Q1 The word "limelight" in the passage is closest in meaning to
- A news
- B university
- C field
- D public eye

Q2 The word "determine" in the passage is closest in meaning to
- A establish
- B alternate
- C abandon
- D decipher

Q3 The word "vehemently" in the passage is closest in meaning to
- A strongly
- B slowly
- C unfortunately
- D somewhat

Reading Skills Guessing Unknown Words

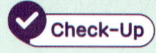 Guess the meaning of the underlined word.

During her life, Meade's findings were very controversial. Many people strongly supported her work while others were vehemently opposed to it.
- A welcome
- B approved of
- C respected
- D divisive

Exercise 6

The Bering Strait Land Bridge

For a long time, anthropologists have acknowledged that the Americas were the last continents people settled. Most of them believe human life began in Africa. From there, it would spread to Asia and Europe and then later to the Americas. They did not, however, know how this happened.

Many of them currently believe they know how early humans settled the Americas. As some believed, these settlers did not sail the Atlantic or Pacific Oceans in boats. Instead, they traversed the Bering Strait Land Bridge. This was a narrow bridge of ice people had crossed between modern-day Siberia and Alaska.

Thousands of years ago, during various ice ages, this bridge connected Asia and North America. However, as temperatures warmed, the water level rose. This caused water to submerge the land bridge, making it vanish. By this time, however, humans had already crossed into the Americas. They would then move all the way down to South America and settle much of the two continents.

settle v to stay; to inhabit
settler n a person who moves to a new place to live; a pioneer
rise v to go up; to increase

Q1 The word "acknowledged" in the passage is closest in meaning to
 Ⓐ known Ⓑ doubted Ⓒ admitted Ⓓ imagined

Q2 The word "traversed" in the passage is closest in meaning to
 Ⓐ swam Ⓑ detoured Ⓒ climbed Ⓓ crossed

Q3 The word "submerge" in the passage is closest in meaning to
 Ⓐ sink Ⓑ melt Ⓒ move Ⓓ transfer

Reading Skills | Guessing Unknown Words

Check-Up Guess the meaning of the underlined word.

This caused water to submerge the land bridge, making it vanish.
 Ⓐ decay Ⓑ disappear Ⓒ evaporate Ⓓ depart

• **Exercise 7** •

Homo Erectus

🎧 05-08

Scientists will usually classify an animal into a genus and species. The genus is the larger group. The species is the more specific categorization. Scientists have named one species of humanoids *Homo erectus*. This was one of the early ancestors of modern man. *Homo* means "man" in Latin, and *erectus* means "upright." Simply put, *Homo erectus* was an early, upright-walking hominoid.

Homo erectus actually looked very much like *Homo sapiens*, "wise man"— the scientific name people have given to humans more modern than *Homo erectus*. First of all, their physical looks are quite similar. This includes the facial structure, height, chest, and length of the arms. *Homo erectus* also had a brain cavity closer in size to *Homo sapiens*.

Finally, scientists have found examples of *Homo erectus* in many places all throughout the world, including Africa, Europe, and Asia. Clearly, like *Homo sapiens*, *Homo erectus* was a wanderer. He lived a nomadic existence and helped populate the world with creatures similar to modern man.

humanoid [n]	a creature similar to a human	cavity [n]	a hole
physical [adj]	relating to the body	wanderer [n]	a nomad; a traveler

Q1 The word "specific" in the passage is closest in meaning to
- Ⓐ precise
- Ⓑ unique
- Ⓒ general
- Ⓓ advanced

Q2 The word "structure" in the passage is closest in meaning to
- Ⓐ size
- Ⓑ arrangement
- Ⓒ coloring
- Ⓓ complexion

Q3 The word "nomadic" in the passage is closest in meaning to
- Ⓐ difficult
- Ⓑ wandering
- Ⓒ crucial
- Ⓓ wonderful

Reading Skills | **Guessing Unknown Words**

 Guess the meaning of the underlined word.

Scientists will usually **classify** an animal into a genus and species.
- Ⓐ sort
- Ⓑ appoint
- Ⓒ award
- Ⓓ replace

• Exercise 8 •

Hunter-Gatherers

Early human societies had no permanent settlements. Instead, the people often wandered from place to place. For this reason, anthropologists have given them the moniker of hunter-gatherers.

As their name suggests, hunter-gatherers survived by using two separate methods. First, they would hunt animals. This was their main method of survival. In fact, this also accounts for their wandering lifestyles. Early hunter-gatherers would often migrate from place to place because they were following packs of animals. Without being able to hunt these animals, they would not have been able to survive.

Gathering was another integral part of their existence. Mostly, they collected fruits, nuts, and berries. They also gathered whatever grains grew wild. This included rice, corn, and wheat.

The hunter-gatherer lifestyle persisted for about two million years. Not until a few thousand years ago, when humans discovered agriculture, did societies begin to settle into permanent locations.

---

permanent adj lasting; forever
account for phr to explain; to justify
lifestyle n a way of living; a routine
wild adj not tame; undomesticated

Q1 The word "moniker" in the passage is closest in meaning to
 Ⓐ classification   Ⓑ name   Ⓒ lifestyle   Ⓓ symbol

Q2 The word "migrate" in the passage is closest in meaning to
 Ⓐ ride   Ⓑ transport   Ⓒ voyage   Ⓓ move

Q3 The word "persisted" in the passage is closest in meaning to
 Ⓐ continued   Ⓑ started   Ⓒ revealed   Ⓓ finished

Reading Skills Guessing Unknown Words

Check-Up Guess the meaning of the underlined word.

Mostly, they collected fruits, nuts, and berries. They also gathered whatever grains grew wild.
 Ⓐ raised   Ⓑ grew   Ⓒ planted   Ⓓ saved

Grammar Point

Auxiliary Verbs

Auxiliary Verb	Uses	Example Sentences
can	- describe a skill or ability - ask for permission	• Folklore can combine many factors. • Can you guess the answer? • Can I go to the restroom?
could	- describe a skill or ability in the past - ask for permission - describe a future possibility	• Humans could construct tools of stone. • Could you get me some water? • I could meet you there tonight.
do, does, did	- used for questions (in the past) - used for negatives (in the past) - used for inversions	• What do you want to do later? • Harry does not enjoy computer games. • Not until the Copper Age did people start to make metal tools.
have, has	- express requirement or obligation - express experience	• You have to finish your homework. • Greg has to call his wife. • Have you ever heard of the story?
may	- express possibility - ask for permission - express a wish	• It may include stories and legends. • May I take a break for a minute? • May you be lucky in your life!
will	- show general truth - use with the future tense	• Scientists will usually classify an animal into a genus and species. • I will see a movie with my friends. • What will you write about?
would	- request permission - describe a continual past action - express uncertainty - express a possibility in the past	• Would you give me a hand? • He would call his dad every morning. • If you were me, what would you do? • It would begin around one million years ago.

Grammar Check-Up

A Choose the correct words.

1 (Can / Have) you tell me what the answer is?

2 Hunter-gatherers (will / would) travel from place to place.

3 The anthropologist (has / will) publish her book in two months.

4 What (did / has) Margaret Meade write about in her books?

5 (Have / Would) you ever read a book on anthropology?

B Choose the correct words for the blanks.

1 *Homo sapiens* _____ not come before *Homo erectus*.
   ⓐ has   ⓑ did   ⓒ will   ⓓ may

2 _____ I talk to you for a minute about this problem?
   ⓐ Will   ⓑ Would   ⓒ May   ⓓ Have

3 We _____ to get to school before eight o'clock.
   ⓐ have   ⓑ could   ⓒ will   ⓓ would

4 In the past, she _____ travel at least once a year.
   ⓐ may   ⓑ can   ⓒ has   ⓓ would

5 Folklore _____ teach ancient people a lot about a culture.
   ⓐ will   ⓑ could   ⓒ have   ⓓ did

C Complete the sentences by filling in the blanks with the best auxiliary verbs in the box. Use each word only once.

| did   could   may   has   will |

1 _____ I go out with my friends for a while?

2 Eric _____ to finish his homework tonight.

3 The students _____ not go on a field trip last week.

4 We _____ watch a movie together this weekend.

5 I _____ play soccer in the past, but I do not do it now.

Vocabulary Review

A Circle the words that best complete the sentences.

1 The water (bridge / **level**) rises when temperatures are warmer.
2 Neanderthals were close (**relatives** / related) of modern humans and other primates.
3 (Culture / **Biology**) is the study of plants and animals.
4 Early humans had (**nomadic** / permanent) lifestyles and constantly wandered around.
5 The shy professor did not like being in the (anonymity / **limelight**) all the time.

B Choose the best words to complete the sentences.

1 Some tribes in South America still hunt by using _____.
   A tips
   B spears
   C settlements
   D animals

2 Most humans were _____ until they learned farming techniques.
   A bipeds
   B primates
   C hunter-gatherers
   D settlers

3 Modern humans have bigger brain _____ than other primates.
   A shapes
   B health
   C cavities
   D looks

4 Many animals that lived in the past have gone _____ and no longer live.
   A extinct
   B endangered
   C rare
   D ancient

5 This unique feature of the culture _____ for thousands of years.
   A migrated
   B meant
   C acknowledged
   D persisted

114

C Choose the words with the closest meanings to the highlighted words.

1. Agriculture was a very important part of life in many early cultures.
   - Ⓐ Farming
   - Ⓑ Tool
   - Ⓒ Crop
   - Ⓓ Age

2. Anthropologists are not really concerned with studying contemporary culture.
   - Ⓐ permanent
   - Ⓑ modern
   - Ⓒ wandering
   - Ⓓ nomadic

3. Very few animals are capable of walking upright.
   - Ⓐ erect
   - Ⓑ influential
   - Ⓒ effective
   - Ⓓ desired

4. Some chimps are able to construct simple tools from bone, wood, and stone.
   - Ⓐ populate
   - Ⓑ submerge
   - Ⓒ encompass
   - Ⓓ make

5. Many primates still live in the jungles of Africa and other place.
   - Ⓐ anthropologists
   - Ⓑ men
   - Ⓒ bipeds
   - Ⓓ apes

D Complete the sentences by filling in the blanks with the best words from the list. Change the forms of the words if necessary. Use each word only once.

| continent | traverse | gender | currently | climate |

1. Humans left Africa and settled in several different _____ over thousands of years.
2. The _____ in places near the equator remains hot all year long.
3. Margaret Meade examined the _____ roles of men and women.
4. They had to _____ the canyon to get to the other side of it.
5. Scientists are _____ studying hundreds of different cultures around the world.

Practice Test

Mummy Making in Ancient Egypt

In ancient Egypt, the weather was hot and dry. It was difficult to bury people because their bodies would not decompose. So thousands of years ago, the Egyptians learned how to make mummies. This process is called mummification.

Mummification allowed the Egyptians to preserve the bodies of the dead. It was a very long process. First, most of the internal organs of the deceased were removed. They were placed in jars. The heart was left in the body though. The body was then covered with natron. This was a kind of salt. It removed all of the moisture from the body. Around seventy days later, the natron was removed, and the body was washed off. Then, it was wrapped in long strips of linen. Amulets and other types of jewelry were added to the body. After that, more linen was wrapped around the body. This completed the process.

The mummy could then be buried. Mummies of pharaohs and their families were often buried in pyramids. ■1 The mummies of wealthy individuals were usually placed in tombs. ■2 In most cases, various treasures were buried along with the mummies. ■3 These included gold, jewelry, weapons, musical instruments, and food and drinks. ■4 The Egyptians believed the deceased would need them in the afterlife.

preserve (v) to save; to keep in good condition
deceased (adj) dead

1 The word "decompose" in the passage is closest in meaning to
   Ⓐ smell bad
   Ⓑ break down
   Ⓒ remove
   Ⓓ disappear

2 According to paragraph 1, people in Egypt made mummies because
   Ⓐ it was important to their religious beliefs
   Ⓑ they wanted to save people's bodies forever
   Ⓒ they felt it was easier than burying them in the desert
   Ⓓ it was hard for them to bury bodies

3 In paragraph 2, why does the author mention "natron"?
   Ⓐ To state that it was added to jars along with internal organs
   Ⓑ To explain how moisture was removed from people's bodies
   Ⓒ To call it a special kind of salt only found in Egypt
   Ⓓ To point out that using it was the last step in mummification

4 Which of the following best expresses the essential information in the highlighted sentence? *Incorrect* answer choices change the meaning in important ways or leave out essential information.
   Ⓐ Bodies were washed with natron and then cleaned off after seventy days.
   Ⓑ In a process that took seventy days, all of the natron was removed from the body.
   Ⓒ It took about seventy days before the natron was removed and the body cleaned.
   Ⓓ The body had to be washed before the natron could be removed from it.

5 The word "These" in the passage refers to
   Ⓐ Wealthy individuals
   Ⓑ Tombs
   Ⓒ Various treasures
   Ⓓ The mummies

6 In paragraph 3, all of the following questions are answered EXCEPT:

- Ⓐ What items were buried in tombs with mummies?
- Ⓑ Why did the Egyptians bury various items with mummies?
- Ⓒ Where were the mummies of pharaohs buried?
- Ⓓ How large were the tombs that wealthy people were buried in?

7 Look at the four squares [■] that indicate where the following sentence could be added to the passage.

Sadly, many of those tombs were later robbed of valuable items, especially the gold.

Where would the sentence best fit?

Click on a square [■] to add the sentence to the passage.

8 *Directions:* An introductory sentence for a brief summary of the passage is provided below. Complete the summary by selecting the THREE answer choices that express the most important ideas in the passage. *This question is worth 2 points.*

The Egyptians made mummies when people died and then buried them in tombs.

-
-
-

Answer Choices

1 The process of making a mummy could take around seventy days.	4 Mummies were often buried with amulets wrapped around their bodies.
2 There were several steps involved in the mummification of a body.	5 Many mummies were buried along with all kinds of valuable items.
3 The Egyptians believed that dead people would go to the afterlife.	6 The Egyptians learned how to make mummies thousands of years ago.

CHAPTER 06

Weather
(Mapping)

1. Weather Fronts
2. Climate
3. El Nino
4. The Tropics
5. Floods and Droughts
6. Winter Weather Conditions
7. Seasonal Changes
8. The Gulf Stream

CHAPTER 6 Weather (Mapping)

Understanding TOEFL Question Types & Reading Skills

1 Question Types — Reference Questions

Reference questions ask you to recognize how some words refer to others in the passage. These questions usually ask about a pronoun and the word or words it refers to. Sometimes the questions ask about other words like *which*, *that*, or *this*. The answer choices will always be a word or words from the passage.

- **Example Reference Questions**
    - The word "X" in the passage refers to ~

- **Useful Tips for Your Success**

    - Make sure
        → you do not confuse feminine and masculine pronouns.
        → you can substitute the answer choice for the pronoun.

    - Don't
        → match a singular pronoun with a plural answer.
        → match a plural pronoun with a singular answer.

Sample Question

Weather Satellites

06-01

People use many methods to predict the weather. One of the best ways is with weather satellites. They orbit the Earth and send back accurate pictures of the planet to meteorologists on the ground. These help weather forecasters make better predictions than using thermometers or barometers. Thanks to satellites, weather forecasting is more accurate than it was in the past.

predict v to forecast; to guess
barometer n a tool that measures the air pressure

Q The word "These" in the passage refers to

Ⓐ Weather forecasts Ⓑ Weather satellites
Ⓒ Accurate pictures Ⓓ Thermometers

2 Reading Skills — Mapping

Mapping is a way to organize information. You draw diagrams to show how all of the ideas in a paragraph or passage relate to each other. When you do this, you can easily notice the connection of each idea to the other.

Check-Up

▸ What is the best answer for the blank below?

Some ways of weather prediction
- Thermometers
- Barometers
- **Weather Satellites**
  - Send pictures of the Earth to meteorologists
  - Can make better _____

Ⓐ predictions Ⓑ pictures Ⓒ satellites Ⓓ thermometers

• **Exercise 1** •

Weather Fronts

🎧 06-02

The weather is constantly changing throughout different places. There are boundaries between different weather conditions. People call them weather fronts. There are several unique kinds of fronts; however, the two most common are warm and cold fronts.

In warm fronts, warm air replaces cold air. Warm fronts sometimes start as thunderstorms, but they usually bring milder weather. They also move more slowly than cold fronts. Finally, warm fronts typically have clear weather following behind them.

In contrast, cold fronts replace warm air in the atmosphere with cold air. They are the fastest moving of all the weather fronts. Cold fronts also bring the most violent weather and always have colder weather following behind them.

front n a zone between two different weather conditions
boundary n a border
thunderstorm n a rainstorm with thunder and lightning

Q1 The word "them" in the passage refers to
Ⓐ different places
Ⓑ boundaries
Ⓒ different weather conditions
Ⓓ weather fronts

Q2 The word "They" in the passage refers to
Ⓐ Warm fronts
Ⓑ Thunderstorms
Ⓒ Cold fronts
Ⓓ Clear weather

Reading Skills **Mapping**

 **Check-Up** What is the best answer for the blank below?

| Weather is constantly changing throughout different places | — | Boundaries between different weather conditions | — | **Weather Fronts** |

Warm Fronts
• start as thunderstorms
• usually bring _____ weather
• clear weather follows behind them

Cold Fronts
• the fastest moving fronts
• bring the most violent weather
• colder weather follows behind them

Other kinds of weather fronts

Ⓐ hot Ⓑ colder Ⓒ milder Ⓓ violent

• Exercise 2 •

Climate

06-03

Most places on the Earth have changing weather and temperature. Over time, people often notice patterns in these changes. Scientists call this climate. The Earth has many climates.

Tropical climates often exist near the equator. They have high temperatures practically all year long. Tropical climates also experience more rainfall than anywhere on the Earth. This can help create areas rich in life. The jungles and the rainforests of Africa and South America exist in tropical climates.

Unlike tropical climates, polar climates are incredibly cold. They usually endure temperatures below freezing for most of the year. They may also have large amounts of snowfall, like near the Arctic Circle. Yet some polar climates, such as Antarctica's, experience almost no snowfall or even rain.

climate n the long-term weather of an area   **tropical** adj very hot and humid   **rich** adj abundant

Q1 The word "This" in the passage refers to
- Ⓐ The equator
- Ⓑ More rainfall
- Ⓒ The Earth
- Ⓓ Life

Q2 The word "They" in the passage refers to
- Ⓐ Tropical climates
- Ⓑ Polar climates
- Ⓒ Temperatures below freezing
- Ⓓ Large amounts of snowfall

Reading Skills | Mapping

Check-Up What is the best answer for the blank below?

Earth has changing weather and temperature → Patterns of changing weather and temperature → **Climate**

Tropical Climates
- exist near _____
- high temperatures and more rainfall
- rich in life
- jungles and rainforests of Africa and South America

Polar Climates
- incredibly cold
- temperatures below freezing
- large amounts of snowfall
- Arctic and Antarctica

Other kinds of climates

- Ⓐ Africa
- Ⓑ the equator
- Ⓒ South America
- Ⓓ the Arctic Circle

Exercise 3

El Nino

Every few years, weather conditions in North and South America change dramatically. Many scientists blame this on El Nino. Unfortunately, they know little about El Nino and its causes.

El Nino is a mysterious weather phenomenon in the Pacific Ocean. The surface water in the tropical Pacific sometimes becomes warmer than normal. This happens because of a combination of factors. The warming then causes the weather to act strangely.

For example, El Nino makes trade winds become weaker. This lets warm water spread throughout the Pacific. So the weather in certain places becomes warmer or colder than normal. They may also experience floods or droughts because of El Nino. In short, it creates many unpredictable weather conditions.

dramatically adv considerably; severely
phenomenon n an event
unpredictable adj random; unable to be guessed

Q1 The word "they" in the passage refers to
- (A) weather conditions
- (B) North and South America
- (C) many scientists
- (D) its causes

Q2 The word "They" in the passage refers to
- (A) Trade winds
- (B) Certain places
- (C) Floods
- (D) Unpredictable weather conditions

Reading Skills — Mapping

Check-Up What is the best answer for the blank below?

Pacific surface water becomes warmer — El Nino
→ Causes weather to act strangely
- _____ become weaker
- Some places have warmer or colder weather
- May have floods or droughts

(A) El Nino (B) Surface water (C) Weather conditions (D) Trade winds

• **Exercise 4** •

The Tropics

🎧 06-05

The equator is the imaginary circle going around the center of the Earth. The tropics are the areas immediately north and south of the equator.

The tropics are usually hotter than other areas on the Earth. Many times, the sun shines straight down on them. This makes the weather generally warm or hot in the tropics all year long. In addition, the tropics usually receive high amounts of rain. Many places have rainy seasons with heavy rainfall.

Many parts of the tropics are covered with rainforests. These can be found in Africa, Asia, and South America. Farther from the equator, there are some tropical deserts. These include the Sahara and the Kalahari.

imaginary adj not real; existing only in the mind
immediately adv directly
shine v to create light

Q1 The word "them" in the passage refers to
- Ⓐ the tropics
- Ⓑ other areas of the Earth
- Ⓒ many times
- Ⓓ high amounts of rain

Q2 The word "These" in the passage refers to
- Ⓐ The tropics
- Ⓑ Rainforests
- Ⓒ Africa, Asia, and South America
- Ⓓ Some tropical deserts

Reading Skills **Mapping**

✓ **Check-Up** What is the best answer for the blank below?

- Are located immediately north and south of the equator

The Tropics

- sun shines straight down
- hotter than other areas on the Earth
- get high amounts of _____

- covered with rainforests
- some tropical deserts

Ⓐ rain   Ⓑ snow   Ⓒ wind   Ⓓ coolness

Chapter ❻ 125

• Exercise 5 •

Floods and Droughts

Water is one of the most important substances for life on the Earth. Because of water, people can survive. However, water can occasionally cause various problems to occur. Two of these are floods and droughts.

Sometimes there is too much water. Most areas throughout the world endure rainy seasons. During them, it often rains heavily for several days. This causes water levels to rise higher than normal. When this happens, floods occur. They can cause enormous damage to the land. Floods often destroy buildings and roads, wash away crops, and sometimes displace or even kill animals, including people.

Meanwhile, sometimes there is not enough rain in a geographical area. Without it, a drought may occur. During a drought, the land becomes dry. Lakes and ponds usually evaporate or experience lower levels. Crops and animals typically die. A drought may last weeks, months, or even years. Only when it rains enough will the drought finally end.

endure [v] to survive; to suffer	displace [v] to move
heavily [adv] very much	evaporate [v] to disappear

Q1 The word "these" in the passage refers to
- Ⓐ the most important substances
- Ⓑ various problems
- Ⓒ floods
- Ⓓ droughts

Q2 The word "them" in the passage refers to

  Ⓐ most areas
  Ⓑ rainy seasons
  Ⓒ several days
  Ⓓ water levels

Q3 The word "it" in the passage refers to

  Ⓐ rain
  Ⓑ a geographical area
  Ⓒ a drought
  Ⓓ the land

Reading Skills Mapping

Check-Up What is the best answer for the blank below?

```
                    Water ── • the most important substance for life
                              • people cannot survive without it
                      │
              Cause various problems
                ╱            ╲
           Floods          Droughts
```

Floods
- during rainy seasons, rains heavily for several days
- water levels rise higher than normal

- cause enormous damage to the land
- destroy buildings and roads
- wash away _____
- displace or even kill animals, including people

Droughts
- not enough rain in a geographical area

- the land becomes dry
- lakes and ponds evaporate or experience lower levels
- crops and animals die
- may last weeks, months, or even years

  Ⓐ crops   Ⓑ animals   Ⓒ individuals   Ⓓ homes

• Exercise 6 •

Winter Weather Conditions

In many places, winter causes severe weather conditions. These can include colder weather and different forms of precipitation. This can create dangerous conditions for people because of the moisture.

Snow is the best-known form of winter precipitation. Snow is simply frozen water. It falls to the ground as six-sided crystals, but it can only fall when the temperature is below freezing.

Sleet is similar to snow, yet it falls to the ground as ice. Sleet begins as snow; however, as it falls to the earth, it passes through air with above-freezing temperatures. This melts the snow and turns it into rain. As it continues falling, it refreezes by going through air with below-freezing temperatures.

Both snow and sleet are dangerous for several reasons. They produce slippery conditions for drivers and therefore help cause many accidents. People exposed to them may suffer severe injuries. They can also damage property if too much falls.

precipitation n rain; snow
freezing n the temperature at which water becomes ice
refreeze v to freeze again
slippery adj icy; slick

Q1 The word "This" in the passage refers to
Ⓐ Winter
Ⓑ Colder weather
Ⓒ Precipitation
Ⓓ The moisture

Q2 The word "it" in the passage refers to

Ⓐ the earth
Ⓑ air
Ⓒ the snow
Ⓓ rain

Q3 The word "them" in the passage refers to

Ⓐ both snow and sleet
Ⓑ several reasons
Ⓒ drivers
Ⓓ many accidents

Reading Skills Mapping

Check-Up What is the best answer for the blank below?

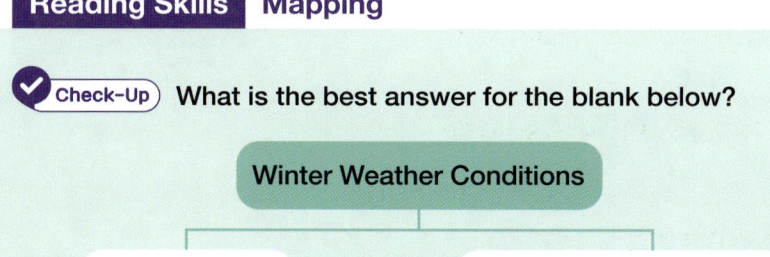

Ⓐ snow　　　Ⓑ water　　　Ⓒ ice　　　Ⓓ rain

Exercise 7

Seasonal Changes

🎧 06-08

The Earth's temperate zones experience seasonal changes throughout the year. These comprise the biggest areas on the planet. The Earth has four different seasons: spring, summer, autumn, and winter. Each season has its own distinct weather, and each lasts approximately four months each year.

As the Earth orbits the sun, it spins on its axis. However, it tilts to the side. Because of this tilting, the sun's rays hit the Earth at different angles. When the sun's rays strike the Earth straight on, the weather is hotter. This causes summer temperatures. When the sun's rays hit the Earth at an angle, it becomes colder, so winter occurs.

While traveling around the sun, different parts of the Earth tilt toward and away from the sun. Therefore the seasons constantly change. In addition, the Northern and Southern hemispheres always experience opposite weather conditions. So when it is summer in the Northern Hemisphere, the Southern Hemisphere experiences winter.

temperate adj mild
distinct adj unique; individual
orbit v to rotate; to go around something
tilt v to lean; to slope

Q1 The word "These" in the passage refers to
- Ⓐ The Earth's temperate zones
- Ⓑ Seasonal changes
- Ⓒ The biggest areas
- Ⓓ Four different seasons

Q2 The first word "it" in the passage refers to

- Ⓐ the Earth
- Ⓑ the sun
- Ⓒ the side
- Ⓓ the weather

Q3 The second word "it" in the passage refers to

- Ⓐ the side
- Ⓑ the Earth
- Ⓒ an angle
- Ⓓ winter

Reading Skills Mapping

Check-Up What is the best answer for the blank below?

```
                    Seasonal Changes

              The Earth spins on its side

     The sun's _____ hit the Earth      Different parts of the Earth tilt at
     at different angles                different times

  Rays hit straight   Rays hit at an    Makes the          Makes the Northern and
  on the Earth in    angle in winter    seasons change     Southern hemispheres
  the summer                                               experience opposite
                                                          weather conditions
```

- Ⓐ seasons
- Ⓑ light
- Ⓒ rays
- Ⓓ energy

• Exercise 8 •

The Gulf Stream

All oceans have currents. These act like rivers inside an ocean. Currents have tremendous effects on the climates of the regions they pass through. The Gulf Stream is one such current.

The Gulf Stream is located primarily in the Atlantic Ocean. It begins in the Gulf of Mexico. But the Gulf Stream quickly leaves it, enters the Atlantic, and follows the coast of the eastern United States northward to Newfoundland, Canada. Then, it moves across the Atlantic Ocean, going toward both northern Europe and western Africa.

The Gulf Stream has many effects on the weather. It makes many places' weather warmer than usual in winter. The Gulf Stream does this by carrying warm water from the Gulf of Mexico. This actually helps affect the weather. For that reason, numerous coastal areas in the eastern U.S. are warmer than areas twenty miles inland. Likewise, islands near the Gulf Stream, such as Bermuda and Martha's Vineyard, have milder climates than other areas at similar latitudes.

primarily adv mostly; largely
coastal adj relating to the coast
milder adj gentler
latitude n the distance north or south of the equator something is

Q1 The word "they" in the passage refers to
Ⓐ rivers
Ⓑ currents
Ⓒ the climates
Ⓓ the regions

Q2 The word "it" in the passage refers to

- Ⓐ the Atlantic Ocean
- Ⓑ the Gulf of Mexico
- Ⓒ the Gulf Stream
- Ⓓ the coast

Q3 The word "This" in the passage refers to

- Ⓐ Winter
- Ⓑ The Gulf Stream
- Ⓒ Warm water
- Ⓓ The Gulf of Mexico

Reading Skills Mapping

 **Check-Up** What is the best answer for the blank below?

Currents
- act like rivers inside an ocean
- tremendous effects on the climates

One of the currents in the world

The Gulf Stream

- located in the Atlantic Ocean
- begins in the Gulf of Mexico
- follows the coast of the eastern United States _____ to Newfoundland, Canada
- moves across the Atlantic Ocean

Many effects on the weather

- makes many places' weather warmer than usual in winter
- numerous coastal areas in the eastern U.S. are warmer than areas twenty miles inland
- Bermuda and Martha's Vineyard have milder climates than other areas at similar latitudes

Ⓐ southward   Ⓑ northward   Ⓒ eastward   Ⓓ westward

Grammar Point

Comparatives and Superlatives

1 Use **comparatives** to describe the similarities or differences between two things. Form comparatives in two ways.

- adjective + -er

big → bigger	sunny → sunnier
nice → nicer	hot → hotter
pretty → prettier	fast → faster

- more + adjective

handsome → more handsome
interesting → more interesting
accurate → more accurate

- Warm fronts are milder than cold fronts.
- Tropical climates are hotter than temperate climates.
- Hurricanes are more violent than rainstorms.
- Weather forecasting is more accurate than it was in the past.

2 Use **superlatives** to describe the similarities or differences between three or more things. Form superlatives in two ways.

- the + adjective + -est

sharp → the sharpest	cold → the coldest
high → the highest	swift → the swiftest
fast → fastest	low → the lowest

- the most + adjective

important → the most important
unique → the most unique
violent → the most violent

- They are the fastest moving of all the weather fronts.
- Mr. Everest is the highest mountain in the world.
- Water is one of the most important substances for life on the Earth.
- Cold fronts also bring the most violent weather.

3 Use **as ~ as** to show that two things are the same. Use **not as ~ as** to show that two things are not the same.

- The barometer is as useful as the thermometer.
- A thunderstorm is not as deadly as a tornado.
- The weather in spring is not as cold as the weather in the winter.

Grammar Check-Up

A Circle the comparative forms of adjectives and underline the superlative forms.

more violent	milder	most useful	deadlier
swiftest	highest	more tremendous	warmest
most different	bigger	colder	most severe
more important	nearer	weakest	most unique

B Choose the correct words.
1 The Gulf Stream has (a greater / the greatest) effect than other ocean currents.
2 Floods are typically (more severe / the most severe) than droughts.
3 Water is (more important / the most important) substance for life.
4 A thermometer is (more useful / the most useful) than a barometer to most people.
5 The (faster / fastest) moving of all the weather fronts is a cold front.

C Check (✔) the correct sentences.
1 ☐ Winter weather such as snow and ice can cause the most severe driving conditions.
2 ☐ Weather satellites predict the weather best than people on the ground can.
3 ☐ Warm fronts create more milder weather than cold fronts do.
4 ☐ El Nino brings more unpredictable weather than other phenomena.
5 ☐ Tropical climates are warmer than the climates in other areas.

D Choose the correct words for the blanks.
1 A typhoon is often _____ than a thunderstorm.
   ⓐ violent   ⓑ violenter   ⓒ more violent   ⓓ the most violent
2 Weather satellites are _____ tool for predicting the weather.
   ⓐ useful   ⓑ more useful   ⓒ usefuller   ⓓ the most useful
3 The water in the Gulf Stream is _____ than the water in the Arctic Ocean.
   ⓐ warmer   ⓑ the warmer   ⓒ more warm   ⓓ the more warm
4 Polar climates have the _____ weather in the entire world.
   ⓐ cold   ⓑ colder   ⓒ coldest   ⓓ most cold

Vocabulary Review

A Circle the words that best complete the sentences.

1 Because of the (flood / drought), there was not enough water in the lakes.
2 Tornadoes can sometimes act in (unpredictable / slippery) manners.
3 Try to avoid getting (refrozen / exposed) to cold weather for a long time.
4 Too much (condition / precipitation) can cause floods to occur in an area.
5 The (equator / tropics) is an imaginary line that goes around the center of the Earth.

B Choose the best words to complete the sentences.

1 Which _____ of weather prediction does that person use?
   A method
   B effect
   C level
   D change

2 The water at the _____ is warmer than the water near the bottom of the ocean.
   A surface
   B climate
   C jungle
   D rainforest

3 The temperature is different depending upon which _____ a person is in.
   A front
   B equator
   C precipitation
   D zone

4 People began to move towns _____ to get away from the typhoon on the coast.
   A immediate
   B inland
   C accurate
   D tremendous

5 The sun's rays hit the Earth at different _____ all throughout the year.
   A hemispheres
   B axes
   C angles
   D conditions

C Choose the words with the closest meanings to the highlighted words.

1. During winter, many parts of Russia experience freezing weather conditions.
   - Ⓐ tropical
   - Ⓑ mysterious
   - Ⓒ polar
   - Ⓓ severe

2. The weather is going to be rainy for the next several days.
   - Ⓐ stormy
   - Ⓑ coastal
   - Ⓒ accurate
   - Ⓓ similar

3. The weather satellite is orbiting high above the Earth.
   - Ⓐ axis
   - Ⓑ planet
   - Ⓒ current
   - Ⓓ boundary

4. The hurricane may strike the land in the next couple of hours.
   - Ⓐ destroy
   - Ⓑ damage
   - Ⓒ endure
   - Ⓓ hit

5. We are experiencing some very mild weather this winter.
   - Ⓐ tropical
   - Ⓑ pleasant
   - Ⓒ seasonal
   - Ⓓ changing

D Complete the sentences by filling in the blanks with the best words from the list. Change the forms of the words if necessary. Use each word only once.

| current | slippery | thunderstorm | hemisphere | rainfall |

1. People call the bottom half of the Earth the Southern _____.
2. There are many different _____ flowing through all of the Earth's oceans.
3. This part of Africa gets a lot of _____ during the summer months.
4. When it snows or sleets, the ground can often become very _____.
5. A _____ is usually much more violent than a simple rainstorm.

Practice Test

Tornadoes

The Earth's weather produces many violent storms. These can include blizzards, hurricanes, typhoons, and cyclones. But one of the most destructive events nature produces is the tornado. A tornado is air that rotates very swiftly in a circle while keeping in contact with the ground. Tornadoes are traumatic events and can cause incredible amounts of damage to land, buildings, and human lives.

Tornadoes often form during thunderstorms although they may appear in less violent weather. They are typically small in size and often have winds rotating at around 130 miles per hour or less. These tornadoes may only be on the ground for a mile or two before they simply disappear. There are thousands of these tornadoes every year. In fact, people are unable to document every case of a tornado appearing simply because they fail to do much damage or they happen in areas where there are no people.

However, there are times when tornadoes may attain wind speeds of more than 300 miles per hour, may stretch for a mile in length, and may stay on the ground for fifty, sixty, or even 100 miles. These super tornadoes can cause millions of dollars in damage and take the lives of hundreds of individuals.

Tornadoes have appeared in all of the world's continents except for Antarctica; however, they most usually occur in the United States. They are particularly common in the Southeast and Midwest parts of the country, appearing most often during the thunderstorms that hit these areas in springtime. **1** Due to their extreme frequency, radar centers keep a look out for tornadoes and are quick to alert local residents when one appears. **2** This has, in recent years, kept the number of lives lost at a minimum. **3** However, tornadoes remain a frequent and deadly product of nature. **4**

---

destructive adj very damaging **document** v to make note of; to record

1   In paragraph 1, why does the author mention "blizzards"?

   Ⓐ To give an example of a powerful storm
   Ⓑ To note they are stronger than hurricanes
   Ⓒ To compare them with tornadoes
   Ⓓ To argue they are less dangerous than tornadoes

2   According to paragraph 1, which of the following is true of tornadoes?

   Ⓐ They are more common than blizzards.
   Ⓑ They always kill many people.
   Ⓒ They can cause injuries to people.
   Ⓓ They do not move very quickly.

3   According to paragraph 2, which of the following is NOT true of tornadoes?

   Ⓐ They are not usually very big.
   Ⓑ Thousands of them occur each year.
   Ⓒ They only form during thunderstorms.
   Ⓓ People do not know about all of them.

4   The word "attain" in the passage is closest in meaning to

   Ⓐ stop
   Ⓑ create
   Ⓒ blow
   Ⓓ reach

5   Which of the following best expresses the essential information in the highlighted sentence? *Incorrect* answer choices change the meaning in important ways or leave out essential information.

   Ⓐ Super tornadoes cause more damage and kill more people than any other storms.
   Ⓑ Super tornadoes might kill many people and cause a lot of damage to property.
   Ⓒ Hundreds of people died, and much property was damaged in the last super tornado.
   Ⓓ A super tornado once killed hundreds of people and damaged a lot of their property.

6 The word "alert" in the passage is closest in meaning to

- (A) talk to
- (B) warn
- (C) call
- (D) await

7 Look at the four squares [■] that indicate where the following sentence could be added to the passage.

In fact, there is a part of the country called Tornado Alley because so many tornadoes occur there.

Where would the sentence best fit?

Click on a square [■] to add the sentence to the passage.

8 *Directions:* Complete the table below to summarize information about tornadoes discussed in the passage. Match the appropriate statements to the characteristics and effects of tornadoes with which they are associated. *This question is worth 3 points.*

TORNADOES

Characteristics

Effects

STATEMENTS

Select 2
•
•

Select 3
•
•
•

Statements

1. They often do damage to buildings and homes.
2. Many radar centers look out for tornadoes.
3. They may kill hundreds of people at times.
4. It is impossible for people to know about every tornado strike.
5. They can get to speeds of several hundred miles per hour.
6. They are usually on the ground for a few miles.
7. They can harm the land they set down on.

CHAPTER 07

Geology
(Identifying Cohesive Devices)

1. The Properties of Gold
2. Alfred Wegener and Continental Drift
3. Coal
4. Caves
5. Strip Mining
6. The Layers of the Earth
7. The Pacific Ring of Fire
8. Glaciation

CHAPTER 7 **Geology** (Identifying Cohesive Devices)

Understanding TOEFL Question Types & Reading Skills

1 Question Types — Sentence Simplification & Insert Text Questions

- *Sentence Simplification questions* ask you to look at a sentence from the passage. Then, you must choose a shorter version of the sentence that has the same meaning. You need to recognize which words are important and which ones you can omit from the sentence.

- *Insert Text questions* ask you to look at a sentence not in the passage. You must then decide where in the passage you could include the new sentence. For this question, you should be able to understand how ideas logically connect to each other.

● Example Sentence Simplification & Insert Text Question

- Which of the following best expresses the essential information in the highlighted sentence? *Incorrect* answer choices change the meaning in important ways or leave out essential information.

- Look at the four squares [■] that indicate where the following sentence could be added to the passage.

[You will see a sentence in bold.]

Where would the sentence best fit?

Click on a square [■] to add the sentence to the passage.

● Useful Tips for Your Success

- Learn to
  - → identify synonyms of various words.
  - → recognize important connector words.

- Don't
  - → choose answers that only provide half of a sentence's meaning.
  - → insert sentences where they make no sense logically.

Sample Question

Earthquakes

Deep underground, the Earth has countless faults. These cracks occasionally move. When this happens, an earthquake will occur, and the ground will begin shaking back and forth. Earthquakes vary in their size and magnitude. <mark>Sometimes people scarcely notice their effects, yet other times earthquakes shake the ground for a long period while causing tremendous damage both to life and property.</mark>

fault *n* a crack; a fissure   **scarcely** *adv* hardly; barely

Q Which of the following best expresses the essential information in the highlighted sentence? *Incorrect* answer choices change the meaning in important ways or leave out essential information.

- Ⓐ People might not notice minor earthquakes, but bigger ones can kill people and destroy buildings.
- Ⓑ Most earthquakes go unnoticed by people even though they can occasionally destroy property.
- Ⓒ Earthquakes typically last a long time, so they can kill many people and destroy their homes.
- Ⓓ In most cases, people do not pay attention to earthquakes since they do not cause much.

2 Reading Skills — Identifying Cohesive Devices

Identifying cohesive devices is an important skill that shows how writers connect different ideas. These cohesive devices allow readers to understand how one idea leads to another. When writers use these ideas, they make their passages more logical and easier to understand.

Check-Up

▶ Choose the best conjunctions in the box below to complete the sentences.

since   before   and   when

These cracks occasionally move. _____ this happens, an earthquake will occur, _____ the ground will begin shaking back and forth.

Chapter **7**   143

• Exercise 1 •

The Properties of Gold

Gold is one of the most precious, yet rarest, elements on the Earth. Because of its value, people have historically used gold as a monetary unit. Gold, however, has many other vital properties, so people use it for very many reasons.

For one, gold is a superb conductor of electricity. Copper and silver actually conduct electricity and heat better. However, gold does not tarnish, so it is more valuable than them in the electronics industry.

1 Gold is also a very malleable element, so people can beat it into many various shapes quite easily. **2** Doctors have used gold effectively in medicine. **3** For example, many dentists use gold for tooth fillings. **4** Other doctors use it for hearing implants in people's ears.

precious adj valuable; expensive
conduct v to move; to transfer
tarnish v to become dull; to become discolored

Q1 Which of the following best expresses the essential information in the highlighted sentence? *Incorrect* answer choices change the meaning in important ways or leave out essential information.

- Ⓐ Gold has several characteristics that help to make it unique.
- Ⓑ Besides money, there are several other reasons people use gold.
- Ⓒ A person with some gold can use it for many different things.
- Ⓓ Gold's characteristics give it many different important uses.

Q2 Look at the four squares [■] that indicate where the following sentence could be added to the passage.

In fact, it has many uses in the healthcare industry.

Where would the sentence best fit?

Reading Skills — Identifying Cohesive Devices

✓ **Check-Up** In the passage, the pronoun "them" in the sentence, "However, gold does not tarnish, so it is more valuable than them in the electronics industry," refers to _____.

- Ⓐ conductor
- Ⓑ copper and silver
- Ⓒ electricity and heat
- Ⓓ electronics industry

• **Exercise 2** •

Alfred Wegener and Continental Drift

People are familiar with maps of the Earth showing seven different continents. However, in the past, there was only one large continent. The reason there are seven continents now is continental drift.

In 1915, the geologist Alfred Wegener published his book *On the Origin of Continents and Oceans*. ■1 He believed there was only one continent in the past. ■2 He called it Pangaea. ■3 He theorized that the upper part of the Earth, the crust, was constantly moving. ■4 So this was the reason Pangaea broke up. Wegener thought it took millions of years for the continents to move apart.

At first, many people refused to accept Wegener's research. However, many geologists continued his research. Now, most people accept that continental drift actually happened.

drift n a movement   **theorize** v to state an opinion   **accept** v to believe as true

Q1 Look at the four squares [■] that indicate where the following sentence could be added to the passage.

His book contained all the research he had conducted over several years.

Where would the sentence best fit?

Q2 Which of the following best expresses the essential information in the highlighted sentence? *Incorrect* answer choices change the meaning in important ways or leave out essential information.

Ⓐ Even today, most people doubt continental drift.
Ⓑ There is not enough proof to support continental drift.
Ⓒ The majority of people believe in continental drift.
Ⓓ Continental drift most likely occurred.

Reading Skills | **Identifying Cohesive Devices**

✓ **Check-Up** Choose the best conjunctions in the box below to complete the sentences.

| so   also   or   however |

1 People are familiar with maps of the Earth showing seven different continents. _____, in the past, there was only one large continent.

2 He theorized that the upper part of the Earth, the crust, was constantly moving. _____ this was the reason Pangaea broke up.

Chapter ❼   145

• **Exercise 3** •

Coal

One common type of fossil fuel is coal. It is a hard, dark-colored rock that formed from peat. Coal is a type of sedimentary rock that was created over the course of millions of years.

There are several types of coal. Each one formed under different conditions. Anthracite is the darkest and hardest coal. **1** It burns for the longest time. **2** Lignite is brown coal that is burned to create electricity. **3** Bituminous coal is another type of coal often used to make electricity. **4** Today, coal is widely used around the world. People use it both to heat buildings and to create electricity. However, burning coal creates pollution, so people hope to reduce the amount of it burned in the future.

fossil fuel n a type of organic material such as oil or gas that can be burned to make energy
peat n decayed plant matter found in damp place
pollution n something that makes the ground, air, or water dirty

Q1 Which of the following best expresses the essential information in the highlighted sentence? *Incorrect* answer choices change the meaning in important ways or leave out essential information.

Ⓐ Most kinds of sedimentary rock such as coal form over millions of years.
Ⓑ One type of sedimentary rock is called coal.
Ⓒ There are many types of coal that form over a long period of time.
Ⓓ It took millions of years for coal, a sedimentary rock, to form.

Q2 Look at the four squares [■] that indicate where the following sentence could be added to the passage.

That is why it is mostly used for heating homes and businesses.

Where would the sentence best fit?

Reading Skills Identifying Cohesive Devices

✓ **Check-Up** In the passage, the pronoun "it" in the sentence, "However, burning coal creates pollution, so people hope to reduce the amount of it burned in the future," refers to _____.

Ⓐ coal
Ⓑ pollution
Ⓒ the amount
Ⓓ the future

• **Exercise 4** •

Caves

07-05

A cave is an underground area with an absence of rock or soil. Typically, caves are big enough for people to move through and explore. Some cave systems can stretch for hundreds of miles underneath the ground.

■1 Caves form in several ways. ■2 One common manner is for surface water to sink below the ground and to dissolve or wash away the soil. ■3 This often creates a void, thereby establishing a cave. ■4 Sometimes caves form simply by the spaces in between falling rocks. Another regular way is for lava from volcanoes to cool while leaving spaces in between the rocks. Altogether, there are thousands of caves throughout the Earth. Many have been explored; nevertheless, many more have not yet been discovered.

absence n a lack
dissolve v to break up

lava n the hot, melted rock that comes from a volcano

Q1 Look at the four squares [■] that indicate where the following sentence could be added to the passage.

One can often find caves formed this way in limestone, a very soft kind of rock.

Where would the sentence best fit?

Q2 Which of the following best expresses the essential information in the highlighted sentence? *Incorrect* answer choices change the meaning in important ways or leave out essential information.

Ⓐ Volcanic rocks sometimes force lava to make caves.
Ⓑ Volcanoes regularly erupt and cause caves to form.
Ⓒ Because of spaces in between rocks, volcanoes have many caves.
Ⓓ Sometimes cooling lava leaves gaps that create caves.

Reading Skills   **Identifying Cohesive Devices**

✓ Check-Up Choose the best conjunctions in the box below to complete the sentences.

> nevertheless   therefore   since   and

1 One common manner is for surface water to sink below the ground _____ to dissolve or wash away the soil.

2 Many have been explored; _____, many more have not yet been discovered.

Chapter ❼   147

• Exercise 5 •

Strip Mining

Throughout history, miners have used many methods to extract valuable minerals and ores from the ground. One such method of mining is strip mining.

Strip mining is common when the mineral being mined is near the surface. One such mineral is coal. First, the miners simply remove the top layer of the soil. ■1 Miners might do this with explosives or simply by digging up the ground. ■2 This exposes the desired mineral, so miners can easily access it. ■3 However, after the mining is complete, the ground is often completely bare, making it useless. ■4

In the past, miners simply left the land alone and did nothing to rehabilitate it. However, nowadays, thanks to government regulations, mining companies must restore the land to make it useful. This will enable people to make use of the land in the future.

extract (v) to remove	bare (adj) naked; nude
expose (v) to uncover	rehabilitate (v) to repair; to restore

Q1 Which of the following best expresses the essential information in the highlighted sentence in paragraph 1? *Incorrect* answer choices change the meaning in important ways or leave out essential information.

Ⓐ There is only one way to mine the ground for minerals and ores.
Ⓑ Miners are still looking for the best method to mine the Earth.
Ⓒ Miners use the same way to mine each kind of mineral and ore.
Ⓓ People have mined the Earth in many different ways over time.

Q2 Look at the four squares [■] that indicate where the following sentence could be added to the passage.

Sometimes they have to use heavy equipment to dig up such big area of land.

Where would the sentence best fit?

Q3 Which of the following best expresses the essential information in the highlighted sentence in paragraph 3? *Incorrect* answer choices change the meaning in important ways or leave out essential information.

    Ⓐ Government regulations exist to control mining companies' actions.
    Ⓑ Mining companies must return the land to its original state because of the law.
    Ⓒ Without various laws, mining companies would not ever restore the land.
    Ⓓ Mining companies do not need laws to make them restore the land.

Reading Skills | **Identifying Cohesive Devices**

Check-Up In the passage, the pronoun "it" in the sentence, "However, after the mining is complete, the ground is often completely bare, making it useless," refers to _____.

    Ⓐ mineral
    Ⓑ mining
    Ⓒ ground
    Ⓓ past

• **Exercise 6** •

The Layers of the Earth

Billions of years ago when the Earth formed, it divided into three distinct layers. Geologists call them the crust, the mantle, and the core; however, scientists only learned about them in the twentieth century. During the past hundred years, they have discovered numerous facts about each layer.

1 The crust, the outermost layer, is anywhere from five to 100 kilometers thick. **2** Everything on Earth's surface comprises part of the crust. **3** Over time, many elements and minerals combined to form it. **4**

The second layer is the mantle. It sometimes is up to 2,900 kilometers thick in places. Heavier metals, such as iron and magnesium, form much of the mantle. It is extremely hot and even moves around occasionally.

1 The innermost layer of the Earth is the core. **2** Actually, it has two parts, the outer core and the inner core. **3** The outer core is liquid because of all the heat and pressure that deep; however, the inner core, made of iron and nickel, is solid. **4**

---

distinct adj different
core n a center
comprise v to make up; to compose
innermost adj deepest

Q1 Which of the following best expresses the essential information in the highlighted sentence? *Incorrect* answer choices change the meaning in important ways or leave out essential information.

- Ⓐ Scientists finally learned about the three parts of the Earth in the last century.
- Ⓑ Geologists know about three parts of the Earth and suspect there may be more.
- Ⓒ In the twentieth century, geologists began to research the crust, the mantle, and the core.
- Ⓓ Geologists know the crust, the mantle, and the core formed during the twentieth century.

Q2 Look at the four squares [■] in paragraph 2 that indicate where the following sentence could be added to the passage.

However, it is usually less thick under the ocean and thicker on land.

Where would the sentence best fit?

Q3 Look at the four squares [■] in paragraph 4 that indicate where the following sentence could be added to the passage.

Of course, no one has ever been to the core because the pressure there would instantly kill a person.

Where would the sentence best fit?

Reading Skills — Identifying Cohesive Devices

Check-Up Choose the best conjunctions in the box below to complete the sentences.

> when   and   because   however

1 Billions of years ago _____ the Earth formed, it divided into three distinct layers.

2 It is extremely hot _____ even moves around occasionally.

• Exercise 7 •

The Pacific Ring of Fire

The Earth's crust is not one complete structure. Instead, many plates have combined to form it. These plates meet one another at locations called faults. Faults are typically geologically unsteady, so many volcanoes have formed, and earthquakes occur near geographical faults. One area with an enormous number of both of these is the Pacific Ring of Fire.

Several faults comprise the Ring of Fire. The best-known one is the San Andreas Fault in California. ■ However, the Ring of Fire is not just in the United States. ■ Actually, it begins in New Zealand, moves north and west toward Indonesia, and then heads north through the Philippines and Japan. ■ It proceeds across the Pacific Ocean into Alaska and subsequently moves southward through North, Central, and South America. ■

There are over 400 volcanoes in the Ring of Fire. Additionally, more than 80% of the Earth's earthquakes happen there. Because of the many faults in the Ring of Fire, the land it covers is quite unstable.

---

unsteady adj unstable
head v to move; to go
proceed v to continue
quite adv very; pretty

Q1 Which of the following best expresses the essential information in the highlighted sentence in paragraph 1? *Incorrect* answer choices change the meaning in important ways or leave out essential information.

Ⓐ An unsteady fault under the ground can cause a volcano to form near it.
Ⓑ The volcanoes and the earthquakes located near faults make them unsteady.
Ⓒ Earthquakes are very common near faults, but volcanoes are not.
Ⓓ Volcanoes form, and earthquakes happen because of unsteady faults.

Q2 Look at the four squares [■] that indicate where the following sentence could be added to the passage.

People know more about it than other faults because of all the severe earthquakes it causes there.

Where would the sentence best fit?

Q3 Which of the following best expresses the essential information in the highlighted sentence in paragraph 3? *Incorrect* answer choices change the meaning in important ways or leave out essential information.

- Ⓐ The faults in the Pacific Ring of Fire help to increase its stability.
- Ⓑ The Pacific Ring of Fire is unstable because of all of its faults.
- Ⓒ The faults are expanding all throughout the Pacific Ring of Fire.
- Ⓓ Because it is unstable, the Pacific Ring of Fire has many faults.

Reading Skills Identifying Cohesive Devices

Check-Up In the passage, the pronoun "It" in the sentence, "It proceeds across the Pacific Ocean into Alaska and subsequently moves southward through North, Central, and South America." refers to _____.

- Ⓐ the Pacific Ring of Fire
- Ⓑ the United States
- Ⓒ New Zealand
- Ⓓ Indonesia

• Exercise 8 •

Glaciation

The Earth's temperature is constantly changing. Sometimes it enters periods of extreme cooling called ice ages. **1** In fact, many currently believe the planet is still in a minor ice age. **2** One feature of ice ages is glaciers. **3** These are enormous accumulations of ice on land. **4** Glaciers can be incredibly long, stretching for miles, and they even move, either going forward or backward.

As temperatures fall, glaciers expand. This is glaciation. Glaciers typically expand only a few inches a day, but in severe cases, they have increased by more than 100 feet a day. They are incredibly thick, so their ice weighs thousands of tons. Therefore, glaciation can dramatically affect the land a glacier covers. For example, glaciers once covered much of the American Midwest. **1** As they receded, they flattened the land. **2** They also carved great holes in the ground. **3** Presently, because of glaciers, the Midwest is flat with few hills or mountains while countless lakes dot the land. **4**

---

minor adj small
feature n a characteristic
expand v to become larger
recede v to move back; to become smaller

Q1 Look at the four squares [■] in paragraph 1 that indicate where the following sentence could be added to the passage.

Many animal species often become extinct in these periods since they cannot handle the extremely cold weather.

Where would the sentence best fit?

Q2 Look at the four squares [■] in paragraph 2 that indicate where the following sentence could be added to the passage.

Some of the bigger holes became the Great Lakes between the United States and Canada.

Where would the sentence best fit?

Q3 Which of the following best expresses the essential information in the highlighted sentence? *Incorrect* answer choices change the meaning in important ways or leave out essential information.

- Ⓐ Glaciers dramatically changed the way the Midwest looks today.
- Ⓑ There are no more glaciers anywhere in the American Midwest.
- Ⓒ The Midwest is a land of few hills but many lakes.
- Ⓓ The glaciers in the Midwest created many hills, mountains, and lakes.

Reading Skills   Identifying Cohesive Devices

Check-Up Choose the best conjunctions in the box below to complete the sentences.

> because   therefore   but   as

1 _____ temperatures fall, glaciers expand.
2 They are incredibly thick, so their ice weighs thousands of tons. _____, glaciation can dramatically affect the land a glacier covers.

Grammar Point

Tenses

Verb Tense	Formation	Example Sentences
Present simple	verb / verb + -s	• The Earth has countless faults. • The weather changes every day. • Snow falls in the winter. • We usually swim in the lake.
Past simple	verb + -ed / irregular	• She predicted the weather. • I attended school yesterday. • Miners simply left the land alone. • No one went to the presentation.
Future simple	will + verb	• An earthquake will occur, and the ground will begin shaking back and forth. • Diamonds will then often rise to the surface. • Will you take a break soon?
Present perfect	have / has + p.p.	• Doctors have used gold effectively in medicine. • They have cost the most money. • She has thought of the answer. • They have purchased some supplies.
Present continuous	be + verb -ing	• It is raining outside. • I am putting on my shirt. • When are they finishing their work?
Past continuous	was / were + verb -ing	• She was shopping yesterday afternoon. • I was sleeping early this morning. • We were taking the train earlier.
Future continuous	will be + verb -ing	• I will be meeting you soon. • It will be snowing in ten minutes. • What will you be doing at five o'clock?

Grammar Check-Up

A Choose the correct words.

1. We (were leaving / **will be leaving**) in just a few minutes.
2. Miners (**used** / use) to do nothing to improve the land in the past.
3. Nowadays, many people (accepted / **have accepted**) Alfred Wegener's ideas.
4. It is highly likely that glaciers (are expanding / **will expand**) in the future.
5. Earthquakes (**continue** / are continuing) to happen around the world every day.

B Choose the correct words for the blanks.

1. Volcanic eruptions _____ diamonds to rise to the top of the ground.
   ⓐ are causing   ⓑ were causing   ⓒ cause   ⓓ causes

2. The Pacific Ring of Fire _____ through many different parts of the Pacific Ocean.
   ⓐ moves   ⓑ is moving   ⓒ will be moving   ⓓ moved

3. Continental drift _____ the continents break up and move apart in the past.
   ⓐ makes   ⓑ was making   ⓒ has made   ⓓ made

4. When glaciers _____, they can make mountains and lakes.
   ⓐ are retreating   ⓑ were retreating   ⓒ will retreat   ⓓ retreated

C Circle the parts of the sentences that are grammatically incorrect.

1. Because the water washes away the ground, it formed a cave decades ago.
   　　　　　ⓐ　　　ⓑ　　　ⓒ　　　　　　　　ⓓ
2. Doctors have use gold to help people in many different ways.
   　　　　　ⓐ　　　ⓑ　　　ⓒ　　　　　　　　ⓓ
3. The volcano is erupting right now, so people leaving the area.
   　　　　　　ⓐ　　　ⓑ　　ⓒ　　　　ⓓ
4. Miners dug in the ground so they can get valuable minerals and ores.
   　　　ⓐ　　　　　　ⓑ　　ⓒ　　　ⓓ

Vocabulary Review

A Circle the words that best complete the sentences.

1 The company (reduced / **published**) the book the geologist wrote.
2 Sometimes water (**dissolves** / extracts) the ground to make a cave.
3 Silver and copper will (**tarnish** / burn), but gold does not.
4 Lava is (**liquid** / complete) rock that is incredibly hot and comes out of volcanoes.
5 Some earthquakes seem to last for a(n) (subsequently / **incredibly**) long time.

B Choose the best words to complete the sentences.

1 Most geologists are _____ with the idea of Pangaea.
   A familiar
   B divided
   C vital
   D unique

2 Several metals are _____, so people can beat them into different shapes.
   A precious
   B rare
   C malleable
   D vital

3 The middle layer of the Earth is the _____.
   A inner core
   B crust
   C mantle
   D outer core

4 Diamonds form _____ because of the enormous pressures there.
   A surface
   B underground
   C volcanoes
   D earthquakes

5 The Earth has several different _____ of soil.
   A accumulations
   B glaciations
   C structures
   D layers

158

C Choose the words with the closest meanings to the highlighted words.

1. Miners remove ore from the ground so others can process it for minerals.
   - Ⓐ extract
   - Ⓑ dissolve
   - Ⓒ proceed
   - Ⓓ wash away

2. The San Andreas Fault is very unstable and can therefore cause earthquakes.
   - Ⓐ dangerous
   - Ⓑ compressed
   - Ⓒ extreme
   - Ⓓ unsteady

3. The oil companies are starting to rehabilitate the land they get oil from.
   - Ⓐ flatten
   - Ⓑ restore
   - Ⓒ extract
   - Ⓓ tarnish

4. The moving of various cracks underground causes earthquakes to occur.
   - Ⓐ elements
   - Ⓑ fillings
   - Ⓒ rocks
   - Ⓓ faults

5. Glaciers created countless lakes all throughout the world when they receded.
   - Ⓐ vital
   - Ⓑ thick
   - Ⓒ precious
   - Ⓓ numerous

D Complete the sentences by filling in the blanks with the best words from the list. Change the forms of the words if necessary. Use each word only once.

| electricity | property | regulation | drift | thick |

1. The ice in a glacier is so _____ that a person cannot cut through it.
2. The volcanic eruption damaged a lot of _____ in the area around it.
3. His home lost _____ in the middle of the heavy thunderstorm.
4. There are many government _____ on how companies can mine the Earth.
5. Continental _____ has changed the way the Earth looks for millions of years.

Practice Test

Methods of Petroleum Extraction

Humans have known about petroleum for thousands of years. While it currently has countless uses, in the past, humans almost never used it. That changed during the Industrial Revolution, when people began inventing machines using petroleum for fuel and during the twentieth century as millions of people began driving cars. The problem they then faced was how to extract the petroleum from the ground.

There are three stages, or steps, in getting petroleum from the ground. The first was the way people most commonly extracted it. They simply sank a pipe into the ground, and the oil came gushing out. However, this was extremely inefficient and wasted lots of oil. So people developed ways to cap the oil to prevent it from spewing everywhere. Nowadays, companies lose virtually no oil in the first stage; however, they only recover about twenty percent of the oil underground.

In the second stage, the company must somehow create pressure to force the petroleum to the surface. It can do this in several different ways. Most commonly, the company pumps water down into the oil field. This helps create the pressure necessary to force the oil to rise. In other situations, the company might pump gas down to push the oil up. This second stage often results in ten percent more oil coming to the surface.

■1 The third stage gets the most petroleum to the surface; however, it is the hardest and most expensive method. ■2 Often, the company somehow heats the oil below. ■3 This makes it easier to recover. ■4 This method enables the company to extract more than fifty percent of the oil in the original field, making it the most effective.

Companies are constantly looking for new ways to extract petroleum. As the Earth's supply of fossil fuels gets lower, it is important for them to extract as much petroleum as possible.

spew v to eject; to send out   **recover** v to acquire; to obtain

1 The word "they" in the passage refers to
   Ⓐ people
   Ⓑ machines
   Ⓒ millions
   Ⓓ cars

2 According to paragraph 1, people needed petroleum during the Industrial Revolution because
   Ⓐ many individuals were driving cars
   Ⓑ they needed to get it out of the ground
   Ⓒ the machines they made needed it
   Ⓓ they required it for transportation

3 According to paragraph 2, which of the following is NOT true of the first stage of petroleum extraction?
   Ⓐ Companies lose the most oil during it now.
   Ⓑ It gets about twenty percent of the oil out.
   Ⓒ It is an inefficient method.
   Ⓓ People have commonly used it.

4 The word "force" in the passage is closest in meaning to
   Ⓐ require
   Ⓑ obligate
   Ⓒ determine
   Ⓓ push

5 According to paragraph 3, which of the following is true of the second stage of petroleum extraction?
   Ⓐ It is the most expensive method.
   Ⓑ It needs something to make the oil go up.
   Ⓒ It recovers less oil than the first stage.
   Ⓓ Most companies are unable to do it.

6. In paragraph 5, why does the author mention "the Earth's supply of fossil fuels"?
   - (A) To emphasize the importance of petroleum
   - (B) To encourage people to use petroleum less often
   - (C) To explain why more extraction methods are necessary
   - (D) To say that people need to find more oil fields

7. Look at the four squares [■] that indicate where the following sentence could be added to the passage.

   For this reason, many companies do not use this method at all.

   Where would the sentence best fit?
   Click on a square [■] to add the sentence to the passage.

8. *Directions:* An introductory sentence for a brief summary of the passage is provided below. Complete the summary by selecting the THREE answer choices that express the most important ideas in the passage. *This question is worth 2 points.*

   The three stages of petroleum recovery help get a large amount of underground oil up to the Earth's surface.

   -
   -
   -

   ### Answer Choices

   1. The final stage is expensive, so many people do not use it.
   2. Early petroleum recovery efforts were very inefficient.
   3. The second stage uses gas or water to recover the oil.
   4. People need to find more ways to recover the Earth's oil.
   5. The third stage can recover over fifty percent of the oil.
   6. The first stage gets only a small percentage of the oil up.

CHAPTER

08

Medicine
(Outlining)

1. Penicillin
2. *Gray's Anatomy*
3. Anesthesia
4. William Harvey
5. Vaccines
6. Organ Transplants
7. Cancer
8. Medical Imaging

CHAPTER 8 Medicine (Outlining)

Understanding TOEFL Question Types & Reading Skills

1 Question Types — Prose Summary & Fill in a Table Questions

- *Prose Summary questions* test your ability to detect the major ideas in the passage. You must be able to find the major ideas and ignore the minor ideas.
- *Fill in a Table questions* ask you to complete a table that classifies various parts of the passage. You must be able to find the major ideas in the passage and then classify them according to the topic.

● Example Prose Summary & Fill in a Table Questions

- An introductory sentence for a brief summary of the passage is provided below. Complete the summary by selecting the THREE answer choices that express the most important ideas in the passage.
- Complete the table below to summarize information about X discussed in the passage. Match the appropriate statements to X with which they are associated.

● Useful Tips for Your Success

- Learn to
  → find the main ideas in the passage.
  → recognize the facts associated with the main ideas.

- Don't
  → pay attention to the minor ideas.
  → become confused between major and minor ideas.

Sample Question

Hippocrates

🎧 08-01

People call Hippocrates the "Father of Medicine." Living in the fifth century B.C., he strongly believed in observing his patients. From his observations, he tried to determine his patients' medical problems. Unlike many others from his time, he thought diseases had natural causes, not supernatural ones. Even today people recall him by reciting the Hippocratic Oath before they become doctors.

determine [v] to find out; to learn   **supernatural** [adj] mystical; paranormal

Q An introductory sentence for a brief summary of the passage is provided below. Complete the summary by selecting the THREE answer choices that express the most important ideas in the passage.

Hippocrates was very influential to the study of medicine.

- Ⓐ He used observation to find his patients' problems.
- Ⓑ He lived in Greece during the fifth century B.C.
- Ⓒ He believed diseases happened for natural reasons.
- Ⓓ Doctors say the Hippocratic Oath because of him.
- Ⓔ Medical school students often study Hippocrates's life.

2 Reading Skills — Outlining

Outlining can identify both the major and minor ideas in a passage. Use outlines to organize all of the ideas in the passage. Then, you can show the relationships between all of these ideas.

Check-Up

▶ Complete the following outline.

I. Hippocrates
   A. The "Father of Medicine"
   B. Tried to observe patients
      1. Would determine problems from _____
      2. Believed in _____ causes of diseases
   C. Doctors recite the Hippocratic Oath today

Exercise 1

Penicillin

Many times, researchers intentionally try to discover certain medicines. However, this was not the case for one of the most important of all antibiotics. In fact, the discovery of penicillin was completely accidental.

In 1928, Dr. Alexander Fleming was working in his laboratory at a hospital. He noticed some bacteria on a plate culture. It had quit growing around a certain area with mold. He investigated more closely and realized the mold was destroying the bacteria.

This was the beginning of penicillin. In the years since, it has become a very widely used drug. Particularly, it saved huge numbers of lives in World War II. These days, doctors use it to fight a large number of infections.

intentionally adv on purpose
antibiotic n a kind of medicine
infection n an illness; a virus

Q1 An introductory sentence for a brief summary of the passage is provided below. Complete the summary by selecting the THREE answer choices that express the most important ideas in the passage.

Dr. Fleming's discovery of penicillin has helped to save many people's lives.

Ⓐ The discovery of penicillin was a complete accident.
Ⓑ Doctors used penicillin during World War II.
Ⓒ In 1928, Dr. Fleming identified penicillin.
Ⓓ Many people take penicillin as a medicine.
Ⓔ Doctors treat many patients with penicillin.

Q2 Complete the table below to summarize information about penicillin discussed in the passage. Match the appropriate statements to the description of penicillin with which they are associated.

PENICILLIN

Discovery

Effects

STATEMENTS

Select 2
•
•

Select 3
•
•
•

Statements

Ⓐ Doctors can treat lots of different diseases with penicillin.
Ⓑ Dr. Fleming was not looking for penicillin when he discovered it.
Ⓒ Doctors used penicillin to save many lives during a time of war.
Ⓓ Penicillin can kill bacteria around it because it is a kind of mold.
Ⓔ Many people usually discover medicines by looking for them.
Ⓕ Since 1928, many people have made use of penicillin as a drug.
Ⓖ It was in 1928 that Dr. Fleming first identified penicillin.

Reading Skills Outlining

Check-Up Complete the following outline.

I Discovery of penicillin
  A. Made by Dr. Alexander Fleming in 1928
  B. Was a _____ that could destroy bacteria

II Effects of penicillin
  A. Has become very widely used
  B. Saved numerous lives during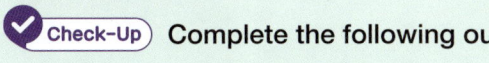
  C. Can fight many different kinds of infections

• **Exercise 2** •

Gray's Anatomy

08-03

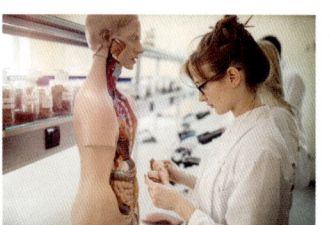

For hundreds of years, people were often skeptical of doctors. Due to a lack of medical training, knowledge, and ability, many doctors provided their patients with extremely poor treatment. In addition, patients often died in the care of doctors.

One thing doctors lacked was a base knowledge of their profession. Dr. Henry Gray sought to provide that knowledge for people. In 1858, he published the book *Gray's Anatomy: Descriptive and Surgical.* People nowadays simply refer to it as *Gray's Anatomy*. This book provided a comprehensive knowledge of the medical profession. Updated several times since its first publication, many today acknowledge the importance of this book in the medical profession. Thanks to this book, many people began trusting their doctors more.

skeptical adj doubtful; disbelieving
comprehensive adj complete; total
trust v to believe; to count on

Q1 An introductory sentence for a brief summary of the passage is provided below. Complete the summary by selecting the THREE answer choices that express the most important ideas in the passage.

***Gray's Anatomy* provided extensive information for doctors to let them treat patients better.**

Ⓐ Dr. Henry Gray published *Gray's Anatomy* in 1858.
Ⓑ Many realize the importance of *Gray's Anatomy* to medicine.
Ⓒ *Gray's Anatomy* was full of medical details.
Ⓓ People continued updating the book to give it more information.
Ⓔ Most people did not trust doctors for the longest time.

Q2 Complete the table below to summarize information about *Gray's Anatomy* discussed in the passage. Match the appropriate statements to the study of medicine before and after *Gray's Anatomy* with which they are associated.

GRAY'S ANATOMY

Medicine before its publication	Select 2 • •
Medicine after its publication	Select 3 • • •

Statements

Ⓐ Dr. Henry Gray published his book in 1858.
Ⓑ Many patients doubted their doctors' abilities.
Ⓒ Patients believed their doctors could help them.
Ⓓ The book gave doctors a base knowledge of medicine.
Ⓔ Doctors did not provide good treatment for their patients.
Ⓕ There was more knowledge available to doctors.
Ⓖ Doctors could do operations much more easily now.

Reading Skills Outlining

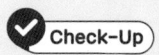 **Complete the following outline.**

I Early medicine
  A. People distrusted doctors
  B. Patients often died because of doctors

II *Gray's Anatomy* written
  A. Dr. _____ published it in 1858
  B. Provided comprehensive knowledge of medicine
    1. Was _____ many times
    2. Has been important to medical profession
    3. Has made patients trust doctors more

Chapter ❽   169

• **Exercise 3** •

Anesthesia

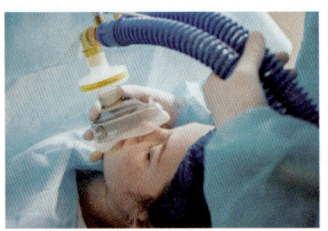

Doctors use drugs called anesthetics to create anesthesia in patients. This prevents patients from feeling pain. As a result, doctors can do all kinds of surgeries on patients.

One type of anesthesia is general anesthesia. It affects the entire body. Doctors can introduce drugs into the body through an IV or by using gas. The drugs make patients unable to move or feel pain. This type of anesthesia lets doctors do major operations on patients.

Local anesthesia blocks pain in a part of the body. It does not make patients unconscious. However, they cannot feel anything in a part of their bodies. Dentists use this on patients. Doctors also use it for eye surgery.

drug n   medicine
patient n   a sick person at a hospital or clinic
IV n   a device used to introduce medicine into the body

Q1 An introductory sentence for a brief summary of the passage is provided below. Complete the summary by selecting the THREE answer choices that express the most important ideas in the passage.

Doctors create anesthesia in patients to do surgery on them.

Ⓐ Doctors may use local anesthesia to block pain in parts of the body.
Ⓑ Anesthetics prevent patients from feeling pain in their bodies.
Ⓒ Before anesthetics were discovered, most surgeries were failures.
Ⓓ General anesthesia affects the entire body and lets doctors do major surgery.
Ⓔ Doctors can use an IV to introduce general anesthetics to the body.

Q2 Complete the table below to summarize information about anesthesia discussed in the passage. Match the appropriate statements to the kind of anesthesia with which they are associated.

ANESTHESIA	STATEMENTS
General anesthesia	Select 3 • • •
Local anesthesia	Select 2 • •

Statements

Ⓐ Patients cannot move after receiving it.
Ⓑ It can have very long-lasting effects.
Ⓒ It can affect the entire body.
Ⓓ It is the more expensive of the two types.
Ⓔ Patients remain awake after being given it.
Ⓕ Doctors may use an IV or gas to give it to patients.
Ⓖ It may be used for eye surgery.

Reading Skills   Outlining

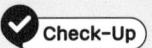 **Complete the following outline.**

I General anesthesia
   A. Affects the entire body
   B. Introduced by an IV or gas
   C. Makes patients _____ or feel pain
   D. Lets doctors do major operations

II Local anesthesia
   A. Blocks pain in a part of the body
   B. Does not make patients unconscious
      1. Cannot feel anything in a part of their bodies
   C. Used by _____ and for eye surgery

• **Exercise 4** •

William Harvey

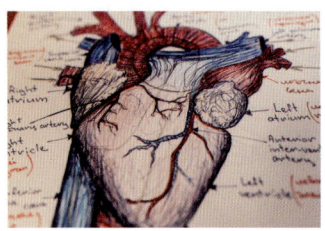

🎧 08-05

The history of medicine has seen many important discoveries. These date back even to the times of Hippocrates and Galen. One important man in the history of medicine was William Harvey. He was a British physician who lived from 1578 to 1657. Harvey did his work on the circulation of the blood.

Importantly, Harvey relied upon the scientific methods of experimentation and observation to make his discovery. First, he experimented on animals. He also made close examinations of how much blood the heart could pump in a day. Through his work, he realized the two ways blood circulates in the body. He also made important discoveries about veins and their contributions to the circulation of the blood.

physician [n] a doctor
circulation [n] a flow; a movement

vein [n] a blood vessel; the part of the body that carries the blood

Q1 An introductory sentence for a brief summary of the passage is provided below. Complete the summary by selecting the THREE answer choices that express the most important ideas in the passage.

William Harvey was important to medicine because of some of his discoveries.

Ⓐ Harvey found out how veins help the body.
Ⓑ Harvey learned about the circulation of blood.
Ⓒ Harvey was as crucial to medicine as Galen was.
Ⓓ William Harvey lived from 1578 to 1657.
Ⓔ Harvey discovered how animals' blood circulates.

Q2 Complete the table below to summarize information about William Harvey discussed in the passage. Match the appropriate statements to the life and work of William Harvey with which they are associated.

WILLIAM HARVEY

Life

Work

STATEMENTS

Select 2
•
•

Select 3
•
•
•

Statements

Ⓐ Harvey used the scientific method to learn.
Ⓑ Harvey was a doctor who lived in England.
Ⓒ He learned about the circulation of blood in the body.
Ⓓ Harvey was a great physician like Galen and Hippocrates.

Ⓔ William Harvey lived from 1578 to 1657.
Ⓕ Harvey made some of medicine's most important discoveries.
Ⓖ He found out the role of veins in the body.

Reading Skills Outlining

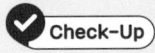 Complete the following outline.

I William Harvey's life
   A. Was a British physician
   B. Lived from 1578 to 1657

II William Harvey's work
   A. Used the scientific method
      1. Used experimentation and observation
      2. Experimented on animals
   B. Learned about _____ of blood
   C. Learned two ways blood circulates
   D. Made discoveries on purposes of _____

• **Exercise 5** •

Vaccines

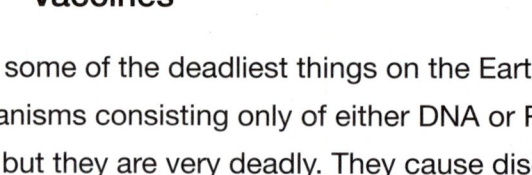

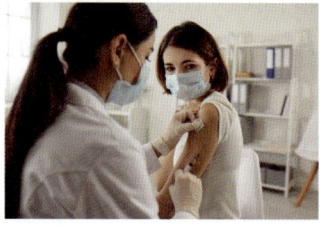

Viruses are some of the deadliest things on the Earth. They are microorganisms consisting only of either DNA or RNA and a protein core, but they are very deadly. They cause diseases such as polio, malaria, chicken pox, measles, and the common cold. These diseases kill millions of people each year. Unfortunately, doctors have never found even one cure for any virus.

However, scientists have created vaccines for viruses. Vaccines help protect the body against a virus. A vaccine typically has a dead or weakened virus in it. The doctor then injects the vaccine in a person's body. The person's body detects the weakened virus and attacks and kills it. It then creates antibodies to fight the virus if it ever returns. In the future, if a person should get that virus, the antibodies will destroy it. Thanks to vaccines, people are safe from many of the deadliest viruses.

consist of [phr] to be made of; to contain
deadly [adj] fatal; lethal
weakened [adj] damaged
inject [v] to insert; to introduce

Q1 An introductory sentence for a brief summary of the passage is provided below. Complete the summary by selecting the THREE answer choices that express the most important ideas in the passage.

Although viruses can be very deadly, vaccines can help protect people from them.

Ⓐ Measles, chickenpox, and polio are some diseases viruses cause.
Ⓑ Vaccines can keep people safe from certain viruses.
Ⓒ Every year, viruses kill incredibly large numbers of people.
Ⓓ DNA or RNA and a protein core are the components of viruses.
Ⓔ Vaccines will attack a virus anytime it invades the body.

Q2 Complete the table below to summarize information about viruses discussed in the passage. Match the appropriate statements to viruses unaffected and affected by vaccines with which they are associated.

VIRUSES	STATEMENTS
Unaffected by vaccines	Select 2 • •
Affected by vaccines	Select 3 • • •

Statements

Ⓐ These viruses cannot harm a person's body at all.
Ⓑ These viruses can kill huge numbers of people yearly.
Ⓒ These viruses get attacked by antibodies in the body.
Ⓓ These viruses leave dead or weakened vaccines in the body.
Ⓔ These viruses can cause many different kinds of diseases.
Ⓕ These viruses can be cured by doctors almost immediately.
Ⓖ These viruses die every time that they return to the body.

Reading Skills Outlining

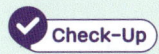 **Complete the following outline.**

I Viruses
   A. Are deadly microorganisms
      1. Made of DNA or RNA and a protein core
   B. Cause many different diseases
      1. Polio, malaria, _____ _____, measles, and the common cold
      2. Can kill millions yearly
      3. Have no known cure

II Vaccines
   A. Protect the body against viruses
      1. Have dead or weakened _____ in it
      2. Injected into the body
      3. Body kills weakened viruses
   B. Create _____ to protect body from viruses
   C. Will destroy the virus if it returns to the body
   D. Have saved the lives of people from deadly viruses

• Exercise 6 •

Organ Transplants

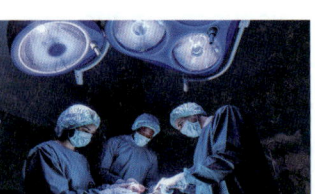

Sometimes people's organs become weak or diseased, or they fail altogether. Without a new organ, they will most likely die. In these cases, doctors perform organ transplants on them.

The first successful organ transplant occurred in 1954 when a doctor transplanted a kidney from one twin to another. Doctors experienced many early failures, especially since patients' bodies often rejected the new organ. In recent years though, doctors have learned very much about transplanting organs. Now, they can successfully transplant hearts, lungs, kidneys, livers, and pancreases. This helps extend people's lives by many years.

In many cases, the organ being transplanted comes from a dead person. But this is not always the case, especially for kidney transplants. In recent years, thousands of people have been waiting for organ transplants. Unfortunately, there are not enough organ donors. Thus, not everyone gets the transplants they need, so many people die before having surgery. And some bodies still reject the organs they receive.

organ n one of the important groups of tissues in the body like the heart, the liver, and the lungs
transplant v to move from one place to another; to relocate
extend v to lengthen
donor n a giver

Q1 An introductory sentence for a brief summary of the passage is provided below. Complete the summary by selecting the THREE answer choices that express the most important ideas in the passage.

Organ transplants help save people's lives, but not everyone can get one of them.

Ⓐ Doctors can now transplant many of the body's organs.
Ⓑ Before 1954, there were no organ transplants done.
Ⓒ Some people die since there are not enough organs for them.
Ⓓ Doctors are trying to learn to transplant every organ in the body.
Ⓔ People survive longer if they can have an organ transplant.

Q2 Complete the table below to summarize information about organ transplants discussed in the passage. Match the appropriate statements to the positive and negative effects of organ transplants with which they are associated.

ORGAN TRANSPLANTS

Positive effects	Select 3 • • •
Negative effects	Select 2 • •

Statements

- Ⓐ A body might not accept a transplanted organ.
- Ⓑ People can survive longer with a transplant.
- Ⓒ The first organ transplant took place in 1954.
- Ⓓ Doctors do not know everything about organ transplants.
- Ⓔ People can have their lives extended.
- Ⓕ Doctors continue learning more about transplanting organs.
- Ⓖ There are sometimes failures during the transplant operations.

Reading Skills Outlining

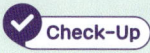 **Check-Up** Complete the following outline.

I Organ transplants
  A. First successful in 1954
  B. Had many early failures
    1. Body would reject new organ
  C. Doctors have learned much about transplanting organs
  D. Can transplant _____, lungs, kidneys, livers, and pancreases

II Organ donors
  A. Organs usually come from _____
  B. Thousands wait for new organs
    1. Often die before geting new organ
    2. Bodies sometimes _____ new organs

• **Exercise 7** •

Cancer

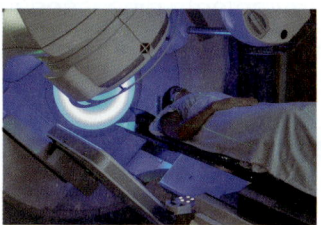

Diseases often attack the human body. Some of the deadliest are the group of diseases people call cancer. There are many kinds of cancer, and they can attack various parts of the body. All cancers usually have the following characteristics: they are very aggressive; they assault various parts of the body; and they can spread to other parts of the body they did not initially attack.

Doctors have learned very much about cancer. They know that abnormal cells with changed genetic material cause most types of cancer. Many types of cancer are extremely deadly. In fact, it causes over ten percent of all deaths.

Luckily, researchers have done much work to fight cancer. They can now defeat many types of it. They use a lot of different methods, including operations, chemotherapy, and radiotherapy. While they have not beaten all types of cancer, it is likely that future breakthroughs will enable people to find cures to the majority of cancers.

---

aggressive adj violent; destructive
assault v to attack
abnormal adj unusual
breakthrough n a discovery; an advance

Q1 An introductory sentence for a brief summary of the passage is provided below. Complete the summary by selecting the THREE answer choices that express the most important ideas in the passage.

Cancer kills many people today, but doctors are learning new methods to fight and defeat it.

- Ⓐ Cancer causes around ten percent of all deaths.
- Ⓑ Radiotherapy is not much use against cancer.
- Ⓒ Doctors hope they can learn new ways to fight cancer.
- Ⓓ Operations and chemotherapy can beat cancer.
- Ⓔ Cancer can aggressively go through a body and kill it.

Q2 Complete the table below to summarize information about cancer discussed in the passage. Match the appropriate statements to the effects and treatments of cancer with which they are associated.

CANCER	STATEMENTS
Effects	Select 3 • • •
Treatments	Select 2 • •

Statements

Ⓐ Researchers need to do more work to learn about cancer.
Ⓑ Cancer sometimes spreads to different parts of the body.
Ⓒ Doctors use chemotherapy to fight against some cancer.
Ⓓ Cancer kills a very large number of people every year.
Ⓔ It is possible for an operation to help fight cancer.
Ⓕ People can get several different types of cancer.
Ⓖ Cancer cells are abnormal with changed genetic material.

Reading Skills Outlining

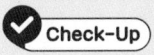 **Complete the following outline.**

I Cancer
   A. Are many different kinds
   B. Is very deadly
   C. Is aggressive when attacking the body
   D. Can _____ to other body parts

II Doctors' knowledge of cancer
   A. Are _____ cells
   B. Have changed genetic material
   C. Causes more than ten percent of all deaths

III Cancer treatments
   A. Doctors can defeat many kinds of cancer
   B. Use _____, chemotherapy, and radiotherapy

• Exercise 8 •

Medical Imaging

Doctors often require internal images of their patients. One way is to use medical imaging. There are several kinds of medical imaging, but two of the most important are CAT scans and MRIs.

A CAT scan is a procedure using X-rays. A CAT scan can produce either two-dimensional X-ray images or three-dimensional views of a person's body. It does this by combining numerous X-ray images on top of one another. Sometimes, doctors inject a dye into the body to provide them with more vivid images. Doctors use CAT scans to provide them with pictures of the internal structures of parts of the body.

An MRI machine uses magnets to look inside the human body. MRIs are actually safer than CAT scans because they use no radiation. They can also provide either two-dimensional or three-dimensional images. The pictures they create can be quite detailed. This is a fairly new technology, having only been around since the 1980s.

---

internal [adj] inner; inside
procedure [n] a process; a method
vivid [adj] detailed; colorful; brilliant
radiation [n] a kind of energy

Q1 An introductory sentence for a brief summary of the passage is provided below. Complete the summary by selecting the THREE answer choices that express the most important ideas in the passage.

CAT scans and MRI machines help doctors look more closely at people's bodies.

- Ⓐ CAT scans are not as expensive to use as MRI machines.
- Ⓑ CAT scans can let doctors see in two or three dimensions.
- Ⓒ MRI machines do not use radiation, so they are quite safe.
- Ⓓ MRI machines can provide good pictures of the body's insides.
- Ⓔ CAT scans give doctors looks at the body's internal structures.

Q2 Complete the table below to summarize information about medical imaging discussed in the passage. Match the appropriate statements to the medical imaging method with which they are associated.

MEDICAL IMAGING	STATEMENTS
CAT scan	Select 2 • •
MRI machine	Select 3 • • •

Statements

Ⓐ Doctors may give the patient a dye before using this machine.

Ⓑ This medical imagining machine relies on magnets to create images.

Ⓒ This machine does not need to use radiation to make pictures.

Ⓓ This is the more expensive of the two medical imaging machines.

Ⓔ X-rays combine to form the image for this medical imaging machine.

Ⓕ The technology for this machine has only been around since the 1980s.

Ⓖ This machine is only capable of providing images in two dimensions.

Reading Skills Outlining

 **Check-Up** Complete the following outline.

I CAT scans
  A. Use _____
  B. Can create two-dimensional or three-dimensional images
  C. Combine X-rays on top of one another
  D. May inject dye first to get images

II MRIs
  A. Rely on _____ to look at the body
  B. Do not need to use _____
  C. Can give two-dimensional or three-dimensional images
  D. Make detailed images
  E. Have been around since the 1980s

Grammar Point

Concord

Singulars and Plurals

1. Use singular verbs for singular subjects and use plural verbs for plural subjects.

   - One of the most incredible is the artificial heart.
   - The animal in her hands is Jason's dog.
   - Doctors use it to fight a large number of infections.
   - Cancer, heart disease, and diabetes are deadly diseases.

2. Some nouns look plural, but they take singular nouns. Many of these words are countries and school subjects.

   > **Countries:** the United States, the Netherlands, the Bahamas, the Maldives
   > **Subjects:** economics, physics, mathematics, politics, statistics

   - The Netherlands is in Europe.
   - The United States has a large amount of land.
   - Physics is my favorite subject.
   - Economics is John's major at college.

3. Words like each and every take singular verbs. Words like most and many take plural verbs.

   - Each of us is going to the party.
   - Every student likes to learn history.
   - Most doctors study at medical school for several years.

4. The number of takes a singular verb. A number of takes a plural verb.

   - The number of hospitals in the city is very small.
   - The number of lives saved was very high.
   - A number of diseases are still not curable.
   - A number of doctors have done research on that illness.

Grammar Check-Up

A Choose the correct words.

1 The Philippines (is / are) an island country in the Pacific Ocean.

2 (Most / Each) person in the room is a student.

3 (The number of / A number of) diseases can kill people very quickly.

4 The doctor and the patient (is / are) both in the emergency room.

5 The CAT scan and the MRI (have / has) helped doctors treat patients for many years.

B Choose the correct words for the blanks.

1 Organ transplants have saved _____ of people's lives.
   ⓐ one   ⓑ most   ⓒ a large number   ⓓ the large number

2 Chicken pox and measles vaccines _____ kept many people from getting sick.
   ⓐ are   ⓑ is   ⓒ has   ⓓ have

3 _____ doctor today takes the Hippocratic Oath before practicing medicine.
   ⓐ Every   ⓑ Most   ⓒ Many   ⓓ Much

4 Politics _____ a field many people are very interested in.
   ⓐ is   ⓑ have   ⓒ has   ⓓ are

5 _____ scientists such as William Harvey have contributed to human knowledge.
   ⓐ A large number   ⓑ Many   ⓒ The large number   ⓓ Every

C Read the following story and fill in the blanks. Change the forms of the words if necessary. Use each word only once.

| every   the number of   want   a number   most of   ask |

Today, Mrs. Lee _____ to take her class on a field trip. _____ student has his or her own idea of where to go. _____ of students think going to the museum will be fun. Many students are thinking of going to the national park. And some of them want to go on a picnic. But _____ them think they should be outdoors. So Mrs. Lee _____ her students to vote on their destination. _____ students in the class is thirty, and twenty vote to go to the park. So they are going to visit the park next week.

Vocabulary Review

A Circle the words that best complete the sentences.

1 Dr. Fleming did not (intentionally / strongly) mean to discover penicillin.
2 Vaccines create (antibodies / viruses) that protect the body from diseases.
3 A doctor should always (recite / observe) patients to find out their problems.
4 We were (skeptical / comprehensive) of her ability since she had just graduated from medical school.
5 All doctors should believe that medical problems have (supernatural / natural) causes.

B Choose the best words to complete the sentences.

1 The boy felt a lot of _____ when he fell and broke his arm.
   A pain
   B cancer
   C method
   D organ

2 If the body rejects an organ, then the operation will _____.
   A wait
   B provide
   C fail
   D extend

3 Doctors often give patients _____ to help them treat minor problems.
   A organs
   B antibiotics
   C transplants
   D cancer

4 He will undergo a special _____ to try to remove the tumor from his body.
   A procedure
   B transplant
   C X-ray
   D vaccine

5 The patient needs _____ to fix the problem in her stomach.
   A infection
   B image
   C virus
   D surgery

C Choose the words with the closest meanings to the highlighted words.

1. The physician tried to help as many patients as he could to get better.
   - A researcher
   - B scientist
   - C patient
   - D doctor

2. The doctors believe they can defeat the illness in the patient's body.
   - A beat
   - B inject
   - C cause
   - D experience

3. Some viruses assault the body quickly and cause incredible amounts of damage.
   - A reject
   - B attack
   - C identify
   - D pump

4. Vaccines can kill certain harmful cells that enter the body.
   - A destroy
   - B produce
   - C extend
   - D weaken

5. The CAT scan gave the doctor a detailed image of the patient's problem.
   - A skeptical
   - B scientific
   - C total
   - D vivid

D Complete the sentences by filling in the blanks with the best words from the list. Change the forms of the words if necessary. Use each word only once.

> investigate   block   publication   protein   unconscious

1. A(n) _____ core is one of the components of a virus.
2. You should _____ the cause of the disease very closely.
3. The boy was _____ the entire time doctors were working on him.
4. This medicine can help _____ the pain in your back.
5. The _____ of this book was very important to the field of medicine.

Practice Test

Alternative Medicine

Many people around the world rely upon Western medicine, but others do not. These people often turn to alternative medicine to treat their problems. These are treatment methods with no scientific basis. Or perhaps scientists have not yet established their effectiveness. However, many users of alternative medicine insist it works. Two of the more popular types of this medicine are herbalism and acupuncture.

Herbalism relies upon the traditional medicine people once used prior to modern medicine. In these cases, the people practicing it rely heavily upon folklore to find cures for their illnesses. These people take remedies made from trees, plants, flowers, roots, and other natural products. In some cases, they may also utilize parts from animals or minerals to make cures. Many cultures have practiced herbalism, including those in India, China, and Greece. Modern scientists have found real benefits in many herbalist cures. But they have failed to prove the scientific value of many of its medicines. This fact has kept herbalism in the category of alternative medicine.

Acupuncture is another kind of alternative medicine. Lately, it has gained many followers worldwide. In this form of medicine, the doctor, called the acupuncturist, inserts needles into various parts of the body to relieve it of pain. Acupuncturists believe there are many pressure points throughout the human body. For example, a place on a person's ear, when pricked with a needle, may help ease pain in the patient's back, knee, or some other body part. While many people firmly believe acupuncture is helpful, as of now, doctors and scientists have determined it has little scientific basis. Nevertheless, there are countless cases of people becoming better right after receiving treatment.

Herbalism and acupuncture are just two of many kinds of alternative medical treatments. While not common now, as scientists learn more about them, more doctors and patients will likely accept them in the future.

---

basis n a foundation

remedy n a cure; medicine

1. In paragraph 1, the author implies that Western medicine
   - Ⓐ is not as effective as alternative medicine
   - Ⓑ is losing popularity to alternative medicine
   - Ⓒ is more expensive than alternative medicine
   - Ⓓ is more scientific than alternative medicine

2. The phrase "prior to" in the passage is closest in meaning to
   - Ⓐ before
   - Ⓑ around
   - Ⓒ near
   - Ⓓ with

3. The word "it" in the passage refers to
   - Ⓐ acupuncture
   - Ⓑ herbalism
   - Ⓒ modern medicine
   - Ⓓ folklore

4. In paragraph 2, the author's description of herbalism mentions all of the following EXCEPT:
   - Ⓐ Where it has been practiced
   - Ⓑ The role folklore has in it
   - Ⓒ The uses of animal parts in it
   - Ⓓ The reasons doctors support it

5. Which of the following best expresses the essential information in the highlighted sentence? *Incorrect* answer choices change the meaning in important ways or leave out essential information.
   - Ⓐ An acupuncturist puts needles into people to heal them.
   - Ⓑ An acupuncturist's needles can sometimes cause pain.
   - Ⓒ Without needles, an acupuncturist can do nothing about pain.
   - Ⓓ Needles go into the body when an acupuncturist is in pain.

6 According to paragraph 3, which of the following is true of acupuncture?

- Ⓐ The doctor always sticks needles in a patient's ear.
- Ⓑ Most doctors believe it is scientifically valid.
- Ⓒ It is always successful at making people feel better.
- Ⓓ More and more people are starting to use it.

7 In paragraph 3, the author implies that acupuncture

- Ⓐ will never be accepted by Western doctors
- Ⓑ may actually help cure people
- Ⓒ needs to use longer needles
- Ⓓ cannot be of help to most people

8 *Directions:* Complete the table below to summarize information about alternative medicine discussed in the passage. Match the appropriate statements to the type of alternative medicine with which they are associated. ***This question is worth 3 points.***

ALTERNATIVE MEDICINE	STATEMENTS
Herbalism	Select 2 • •
Acupuncture	Select 3 • • •

Statements

1 This is becoming more popular all around the world.
2 It uses plants, trees, and flowers to make cures for problems.
3 Cultures in Greece and India have practiced it.
4 Doctors often use it together with Western medicine.
5 Doctors put needles in the body to ease a person's pain.
6 It depends upon pressure points in parts of the body.
7 Scientists have completely established its effectiveness.

Actual Test

Actual Test 1

Caves

Caves are large, natural holes in the ground that are large enough for humans to enter. Many are found in mountains. Others are found in other places in the ground. Some caves may be tiny. Others, such as Mammoth Cave in the United States, may extend for hundreds of kilometers. There are several types of caves. They each form in different ways. Three common types are solution caves, lava caves, and sea caves.

Solution caves are created by the effects of groundwater. Water seeps into cracks into the ground. Over time, it erodes the rocks and washes them away. Many solution caves are found in limestone because it is easily eroded. Yet water can sometimes erode other rocks, including marble, dolomite, and gypsum. These caves take a long time to form. Some are created over millions of years, yet they can be quite extensive.

Lava caves exist in places with past or present volcanic activity. They form after a volcano erupts. When lava flows, it often moves in streams. These streams can drain, which leaves long, hollow tubes under the ground. People used them as burial sites in the past. Some people even lived in them. There are many lava caves in Hawaii, Japan, Italy, and Kenya.

Sea caves are formed by the power of ocean tides. As waves beat against cliffs at the ocean shore, they erode the land. Over time, cracks occur. Slowly, the cracks become larger until caves form. **1** Most sea caves are filled with water, especially at high tide. **2** They are popular places for people to see, but they are also incredibly dangerous. **3** Many swimmers and scuba divers have died after getting lost in them. **4** New Zealand, Greece, and England all have sea caves.

---

hollow [adj] having a hole in the middle
high tide [n] the time when the ocean is at its highest level

1. In paragraph 1, why does the author mention "Mammoth Cave"?
   - Ⓐ To explain the way that it formed
   - Ⓑ To provide its precise location
   - Ⓒ To name a kind of solution cave
   - Ⓓ To point out how large it is

2. In paragraph 1, the author's description of caves mentions all of the following EXCEPT:
   - Ⓐ The places where caves are found
   - Ⓑ The ways caves are formed
   - Ⓒ Some different types of caves
   - Ⓓ The definition of a cave

3. The word "seeps" in the passage is closest in meaning to
   - Ⓐ remains
   - Ⓑ drops
   - Ⓒ approaches
   - Ⓓ oozes

4. In paragraph 2, the author implies that solution caves
   - Ⓐ form in limestone more often than in marble
   - Ⓑ are the most popular caves for explorers
   - Ⓒ usually have different rock formations in them
   - Ⓓ may go deep under the ground

5. The word "them" in the passage refers to
   - Ⓐ these streams
   - Ⓑ long, hollow tubes
   - Ⓒ burial sites
   - Ⓓ some people

6 According to paragraph 3, lava caves form because

- Ⓐ water erodes holes in cooled lava
- Ⓑ volcanoes shoot out large amounts of water
- Ⓒ volcanoes erupt and shoot out lava
- Ⓓ heated rocks melt holes underground

7 The phrase "beat against" in the passage is closest in meaning to

- Ⓐ smash into
- Ⓑ move toward
- Ⓒ go under
- Ⓓ flow against

8 According to paragraph 4, which of the following is true of sea caves?

- Ⓐ They can be found in cliffs alongside lakes.
- Ⓑ They form through the process of erosion.
- Ⓒ They are only found in countries that have islands.
- Ⓓ They are filled with water at all times.

9 Look at the four squares [■] that indicate where the following sentence could be added to the passage.

They cannot find their way out and then drown after running out of air.

Where would the sentence best fit?
Click on a square [■] to add the sentence to the passage.

10 *Directions*: Complete the table below to summarize information about caves discussed in the passage. Match the appropriate statements to the type of cave with which they are associated. ***This question is worth 3 points.***

CAVES

Solution Caves

- Select 3
-
-
-

Lava Caves

- Select 2
-
-

Sea Caves

- Select 2
-
-

Statements

1. Can be found in both Japan and Kenya
2. May be thousands of kilometers long
3. May take millions of years to form
4. Are only found in the sides of mountains
5. Can be filled with water at times
6. Can form in gypsum or dolomite
7. Were used to bury people in at times
8. Can extend very far
9. Sometimes have people die in them

Actual Test 2

Prosthetic Limbs

At times, people may lose limbs such as arms, hands, legs, or feet. This may happen due to accidents, war, or illnesses. **1** In the past, those individuals could do nothing to replace their missing limbs. **2** Today, doctors can attach prosthetic limbs to people's bodies. **3** Some of them can function almost like regular body parts. **4**

Prosthetic limbs are not new. They are at least 3,000 years old. Archaeologists unearthed a mummy from ancient Egypt that had a wooden toe. The ancient Greeks and Romans also used wood to make primitive prosthetic limbs. Pirates were also notorious for having peg legs, which were made of wood. Some that had missing hands had hooks attached to their bodies to replace them. These limbs were all usable but did not restore many lost functions to their users.

Advances were made in Europe from the 1400s to the 1800s. Engineers used wood, leather, and metal to make various types of prosthetic limbs. Prosthetic fingers could pick up and hold objects. Other limbs could bend and move in various directions. In the 1900s, there were many wars, including World War I and World War II, and millions of soldiers suffered injuries in them. Many lost limbs. This encouraged scientists to make improvements in prosthetic technology.

Today, prosthetic limbs are made of state-of-the-art materials. They often look like the actual missing limbs. Many allow their users to function like they did before they lost their limbs. Some can even be controlled by thought. These limbs are expensive, yet it is likely that the cost will decline in the future as the technology improves.

unearth [v] to dig up
state-of-the-art [adj] being advanced and sophisticated

1. In paragraph 1, the author's description of prosthetic limbs mentions which of the following?
   - Ⓐ How they are attached to people
   - Ⓑ What functions they do not have
   - Ⓒ Why people may need them
   - Ⓓ Which body parts they usually replace

2. In paragraph 2, why does the author mention "The ancient Greeks and Romans"?
   - Ⓐ To claim prosthetic limbs were made in those places
   - Ⓑ To argue that they invented the first prosthetic limbs
   - Ⓒ To describe the types of prosthetic limbs they made
   - Ⓓ To explain why they needed to have prosthetic limbs

3. The word "notorious" in the passage is closest in meaning to
   - Ⓐ untrusted
   - Ⓑ remembered
   - Ⓒ noticeable
   - Ⓓ infamous

4. The word "them" in the passage refers to
   - Ⓐ peg legs
   - Ⓑ missing hands
   - Ⓒ hooks
   - Ⓓ their bodies

5. In paragraph 3, the author uses "wood, leather, and metal" as examples of
   - Ⓐ kinds of materials used only in Europe in the 1400s
   - Ⓑ materials prosthetic limbs were once made from
   - Ⓒ the cheapest materials used to make prosthetic limbs with
   - Ⓓ the most common materials used by soldiers

6 Which of the following best expresses the essential information in the highlighted sentence? *Incorrect* answer choices change the meaning in important ways or leave out essential information.

   Ⓐ Some of the biggest wars in history were fought during the 1900s.
   Ⓑ Millions of soldiers took part in battles in various wars in the twentieth century.
   Ⓒ Large numbers of soldiers were injured in the many wars in the 1900s.
   Ⓓ World War I and World War II both took place during the 1900s.

7 According to paragraph 4, which of the following is true of prosthetic limbs in the present day?

   Ⓐ They do not cost too much money for most people.
   Ⓑ They cannot restore every missing function to their users.
   Ⓒ They can look like the limbs they are replacing.
   Ⓓ They have been steadily declining in price.

8 In paragraph 4, the author implies that prosthetic limbs

   Ⓐ will be cheaper in the future than they are now
   Ⓑ can be attached to people by surgery
   Ⓒ make people stronger than they were before
   Ⓓ are made from the same materials used in the past

9 Look at the four squares [■] that indicate where the following sentence could be added to the passage.

   For example, doctors may have to cut off body parts when people get injured.

   Where would the sentence best fit?
   Click on a square [■] to add the sentence to the passage.

10 Directions: An introductory sentence for a brief summary of the passage is provided below. Complete the summary by selecting the THREE answer choices that express the most important ideas in the passage. *This question is worth 2 points.*

People have used prosthetic limbs to replace missing body parts for thousands of years.

-
-
-

Answer Choices

1. It can be too expensive for many people to buy quality prosthetic limbs.
2. The technology for prosthetic limbs got better in the twentieth century.
3. People in ancient Egypt, Greece, and Rome sometimes have prosthetic limbs.
4. Most prosthetic limbs today are made from wood or metal.
5. Pirates were some of the first people to replace their missing body parts.
6. Modern-day prosthetic limbs provide their users with many functions.

Actual Test 3

Rainforests

Rainforests are thick with trees and other vegetation and grow in areas that get lots of rain. **1** Tropical rainforests are the best known. **2** Yet there are several other types of rainforests. **3** Each has its own unique characteristics. **4**

Temperate rainforests grow in cool regions. These rainforests may see four unique seasons each year. Some are found in southern Australia as well as in the northwestern United States. In Southeast Asia, there are monsoon rainforests. These forests get a dry season each year. Their trees also lose leaves annually. Finally, there are montane rainforests. These grow in areas with mountains and are almost continuously covered with clouds. They are located in many places, including South America and Africa.

As for tropical rainforests, they are located in the tropics. This is the region directly north and south of the equator. There are tropical rainforests in Southeast Asia, Africa, Australia, and South and Central America. The Amazon Rainforest in South America is the largest rainforest in the world. Tropical rainforests are divided into four parts. They are the emergent layer, the canopy, the understory, and the forest floor.

The emergent layer is at the top. It can be more than fifty meters high. It receives the most sunlight. Birds, monkeys, and insects live there. The canopy, where the highest trees are, is next. The understory is the third layer. It has smaller trees as well as shrubs, vines, and other types of plants. Snakes, lizards, small mammals, and birds live there. It receives less sunlight because the leaves in the canopy obstruct most of it. The forest floor is dark as almost no light reaches it. Few plants grow there because of that. Large mammals such as tigers, jaguars, and anteaters live there. So do numerous lizards, amphibians, and insects.

temperate adj moderate   **monsoon** n a season in which strong winds blow and heavy rain falls

1. According to paragraph 1, which of the following is true of rainforests?
   - Ⓐ They cannot survive in cold temperatures.
   - Ⓑ They get rain almost every day of the year.
   - Ⓒ They have large numbers of trees.
   - Ⓓ They have the world's tallest trees.

2. The word "continuously" in the passage is closest in meaning to
   - Ⓐ nonstop
   - Ⓑ periodically
   - Ⓒ entirely
   - Ⓓ heavily

3. In paragraph 2, what does the author imply about monsoon rainforests?
   - Ⓐ They have trees that provide lots of different fruits.
   - Ⓑ They cover most of the land in Southeastern Asia.
   - Ⓒ They have more clouds than montane rainforests.
   - Ⓓ They do not get rain during some parts of the year.

4. According to paragraph 2, where can montane rainforests be found?
   - Ⓐ In Africa
   - Ⓑ In the United States
   - Ⓒ In Australia
   - Ⓓ In Europe

5. In paragraph 3, why does the author mention "The Amazon Rainforest"?
   - Ⓐ To discuss its four parts
   - Ⓑ To compare it to another rainforest
   - Ⓒ To call it important
   - Ⓓ To refer to its size

6 In paragraph 3, the author's description of tropical rainforests mentions all of the following EXCEPT:

Ⓐ How many layers they have
Ⓑ Where many of them can be found
Ⓒ Why they are important to people
Ⓓ What the world's biggest one is

7 The word "obstruct" in the passage is closest in meaning to

Ⓐ block
Ⓑ absorb
Ⓒ utilize
Ⓓ detour

8 The word "it" in the passage refers to

Ⓐ sunlight
Ⓑ the canopy
Ⓒ the forest floor
Ⓓ light

9 Look at the four squares [■] that indicate where the following sentence could be added to the passage.

In addition, they occupy more land than the other types of rainforests do.

Where would the sentence best fit?
Click on a square [■] to add the sentence to the passage.

10 *Directions:* An introductory sentence for a brief summary of the passage is provided below. Complete the summary by selecting the THREE answer choices that express the most important ideas in the passage. *This question is worth 2 points.*

There are several types of rainforests, which all have characteristics that make them unique.

-
-
-

Answer Choices

1. It is possible to find temperate rainforests in cooler regions.
2. There are more montane rainforests than there are monsoon rainforests.
3. Large mammals tend to live on the forest floor.
4. Tropical rainforests have four different layers in them.
5. Places in Southeastern Asia have several kinds of rainforests in them.
6. Various types of animals live in each layer of a tropical rainforest.

Publisher Kyudo Chung
Editors Woonhee Park, Sangik Cho
Author Michael A. Putlack
Designers Minji Kim, Yeji Kim

First published in February 2008 by Happy House
Second edition first published in June 2023 by Darakwon, Inc.
Darakwon Bldg., 211, Munbal-ro, Paju-si, Gyeonggi-do 10881
Republic of Korea
Tel: 82-2-736-2031 (Ext. 250)
Fax: 82-2-732-2037

Copyright © 2008 Happy House, 2023 Darakwon

All rights reserved. No part of this publication may be reproduced, stored in a retrieval system, or transmitted in any form or by any means, electronic, mechanical, photocopying or otherwise, without the prior consent of the copyright owner. Refund after purchase is possible only according to the company regulations. Contact the above telephone number for any inquiries. Consumer damages caused by loss, damage, etc. can be compensated according to the consumer dispute resolution standards announced by the Korea Fair Trade Commission. An incorrectly collated book will be exchanged.

ISBN 978-89-277-8059-5 14740
        978-89-277-8056-4 14740 (set)

www.darakwon.co.kr

Photo Credits
Shutterstock.com

Components Main Book / Answer Key
9 8 7 6 5 4 3   25 26 27 28 29

High Score
iBT TOEFL READING For Junior

2nd Edition

Intermediate

Answer Key

DARAKWON

CHAPTER 1 Chemistry

Understanding TOEFL Question Types & Reading Skills
p.14

1 Question Types ▶ Sample Question
Ⓑ

해석 화합물 분해하기

어떤 이들은 화합물을 전기 분해 요법을 사용하여 근본 원소로 분해한다. 흔히 물에서 수소를 추출하기 위해 전기 분해 요법을 사용한다. 일단 물 한 컵이 있어야 한다. 그런 다음, 두 개의 전극 내지 전기판을 물에 넣어야 한다. 그 다음으로는 물 속으로 전류를 흘려 보내야 한다. 그러면 물은 수소와 산소로 나누어질 것이다.

2 Reading Skills ▶ Check-Up
1 electrodes
2 hydrogen, oxygen

• Exercise 1 •
p.16

정답 Q1 Ⓑ Q2 Ⓒ

해석 마리 퀴리

마리 퀴리는 역사상 가장 위대한 화학자 중 한 사람이었다. 그녀는 1867년에 폴란드에서 태어났으나 대부분의 연구를 프랑스에서 했다. 그녀는 1891년에 그곳으로 이주하였고 프랑스 소르본느 대학에서 수학하였다. 그녀와 남편 피에르는 함께 연구를 진행했다. 그들은 서로에게 매우 훌륭한 동료였다.

사실 그들은 공동 연구 도중 두 가지 원소를 발견했다. 첫째로, 1898년에 폴로늄 원소를 발견하여 명명하였다. 이후 같은 해에 라듐 또한 발견하였다. 피에르는 1906년에 사망했지만, 마리는 화학 연구를 계속했다. 마리의 연구는 매우 성공적이어서 그녀는 노벨상을 두 번 수상했다. 그녀는 1903년에 노벨 물리학상을, 1911년에는 노벨 화학상을 받았다. 그녀의 생애는 실로 대단히 성공적이었다.

Reading Skills
2, 4, 1, 3

• Exercise 2 •
p.17

정답 Q1 Ⓓ Q2 Ⓑ

해석 녹

많은 건물 및 구조물들은 철과 강철로 만들어져 있다. 이들은 적절히 관리되는 것이 중요한데, 그 이유는 철과 강철에 모두 녹이 생길 수 있기 때문이다. 녹은 적색이나 적황색을 띠는 피막으로 금속에서 나타날 수 있다.

녹은 화학 반응 때문에 형성된다. 녹은 철이나 강철이 수소 및 산소 원자에 노출되는 경우에 생긴다. 보통은 금속이 물에 노출될 때 이러한 일이 발생한다. 그 이유는 물이 수소와 산소 원자로 구성되어 있기 때문이다. 물이 금속에 닿으면 이 둘이 결합하기 시작한다. 이로써 산화라고 불리는 화학 반응이 시작된다. 시간이 지나면 금속의 색이 변하여 적황색이나 적색을 띠게 된다. 녹이 슬면 금속이 약해져서 부서질 수 있다.

Reading Skills
1 oxidation
2 brittle

• Exercise 3 •
p.18

정답 Q1 Ⓒ Q2 Ⓑ

해석 저온 살균법

과거에는 우유와 같은 액체를 장기간 보존할 수 없었다. 시간이 지나면 여러 액체는 해로운 박테리아나 심지어 바이러스까지 키웠냈다. 만약 사람들이 그런 것을 마시면 크게 탈이 날 것이다. 그러나 1862년, 루이스 파스퇴르가 액체를 안전하게 만드는 처리 방법을 개발해 냈다. 그는 이 방법을 저온 살균법이라 이름 붙였다.

저온 살균법은 액체를 그 액체의 끓는점 이상으로 가열하는 방법을 썼다. 이 방법을 사용해 바이러스, 세균, 박테리아, 그리고 기타 해로운 미생물들을 대부분 제거할 수 있었다. 이를 통해 사람들은 다양한 액체를 더 긴 시간 동안 보존할 수 있게 되었다. 1886년엔 우유가 처음으로 저온 살균되었다. 저온 살균된 우유를 냉장 보관하면, 그것은 2주에서 3주 동안 상하지 않은 상태를 유지할 수 있다. 그 후, 누군가가 초저온 살균법을 개발해 냈다. 이 방법을 이용하면 우유를 3개월까지도 보존할 수 있다.

Reading Skills
1, 3, 4, 2

• Exercise 4 •
p.19

정답 Q1 Ⓑ Q2 Ⓒ

해석 전지

오늘날 사람들은 여러 가지 이유로 전지를 사용한다. 전지는 오랜 시간 동안 에너지를 효율적으로 저장한다. 그러나 전지는 상당히 최근에 발명된 것이다. 그리고 발명된 이래 많은 변화를 겪어 왔다.

1798년, 알레산드로 볼타가 최초의 전지를 발명했다. 그 전지에는 다량의 아연과 판지, 구리가 들어 있었다. 그 전지는 그다지 효율적이지는 않았다. 한 가지 예로, 그것은 너무 쉽게 부식되었다. 그래서 존 다니엘이 볼타의 전지를 개량했다. 1836년, 그는 부식되지 않는 전지를 개발했다.

19세기에 들어서 개발된 것이 몇 가지 더 있었다. 그러나 결정적인 것은 1888년에 개발되었다. 그해에 독일인인 카를 가스너가 건전지를 발명했다. 이것은 오늘날 사람들이 사용하는 구리-아연 전지와 유사했다. 마침내 1896년에는 기업에서 소비자들에게 전지를 판매하기 시작했다.

Reading Skills
1 1836
2 Carl Gassner

• Exercise 5 •
p.20

정답 Q1 Ⓓ Q2 Ⓑ Q3 Ⓒ

해석　　**고대 그리스 시대의 화학**

사람들은 보통 화학을 현대 과학이라고 생각한다. 그러나 알고 보면 화학은 수백 년 전부터 있었다. 사실, 고대 그리스인들이 최초로 화학을 연구한 사람들에 속한다.

데모크리토스는 기원전 5세기에 고대 그리스에 살았다. 그는 원자가 모든 물질을 구성한다고 믿었다. 그는 원자가 존재하는 것 중 가장 작은 물질이라고 생각했다. 그 후 기원전 300년경, 철학자인 아리스토텔레스가 물질에 대해 독자적인 주장을 펼쳤다. 그는 흙, 공기, 물, 불이라는 네 가지 원소만이 존재한다고 믿었다.

아리스토텔레스 이후, 서기 7세기까지는 연금술이 꽤 인기를 얻게 되었다. 연금술사들은 여러 가지 물질의 형태를 변형시키려고 노력했다. 특히, 그들은 납과 같은 금속을 금으로 바꾸고 싶어 했다. 그들은 현자의 돌을 만들어내려고 끊임없이 시도했다. 전설에 의하면, 현자의 돌은 금속을 금으로 바꿀 수 있었다. 안타깝게도 그들은 그것을 전혀 발명해 내지 못했다. 그렇지만, 초기의 연금술사들은 많은 물질들의 화학적 성질에 대해 많은 것을 알아냈다.

Reading Skills

3, 1, 2, 4

• Exercise 6 • ──────────── p.22

정답　Q1 Ⓑ　Q2 Ⓐ　Q3 Ⓓ

해석　　**원소의 발견**

지구상에는 자연적으로 발생하는 원소가 92개 있다. 그러나 사람들이 그 원소들을 발견하는 데는 수백 년이 걸렸다. 사실, 화학자들이 마지막 자연 원소를 발견한 것은 20세기 들어서였다. 또한 수많은 합성 원소들이 21세기에도 만들어지고 있다.

고대 사회에서는 몇 가지 원소만이 알려져 있었다. 금과 은, 구리, 철, 탄소가 이 원소들이다. 이러한 원소들은 수천 년 전에 발견되었다.

그러나 1250년이 되어서야 그 다음 원소에 대해 알아내게 되었다. 그 원소는 비소였다. 알베르투스 마그누스가 그것을 발견했다. 그 이후, 서서히 더 많은 원소들이 발견되기 시작했다. 1766년, 헨리 캐번디쉬가 수소를 발견했고, 몇 년 후 1774년에 조지프 프리스틀리가 산소를 발견했다. 이 둘은 모든 원소들 중 가장 중요한 것으로 꼽힌다.

그 후 19세기와 20세기 두 세기 동안, 현대적이며 더 발전한 장비 덕분에 화학자들은 수많은 원소들을 찾아내기 시작했다. 그들이 더 이상의 자연 원소를 찾아내기는 어려울 것으로 보인다. 그러나 새로운 인공 원소들을 더 만들어내는 것은 가능할지도 모른다.

Reading Skills

1　Albertus Magnus
2　Joseph Priestley
3　nineteenth, twentieth

• Exercise 7 • ──────────── p.24

정답　Q1 Ⓐ　Q2 Ⓒ　Q3 Ⓒ

해석　　**알프레드 노벨**

19세기에 건설업과 광산업은 매우 위험한 직업이었다. 많은 사람들이 그 일에 종사하다가 죽었으며, 대규모의 토목 공사를 완수하려면 오랜 시간이 걸렸다. 그러던 중 한 사람이 이 모든 것을 바꿔 놓았다. 그의 이름은 알프레드 노벨이었다.

알프레드 노벨은 1833년에 태어났다. 그의 아버지가 기술자였기 때문에 그 분야는 자연스럽게 노벨의 관심을 끌었다. 1846년에 이탈리아의 한 과학자가 니트로글리세린을 발명했다. 이것은 굉장히 강력했지만, 매우 불안정하고 폭발력이 있었다. 1849년, 노벨은 그 발명가를 만났고, 니트로글리세린으로 실험을 시작했다. 그는 그것을 좀 더 안정성 있게 만들고 싶었다.

슬프게도, 1864년에 노벨의 남동생 에밀이 실험 도중 니트로글리세린이 폭발하여 죽었다. 이 일로 노벨은 더욱 열심히 연구하게 되었다. 1867년, 그는 드디어 액체 상태인 니트로글리세린을 고체 형태로 만들게 되었다. 그는 그것을 다이너마이트라고 명명했다. 다이너마이트는 훨씬 더 안정적이었다. 다이너마이트의 발명은 전 세계의 건설업과 광산업에 이바지했다. 정말 많은 사람들이 다이너마이트를 사용했기 때문에, 그로 인해 노벨 또한 굉장한 부자이자 성공한 사람이 되었다.

Reading Skills

3, 2, 4, 1

• Exercise 8 • ──────────── p.26

정답　Q1 Ⓑ　Q2 Ⓓ　Q3 Ⓑ

해석　　**원소 주기율표**

오늘날 대부분의 고등학생들이 원소 주기율표를 공부한다. 그런데 그것은 오랜 세월에 걸쳐 수없이 많이 바뀐 것이다. 이제는 대부분의 화학자들이 원소 주기율표가 완전하다고 여긴다. 그러나 항상 그랬던 것은 아니다.

앙투안 라부아지에는 1789년에 최초의 주기율표를 만들었다. 그의 주기율표에는 33개의 원소만 포함되어 있었고, 그는 그 원소들을 금속과 비금속으로만 분류했다. 그 다음으로 기여한 사람은 옌스 야코브 베르셀리우스였다. 그는 원소에 문자를 붙여 기호 역할을 하게 하였으며 일부 원소들의 원자량을 측정했다. 1864년엔 존 뉴랜즈가 60개 가량의 기존 원소들을 원자량에 따라 배열했다.

그러나 1869년, 드미트리 멘델레예프가 원소 주기율표의 진정한 창시자로 등장했다. 그가 만든 주기율표는 원소를 원자량에 따라 배열한 것이었다. 그렇지만 그는 다른 원소들이 있어야 한다고 생각하는 자리를 비워 놓았다. 나중에 사람들이 그 원소들을 발견해 냈다. 그는 또한 원자들을 그 특성에 따라 배열했다. 그가 만든 주기율표가 지금의 학생들이 배우는 바로 그것이다.

Reading Skills

1　Antoine Lavoisier
2　John Newlands
3　1869

Grammar Point p.28

✓ Grammar Check-Up

A
1. Many
2. lots of
3. Some
4. a few
5. A lot of

B
1. any
2. many
3. a lot of
4. some
5. few

C some, much, few of, Many, lots of, a few of, any, few

Vocabulary Review p.30

A
1. brittle
2. legend
3. continued
4. reaction
5. stable

B 1 ⒝ 2 ⒟ 3 ⒜ 4 ⒜ 5 ⒞

C 1 ⒞ 2 ⒜ 3 ⒟ 4 ⒟ 5 ⒜

D
1. resemble
2. partners
3. maintain
4. consumers
5. identify

Practice Test p.32

1 ⒝ 2 ⒜ 3 ⒝ 4 ⒞ 5 ⒟
6 ⒟ 7 ■1 8 Physical Changes: ④, ⑥
Chemical Reactions: ①, ②, ⑦

해석   물리적 변화 및 화학적 변화

물질은 항상 변화를 겪는다. 이러한 변화는 때때로 물리적 변화이다. 혹은 화학적 변화인 경우도 있다.

다양한 유형의 물리적 변화가 존재한다. 이는 물질의 상태 변화와 관련된 것일 수 있다. 예를 들어 얼음이 녹아서 물이 되는 경우는 물리적 변화이다. 얼음이 단순히 고체에서 액체로 바뀐 것이다. 하지만 얼음의 화학적인 특성은 전혀 변하지 않았다. (그것은 여전히 두 개의 수소 원자와 한 개의 산소 원자로 이루어져 있다.) 또 다른 물리적 변화로 어떤 사람이 종이 한 장을 찢어 조각을 내는 경우를 들 수 있다. 종이 자체의 화학적 상태는 변하지 않았다. 하지만 종이의 형태가 바뀌었다.

그렇지만 화학적 변화는 물리적 변화와는 다르다. 화학적 변화는 하나 이상의 물질이 다른 물질로 변화할 때 일어난다. 물질 내 원자들 간의 화학적 결합이 변할 때 이러한 변화가 일어난다. 매우 다양한 종류의 화학 반응이 존재한다. 잘 알려진 것 중의 하나가 광합성이다. 그것은 식물이 스스로 양분을 만들기 위해 사용하는 과정이다. 식물은 이산화탄소와 물을 흡수한 다음, 햇빛을 이용해 이를 포도당과 산소로 바꾼다. 화학 반응은 열에 의해 자주 발생한다. 예컨대 자동차에서 가솔린이 연소되는 것은 화학 반응이다. 오븐에서 케이크를 굽는 것도 또 다른 화학 반응을 일으킨다. 이러한 경우들에서, 다양한 물질들이 열에 의해 변화하여 새롭고 전혀 다른 물질이 된다.

CHAPTER 2 Biology

Understanding TOEFL Question Types & Reading Skills p.36

1 Question Types ▶ Sample Question
ⓒ

해석   생태계

생태계란 식물과 동물이 함께 살아가는 영역이다. 생태계에는 여러 다양한 형태가 있다. 사막 생태계 같은 곳은, 동물이 생존하기 어려운 장소이다. 비가 거의 내리지 않고 그곳에 사는 동물도 거의 없다. 그러나 해양 생태계는 생명체가 풍부하다. 정말 다양한 종의 동물들이 그곳에 살고 있으며 동물들이 먹을 먹이도 풍부하다.

2 Reading Skills ▶ Check-Up
ⓑ

• Exercise 1 • 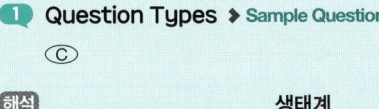 p.38

정답 Q1 ⒜   Q2 ⒝

해석   유전자 변형 식품

이 세상의 어떤 지역에서는 농작물이 잘 자라지 않는다. 아마도 강수량이 부족하거나 토양이 아주 척박할 것이다. 게다가, 어떤 경우에는 질병과 해충으로 인해 식물이 죽기도 한다. 이러한 문제들 때문에 생물학자들은 식물의 유전자 구조를 변형시켜 유전자 변형(GM) 농작물을 개발하는 연구를 진행하고 있다.

과학자들은 여러 종류의 유전자 변형 옥수수를 만들어냈다. 이 옥수수는 보통 질병에 내성이 있다. 어떤 경우에는 유전자 변형 옥수수가 작물을 더 튼튼하고 건강하게 만들 수도 있다. 또 다른 유전자 변형 옥수수는 일반 옥수수 작물보다 낟알을 더 많이 생산해낼 수 있다.

콩 또한 인기 있는 유전자 변형 식품이다. 유전자 변형 콩은 영양가가 높은 경우가 많다. 어떤 것은 척박한 토양에서도 잘 자랄 수 있다. 농부들 또한 살충제 사용량을 줄일 수 있어서 유전자 변형 콩을 좋아한다.

Reading Skills

ⓐ

• Exercise 2 — p.39

정답 Q1 ⓒ   Q2 ⓓ

해석　　　　　　　산호초

산호는 화석화된 개체로, 딱딱한 수생 식물처럼 생겼다. 산호초는 산호가 함께 모여 성장하는 커다란 무리이다. 산호초는 거초와 보초, 두 종류가 있다.

거초는 가장 흔한 종류이다. 거초는 연안 바로 가까이에서 살아가며 해안에서 멀어지면서 넓게 펼쳐져 자라는 경향이 있다. 거초는 플로리다 연안 앞바다와 같은 얕은 물에서 서식한다.

보초는 또 다른 산호초의 형태이다. 보초는 대륙붕을 따라 성장하는 것으로 알려져 있어, 바다를 사이에 두고 본토와 떨어져 있다. 보초는 보통 연결되어 있지 않으나, 대신 서로 가까운 곳에 자리잡은 산호 군락이다. 오스트레일리아의 대보초(그레이트 배리어 리프)가 이러한 보초의 대표적인 예이다.

Reading Skills

ⓓ

• Exercise 3 — p.40

정답 Q1 ⓒ   Q2 ⓒ

해석　　　　　　　유대류

유대류는 300종 이상이 존재한다. 여기에는 캥거루, 코알라, 웜뱃, 주머니쥐 등과 같은 동물들이 포함된다. 유대류는 포유 동물이지만, 포유류의 모든 특징을 공유하지는 않는다. 실제로 유대류는 몇 가지 차이점을 보인다.

주요한 차이점은, 포유 동물과 달리, 유대류 새끼들은 발달되지 않은 상태로 태어난다는 점이다. 이러한 작은 새끼들은 태어난 후 어미의 배에 있는 주머니로 기어 들어간다. 그곳에서 새끼들은 젖을 먹고 발달을 지속한다. 유대류 새끼들은 또한 귀와 뒷다리가 없이 태어난다. 또한 볼 수도 없다. 유대류는 포유 동물보다 체온이 낮다. 또한 더 적은 지역에 분포해 산다. 포유 동물은 전 세계 각지에서 찾아볼 수 있다. 유대류는 주로 오스트레일리아와 아메리카 대륙에서 발견된다.

Reading Skills

ⓑ

• Exercise 4 — p.41

정답 Q1 ⓒ   Q2 ⓓ

해석　　　　　　　미생물

지구상에는 아주 작은 동물들이 많이 있다. 사실, 현미경의 도움 없이는 이러한 생명체들을 볼 수조차 없을 때도 있다. 생물학자들은 이러한 동물들을 일컬어 미생물이라고 한다. 미생물에는 박테리아와 균류 등 여러 가지 다양한 종류가 있다.

박테리아는 일반적으로 단세포 생물이다. 박테리아는 바이러스 다음으로 지구상에서 가장 작은 생명체이다. 박테리아는 공기를 포함하여, 어떤 곳에서든 살 수 있는데, 다만 생존을 위해서는 물이 필요하다. 박테리아는 또한 놀라울 정도로 빠르게 번식할 수 있다.

균류도 마찬가지로 단세포인 경우가 많다. 균류는 주로 흙과 죽은 물질 속에서 산다. 그렇지만 균류는 생태계에 중요한 존재인데 왜냐하면 균류가 쓰레기를 분해하여 쓸모 없거나 불필요한 생산물을 없애기 때문이다. 그러므로 사람들은 박테리아와 균류를 좋아하지 않을지 모르지만, 그래도 그것들은 여전히 중요한 존재들이다.

Reading Skills

ⓓ

• Exercise 5 — p.42

정답 Q1 ⓓ   Q2 ⓐ   Q3 ⓒ

해석　　　　　　　현미경

수백 년 동안 인류는 야생 상태에서 식물과 동물을 관찰했다. 사람들은 그것들에 대해 더 많은 것을 알아내길 간절히 원했지만, 그것들을 면밀하게 연구하기란 어려웠다. 과학자들은 관찰하고 있는 대상이 더 커 보이게 하는 도구가 필요했다.

이러한 필요에 의해 사람들은 현미경을 발명하게 되었다. 가장 일반적인 종류는 복합 현미경이다. 그것은 또한 가장 저렴하다. 그것은 빛을 이용하여 2차원 영상을 만들어낸다. 복합 현미경은 영상을 아주 많이 확대할 수 있지만, 항상 선명하지는 않다.

또 다른 종류로는 해부 현미경이 있다. 해부 현미경 또한 빛에 의존하지만, 그것은 대상을 3차원으로 보여줄 수 있다. 생물학자들은 이 현미경을 해부한 동물을 보는 데 이용한다. 아쉽게도 해부 현미경은 확대율이 낮아서 세포 하나하나를 보여주지는 못한다.

전자 현미경이 최첨단 모델이다. 이 현미경은 구입하는 데 돈이 매우 많이 든다. 그것은 2차원 또는 3차원 영상을 보여줄 수 있고 영상을 아주 선명하게 확대할 수 있다. 그러나 전자 현미경은 영상을 컬러가 아닌 흑백으로만 보여준다.

Reading Skills

ⓒ

• Exercise 6 — p.44

정답 Q1 ⓒ   Q2 ⓒ   Q3 ⓑ

해석　　　　　　　광합성

광합성이란 식물이 햇빛을 흡수하여, 생존하는 데 이용할 에너지로 햇빛을 전환하는 방식을 말한다. 광합성의 과정은 모든 식물에서 동일하게 작용한다. 이 화학 작용 과정에서, 식물은 이산화탄소와 물, 햇빛 에너지를 필요로 한다. 그런 다음 광합성을 통해, 식물은 이런 것들을 설탕의 일종인 포도당과 물, 산소로 변환한다. 이들 세 가지 생산물은 모두 중요하다.

첫째로, 식물은 스스로 포도당을 만들어낸다. 이것은 본질적으로 식물의 양분이 된다. 포도당이 없으면 식물은 죽을 것이다. 포도당은 식물의 여러 기관으로 가서 식물에 에너지를 제공한다.

그 다음 생산물은 물이다. 식물은 광합성의 부산물로서 물을 생산해 낸다. 물론, 물은 지구상의 모든 생명체에게 중요하다. 물이 없다면 모든 생명체가 사라질 것이다. 식물은 그 물을 재사용하기도 하고, 물 자체가 증발하기도 하며 또는 어떤 다른 방식으로든 사라진다.

마지막으로, 식물은 또한 산소를 배출한다. 인간이 생존하는 데는 산소가 필요하기 때문에 이것은 중요한 일이다. 다른 대부분의 동물들도 마찬가지다. 따라서 광합성이 없다면 지구상의 대다수 생명체가 죽을 것이다.

Reading Skills

Ⓑ

• **Exercise 7** • ────────────────── p.46

정답 Q1 Ⓑ   Q2 Ⓐ   Q3 Ⓓ

해석   생물 연료

사람들은 여러 가지 다양한 형태의 에너지를 사용한다. 일반적인 종류로는 생물 연료가 있다. 생물 연료는 바이오매스에서 나온다. 바이오매스는 살아 있거나 혹은 최근에 죽은 것은 무엇이든 해당된다. 생물 연료를 생산하는 데는 몇 가지 다른 방식들이 있다.

첫 번째 방식은 다양한 종류의 바이오매스를 연소시키는 것이다. 목재가 가장 흔히 사용되는 바이오매스지만, 옥수수, 사탕수수, 콩 등 어떤 농작물이든 연소시켜 사용할 수도 있다. 또한 산업 폐기물과 농업 폐기물을 이용하여 에너지를 만들어 낼 수도 있다.

생물 연료를 더 많이 얻는 또 다른 방법은 성장이 빠른 나무를 길러 목재로 쓰는 것이다. 포플러와 버드나무는 단 몇 년 만에 굉장히 높이 자랄 수 있다. 스위치그라스도 성장이 빠른 식물로서, 그것을 빨리 키워 생물 연료로 사용할 수 있을 것이다.

마지막으로, 썩어가는 젖은 쓰레기에서 생물 가스가 생산되고 있다. 과학자들은 동물의 똥과 오물에서 생물 가스를 만들어낼 수 있다. 또한 쓰레기 매립지에서 썩고 있는 쓰레기에서 만들어지는 생물 가스를 포집할 수도 있다. 요컨대, 생물 연료는 화석 연료에 대한 인류의 의존도를 감소시키는 데 도움을 줄 것으로 보인다.

Reading Skills

Ⓐ

• **Exercise 8** • ────────────────── p.48

정답 Q1 Ⓓ   Q2 Ⓓ   Q3 Ⓐ

해석   식물학의 역사

생물학은 생명체에 관한 학문이다. 생물학에는 여러 다양한 분야가 있다. 그중 대중적인 분야로는 식물학이 있다. 식물학자는 식물과 식물의 삶에 대해 연구한다. 오랜 세월 동안, 식물학자들은 다양한 방법을 사용하여 식물을 연구해 왔다.

과거에는 사람들이 시행착오의 방법에 의존했다. 그들은 독성이 있는 식물을 피하고 건강에 좋고 안전한 식물을 먹도록 배웠다. 그들은 자신들의 지식을 부족의 전승 지식을 통해 다음 세대에게 전수해 주었다. 부족의 원로들은 박식한 식물학자가 되어 식물을 질병 치료제나 치료 요법으로 이용할 수도 있게 되었다.

그러나 현대의 식물학자들은 이 분야의 연구를 위해 다른 방식들을 이용한다. 그들은 실험실에서 조사를 하고 첨단 장비를 이용해 식물에 대한 연구를 수행한다. 그들은 과학적 방식에 의존해 식물을 연구한다. 많은 식물학자들이 식물의 유전자 구조까지 연구하고 있으며, 그에 따라 어떤 이들은 식물의 세포 구조를 변형시킬 수도 있다. 현대의 식물학자들은 부족의 원로들과는 다르지만, 둘 다 관심사는 같은 것에 있다: 바로 식물에 대한 학습이다.

Reading Skills

Ⓒ

Grammar Point   p.50

✓ Grammar Check-Up

Ⓐ 1 ⓑ   2 ⓒ   3 ⓐ   4 ⓓ

Ⓑ 1 decompose
    2 live
    3 alter
    4 eat
    5 create

Ⓒ 1 ⓒ   2 ⓓ   3 ⓐ

Vocabulary Review   p.52

Ⓐ 1 Microorganisms
    2 modified
    3 develop
    4 desert
    5 reef

Ⓑ 1 Ⓑ   2 Ⓒ   3 Ⓓ   4 Ⓐ   5 Ⓑ

Ⓒ 1 Ⓑ   2 Ⓓ   3 Ⓓ   4 Ⓐ   5 Ⓑ

Ⓓ 1 invent
    2 resist
    3 share
    4 fringing
    5 decompose

Practice Test   p.54

1 Ⓒ   2 Ⓐ   3 Ⓐ   4 Ⓑ   5 Ⓐ
6 Ⓓ   7 ④   8 Infectious Diseases: ②, ⑦
Noninfectious Diseases: ③, ④, ⑥

해석   수목병

식물도 인간처럼 질병으로 고통 받을 수 있다. 식물은 전염성 질병과 비전염성 질병 모두를 겪을 수 있다.

전염성 질병은 한 식물에서 다른 식물로 옮겨갈 수 있다. 이는 바이러스뿐 아니라 기타 요인들, 즉 박테리아, 균류, 벌레 등에 의해 발생할 수 있다. 이들은 종종 바람, 곤충, 혹은 심지어 농장의 기기에 의해 다른 식물들에 퍼진다. 이러한 질병은 잎을 변색시킬 수 있다. 또한 식물이 이상한 형태로 자랄 수도 있다. 어떤 경우에는 식물을 고사시키기도 한다. 많은 경우, 멀리까지 확산되어 수많은 식물들을 죽게 만들 수 있다. 예를 들어 1800년대 아일랜드에서는 하나의 균류 때문에 많은 감자 작물들이 고사했다. 이것은 아일랜드 감자 기근의 직접적인 원인이 되었다.

식물의 비전염성 질병은 한 식물에서 다른 식물로 전염되지 않는다. 하지만 마찬가지로 이 때문에 식물들이 심한 병에 걸릴 수 있다. 이는 환경적인 요인 때문에 빈번히 발생한다. 예를 들어 토양에 양분이 부족하면 식물이 병에 걸릴 수 있다. 물이 너무 많거나 너무 적어도 문제가 발생할 수 있다. 대기 오염뿐만 아

니라 살충제와 같은 화학 물질에 의해서도 비전염성 질병이 나타날 수 있다. 산성비 역시 식물들이 병에 걸리는 또 다른 원인이다. (산성비가 내리면, 그 안의 유해한 물질 때문에 식물이 심한 병에 걸릴 수 있다.) 많은 경우, 식물들은 비전염성 질병에 의해 생기는 문제들 때문에 죽는다.

CHAPTER 3 Culture

Understanding TOEFL Question Types & Reading Skills
p.58

1 Question Types ▶ Sample Question
Ⓑ

해석   문화의 세계화

세계화 덕분에 문화는 여기저기로 퍼져나가고 있다. 이는 일반적으로 긍정적인 영향을 끼친다. 사람들은 재미있는 외국 영화를 보거나 다른 언어로 된 책을 읽는다. 또한 다른 나라에 방문하고, 매력적이며 새로운 곳에서 살기도 한다. 그러나 세계화는 부정적인 영향도 어느 정도 있다. 어떤 이들은 자신들의 문화가 사라지고 있다고 느낀다. 그리고 다양한 나라에서 온 사람들이 자신의 다양성을 상실하고 있다. 모두가 비슷해지고 있는 것이다.

2 Reading Skills ▶ Check-Up
Ⓐ

• Exercise 1 •
p.60

정답 Q1 Ⓑ Q2 Ⓐ

해석   단일문화주의와 다문화주의

어떤 나라의 국민들은 단일 인종 집단으로 구성되어 있다. 사회학자들은 이를 가리켜 단일문화주의라고 한다. 예를 들어, 일본과 한국, 캄보디아와 같은 나라들이 단일문화권이다. 그들은 문화적 단일성의 정도가 높다. 이러한 나라의 국민들 대다수는 같은 언어를 사용한다. 또한 원주민 대부분이 구속력 있는 특정한 문화 규범을 따른다.

다문화권 국가들도 있다. 이러한 나라들에는 여러 다양한 인종 집단 출신의 사람들이 섞여 살고 있다. 캐나다와 영국, 오스트레일리아와 같은 나라들이 다문화권이다. 그들은 대체로 그들의 영토 내에서 살고 있는 사람들의 다양성을 기쁘게 받아들인다. 그런 나라들은 특정한 문화 규범을 따르긴 하지만, 다른 곳에서 온 사람들이 그들만의 문화를 보존하길 권장한다. 이렇게 함으로써 그들의 문화는 더 다양해진다.

Reading Skills

D, S, S, D

• Exercise 2 •
p.61

정답 Q1 Ⓑ Q2 Ⓓ

해석   결혼생활의 변화

사실상 거의 모든 문화에는 어떤 결혼생활의 전통이 있다. 그러나 오랜 세월 동안 결혼생활은 아주 많이 변했다.

전통적으로 전 세계 대부분의 문화에서는 남편이 결혼생활의 우위를 차지했다. 남편은 중요하고 구속력 있는 결정을 했다. 남편만 일을 하는 경우도 많았다. 아내는 보통 아이들을 키우고 가사를 돌보는 일을 했다. 본질적으로 여성은 이등 시민과 같은 존재였다.

오늘날에는 페미니즘 덕분에 현대의 결혼생활이 동등한 협력관계인 경우가 많다. 남편과 아내가 보통 둘 다 직업을 갖는다. 때로는 남편의 벌이가 적고 아내가 고소득 직업을 가진 경우도 있다. 또한, 남편과 아내가 둘 다 가정 내 의사결정을 한다. 우위를 차지하는 사람은 없고, 둘 다 결혼생활에서 협력자로서 함께 역할을 한다.

Reading Skills

Ⓒ

• Exercise 3 •
p.62

정답 Q1 Ⓐ Q2 Ⓒ

해석   카우보이

19세기에 카우보이들은 미국 문화의 중요한 일부분이 되었다. 그들은 서부에서 살며 주로 목장에서 일했다. 카우보이에 관해 전해진 많은 이야기들이 사실이긴 하지만, 그들에 관해서 과장된 신화는 셀 수 없이 많다.

카우보이들은 목장주를 위해 말들과 소떼를 돌보았다. 그들은 쉬는 시간이 거의 없이 녹초가 되도록 오랜 시간 동안 일했다. 그들은 상당히 개인주의적이었으며 모든 일을 스스로 처리하도록 배웠다.

그러나 영화 덕분에 카우보이에 관해 잘못된 이야기들이 수없이 많이 생겨났다. 많은 이들이 카우보이는 피에 굶주린 살인자 내지 총잡이였다고 생각한다. 사실, 그들은 다른 이들과 거의 싸우지도 않았고 살인도 하지 않았다. 영화에서 보여주는 것처럼 아메리카 원주민들을 공격하고 죽이지도 않았다. 그리고 카우보이들의 삶은 특별히 매력적이지도 않았다; 그보다는 대다수가 단촐한 삶을 살았다.

Reading Skills

D, D, S, S

• Exercise 4 •
p.63

정답 Q1 Ⓓ Q2 Ⓑ

해석   유교와 불교

종교와 철학은 국가와 그 문화에 크게 영향을 주는 경우가 많다. 그 두 가지 예가 유교와 불교이다. 이 둘은 아시아의 여러 국가들에 아주 강력하게 작용한다.

유교는 사람들 사이의 관계를 중요시한다. 유교에는 사람들이 따라야 할 종교적인 의식이 많으면서도 또한 다른 이들에게 헌신할 것을 강조한다. 유교는 중국에서 시작해 다른 여러 나라들로 퍼졌다. 일본과 한국, 대만이 그 영향을 받은 나라들이다. 유교 때문에 그들의 문화는 매우 많은 변화를 겪었다.

반면 불교는 평화와 자비, 지혜를 강조한다. 불교에 따르면 모든 이들이 평등하며, 모든 이들이 행복을 추구하고 행복한 삶을 살 수 있다. 불교는 인도에서 유래하였으나 중국과 한국, 일본, 베트남으로 퍼져 그 나라 국민과 문화에 영향을 끼치고 있다.

Reading Skills

Ⓓ

• **Exercise 5** • ─────────────────────── p.64

정답 Q1 Ⓒ   Q2 Ⓐ   Q3 Ⓑ

해석   도시 환경과 시골 환경

문명화가 시작된 이래로 대부분의 사람들은 도시 혹은 시골 환경에서 살고 있다. 도시 환경은 도시이다. 시골 환경은 전원 지대에 있는 지역이다. 이 두 지역은 많은 차이점을 나타낸다.

가장 명백한 차이는 인구이다. 도시 지역에는 인구가 많다. 오늘날 도시에는 수백만 명의 주민들이 살고 있다. 도쿄, 카이로, 상하이와 같은 대도시에는 2천만 명의 사람들이 그 주변에 거주할 수도 있다. 시골 지역은 인구 밀도가 훨씬 더 적다. 따라서 사람들은 서로 멀리 떨어져 산다. 그들은 보통 주택에서 산다. 도시에서는 대부분의 사람들이 아파트에서 생활한다. 아파트 한 건물에는 수백 혹은 수천 명의 사람들이 그 안에서 생활할 수도 있다.

시골 지역은 조용한 편이다. 또한 대기 오염도 훨씬 덜하다. 시골 지역에 사는 사람들은 자가용을 소유하는 경우가 많다. 하지만 도시에 사는 많은 사람들은 대중교통에 의존한다. 그들은 버스와 지하철, 기차를 타고 목적지에 도착한다. 도시는 또한 꽤 위험할 수 있다. 도시의 범죄율은 시골 지역에 비해 훨씬 더 높다.

Reading Skills

S, D, D, D

• **Exercise 6** • ─────────────────────── p.66

정답 Q1 Ⓐ   Q2 Ⓒ   Q3 Ⓐ

해석   민속 문화

인종 집단 혹은 지리적 영역에 따라 많은 사람들이 특정한 전통을 유지하며 살아간다. 세상은 비록 변화하고 있지만, 그들은 대체로 자신들의 전통을 지킨다. 이러한 것을 민속 문화라 한다. 민속 문화는 여러 다양한 방식으로 나타날 수 있다.

가장 흔한 방식 중 하나가 음악과 함께 나타나는 것이다. 미국의 애팔래치아 산맥 지방에 사는 어떤 이들은 다음 세대에게 블루그래스 음악을 전승해 준다. 또한 하와이 제도의 사람들은 우쿨렐레와 같은 악기를 기반으로 한 고유한 민속 음악을 갖고 있다. 그리고 오스트레일리아 원주민들은 전통 악기인 디저리두를 사용한 음악을 대물린다.

민속 문화의 또 다른 종류로 미술 공예가 있다. 캐나다와 북극 지역의 여러 나라에 사는 이누이트 족은 뼈와 돌, 상아를 이용해 조각 입상을 만든다. 중서부 지역의 많은 미국인들은 고유의 퀼트 제품을 꿰매 만든다. 심지어 일본의 오리가미도 민속 문화의 한 종류이다. 오리가미란 종이를 접어 다양한 작품으로 만드는 것이다.

Reading Skills

Ⓐ

• **Exercise 7** • ─────────────────────── p.68

정답 Q1 Ⓐ   Q2 Ⓑ   Q3 Ⓐ

해석   할리우드 영화와 볼리우드 영화

대부분의 사람들이 영화를 생각할 때, 할리우드를 떠올린다. 할리우드는 캘리포니아의 한 도시로, 그 근처에서 많은 영화를 찍는다. 인도에도 볼리우드가 있다. 볼리우드 역시 많은 영화를 제작한다.

대부분의 사람들은 할리우드 영화에 대해 긍정적인 이미지를 갖고 있다. 남녀 영화 배우들은 정말 눈부시게 매력적이고, 액션 영화에 사용되는 특수 효과들은 놀라운 정도이다. 그러나 그 영화들은 항상 영어로 만들어져서 외국 관객들이 혼란을 겪는 경우도 있다. 그리고 어떤 경우, 할리우드 영화들은 너무 폭력적이고 욕설이 난무하기도 한다.

볼리우드 영화는 인도의 뭄바이 근처 지역에서 만들어진다. 그러나 볼리우드는 실제 장소가 아니다. 볼리우드는 매년 1,000편이 넘는 영화를 제작한다. 영화는 힌디어와 우르두어, 영어로 만들어진다. 볼리우드 영화는 대부분 뮤지컬로 노래와 춤이 많이 등장한다. 볼리우드 영화는 할리우드 영화만큼 인기 있지는 않다. 그래도 많은 사람들이 즐겨 본다.

Reading Skills

D, S, S, D

• **Exercise 8** • ─────────────────────── p.70

정답 Q1 Ⓑ   Q2 Ⓑ   Q3 Ⓒ

해석   식민지화를 통한 문화 전파

역사를 통틀어 국가들은 항상 서로를 식민지로 삼아 왔다. 적국을 상대로 전쟁에서 승리함으로써 식민지로 삼는 경우가 많았다. 이를 통해 국가들은 자신들의 문화를 다른 지역에 전파할 수 있었다.

대부분의 사람들은 식민지화에 대해 부정적인 견해를 갖고 있다. 그러나 어떤 사람들은 식민지화가 식민지 지역에 긍정적인 영향을 어느 정도 미칠 수 있다고 주장한다. 어떤 경우 식민지 개척자들은 자신들의 새로운 기술을 가져오기도 한다. 그래서 식민지 국가가 더 발전하게 될 수도 있다. 그에 더해, 정복 국가는 다른 국가의 기반 시설을 구축하기도 한다. 예를 들면 도로와 철도를 건설할 수도 있는 것이다. 식민지 개척자들은 또한 식민지 국가의 교육과 정치 체제를 개선할 수도 있다.

물론 사람들이 식민지화에 반감을 갖는 데는 많은 이유가 있다. 한 가지 이유는, 굴복한 나라가 자주성을 잃는다는 것이다. 식민지가 되었으니 더 이상 독립된 나라가 아니다. 또한, 많은 식민지들이 그들만의 고유한 문화를 잃기 시작한다. 그들은 또한 자신들만의 고유한 체제를 바꾸고 싶지 않을 수도 있다. 많은 이들이 새로운 것을 받아들이기보다는 자신들만의 고유한 전통과 방식을 지키고 싶어 한다.

Reading Skills

Ⓒ

Grammar Point   p.72

✓ Grammar Check-Up

A 1 exciting
   2 amazed
   3 respected
   4 globalized
   5 striking

B 1 ⓑ   2 ⓑ   3 ⓓ

C interested, written, exhausting, interesting, influenced, published

Vocabulary Review   p.74

A 1 railroads
   2 opponents
   3 dominated
   4 monocultural
   5 globalization

B 1 ⓒ   2 ⓐ   3 ⓑ   4 ⓑ   5 ⓑ

C 1 ⓓ   2 ⓑ   3 ⓓ   4 ⓑ   5 ⓐ

D 1 Feminism
   2 produce
   3 infrastructure
   4 cowboys
   5 dwell

Practice Test   p.76

1 ⓒ   2 ⓑ   3 ⓑ   4 ⓐ   5 ⓑ   6 ⓓ
7   8 ②, ④, ⑥

해석   **로마 제국의 문화 유산**

서기 2세기에 로마 제국의 영토는 가장 넓었다. 로마는 서유럽의 대부분 지역에 걸쳐 있었는데, 이는 오늘날의 이탈리아와 프랑스, 스페인 및 포르투갈과 영국과 독일의 일부, 북아프리카 일부 지역, 그리고 동유럽과 중동의 많은 지역에 해당한다. 로마는 역사상 가장 거대한 제국 중 하나였다. 그러나 5세기 말 유럽에서 로마 제국은 사라졌고 동쪽 지역에 비잔틴 제국만이 남았다. 그럼에도 불구하고 로마는 유럽의 문화에 여러 면에서 중요한 영향을 끼쳤다. 그중 두 가지가 언어와 기독교의 도입이다.

로마 제국의 시민들은 라틴어를 사용했다. 지금은 사용하지 않는 사어(死語)이지만 한때 교양 있는 사람들은 모두 라틴어를 사용했다. 그리고 많은 현대의 언어들이 라틴어에서 진화했다. 로망스어인 이탈리아어, 프랑스어, 스페인어가 모두 라틴어와 유사하다. 사실, 이 언어들은 라틴어에서 직접 파생되었다. 그 언어들은 로마 제국이 멸망한 뒤에야 발달한 것으로, 이들 서로 다른 나라의 국민들 사이에는 접촉할 일이 적었다. 심지어 영어는 라틴어에서 직접 파생된 것은 아니지만, 라틴어에서 차용한 단어들이 정말 많다.

로마 제국의 가장 중요한 유산 중 하나는 아마도 기독교였을 것이다. 네로와 같은 초기의 로마 황제들은 기독교인들을 처형했으나 콘스탄티누스 대제는 330년대에 최초의 기독교인 황제가 되었다. (그는 죽기 직전에 세례를 받았지만, 몇 년 전부터 이미 기독교인이었다.) 그를 따라, 사실상 모든 로마 황제들이 기독교인이었다. 기독교는 이후에 거대한 제국 전체로 급속하게 퍼졌으며, 유럽 국가들은 오늘날까지도 대부분 기독교 국가로 남아 있다. 기독교의 도입은 이들 지역에 살고 있는 사람들을 개화시키는 효과를 가져왔고, 로마 멸망 후 중세 암흑기에 문화와 지식을 보존하려 했던 사람들은 기독교 수도사들이었다.

로마는 많은 영향을 끼쳤지만, 언어와 기독교는 그중 가장 중요한 것들이었다. 이 두 가지가 없었다면 세상은 매우 다른 모습이었을 것이다.

CHAPTER 4 Music

Understanding TOEFL Question Types & Reading Skills   p.80

1 Question Types ▸ Sample Question
Ⓐ

해석   **음유 시인들**

중세 시대에 음악은 매우 인기가 있었다. 사람들은 특히 노래 부르는 것을 좋아했다. 그래서 음유 시인들이 이 도시 저 도시를 다니며 사람들에게 노래를 불러 주기 시작했다. 노래를 작곡하고 부르는 것이 음유 시인들의 전문 분야였다. 그들은 기사도에 대해서, 그리고 기사들과 귀족들의 위대한 공적에 대해 노래하곤 했다. 귀족들은 대개 음유 시인들의 노래를 좋아했으므로, 그들은 성과 궁궐에서 음악을 연주하는 일이 많았다.

2 Reading Skills ▸ Check-Up
C, E

• Exercise 1 •   p.82

정답 Q1 Ⓓ   Q2 Ⓐ

해석   **서사시와 음악**

많은 문화권에 긴 시들의 모음, 즉 서사시가 존재한다. 이러한 시들은 영웅들의 위대한 공적에 관련된 이야기들을 다루고 있다. 유명한 서사시 중에는 고대 그리스의 *일리아드*와 *오디세이*, 메소포타미아의 *길가메시*, 앵글로색슨의 *베오울프*가 있다. 그러나 이러한 서사시의 대부분은 길이가 수천 줄에 달했다. 따라서 대부분의 사람들이 문맹이었기 때문에 서사시를 읽는다는 것은 어려운 일이었다.

사람들은 이러한 시들을 기억하기 위해 더 나은 다른 방법을 생각해 내야 했고, 그래서 어떤 이들은 그것을 노래하기로 했다. 시를 노래로 부르면 기억하기가 더 쉬웠다. 그에 따라 서사시를 듣는 것은 오락거리의 초기 형태가 되었다. 식사 후, 사람들은 위대한 업적에 대한 이야기들을 누군가가 노래로 부르는 것을 듣곤 했다.

Reading Skills

1 E, C 2 E, C

• Exercise 2 • ───────── p.83

[정답] Q1 Ⓓ Q2 Ⓑ

[해석]
관악기

세계에서 가장 오래된 악기로는 관악기가 있다. 고고학자들은 수천 년 전 원시시대 사람들이 만들었던 뼈로 된 피리를 발견했다. 관악기는 공기를 이용해 소리를 만든다. 공기는 사람의 입에서 나온다. 관악기에는 여러 종류가 있다.

여러 가지 목관 악기가 있다. 여기에는 플루트, 클라리넷, 색소폰이 포함된다. 금관 악기 역시 관악기로 간주된다. 트럼펫, 트롬본, 튜바가 여기에 해당된다. 금관 악기는 보통 황동으로 만들어진다. 목관 악기는 나무나 금속으로 만들어진다. 이 두 가지 유형의 악기들은 서로 다른 소리를 만들어낸다. 하지만 연주 방식은 상당히 유사하다. 연주자들이 악기에 공기를 불어 넣는다. 그러면 악기가 음악을 만들어낸다.

Reading Skills

1 C, E 2 C, E

• Exercise 3 • ───────── p.84

[정답] Q1 Ⓐ Q2 Ⓓ

[해석]
존 윌리엄스

초창기 영화들은 무성 영화였다. 그러나 기술이 급속도로 발전했다. 이 때문에 영화 감독들은 영화에 소리를 입힐 수 있게 되었다. 감독들은 영화에 음성도 입히고 사운드트랙도 넣는 일이 많았다. 사운드트랙은 영화에 함께 나오는 악곡을 말한다. 오랜 세월 동안 사운드트랙은 다양한 영화들과 함께 연상되는 일이 많아졌다.

존 윌리엄스는 세계적으로 가장 유명한 사운드트랙들을 작곡했다. 어떤 것들은 영화 *조스*에 나오는 주제곡처럼 단순하다. 또 어떤 것들은 영화 *스타워즈*에 삽입된 서곡처럼 감격적이다. 윌리엄스가 사운드트랙을 작곡한 수많은 영화들이 흥행에 성공했다. 그 결과 그는 유명해졌다. 지금까지 그의 앨범은 수백만 장이 팔렸다.

Reading Skills

1 E, C 2 C, E

• Exercise 4 • ───────── p.85

[정답] Q1 Ⓑ Q2 Ⓒ

[해석]
볼프강 아마데우스 모차르트

역사상 가장 뛰어난 음악가 중 한 사람으로 볼프강 아마데우스 모차르트가 있었다. 1756년에 태어난 모차르트는 신동이었다. 세 살 때 피아노를 연주하는 법을 배운 그는 다섯 살 때 작곡을 시작했다. 그의 천재성 덕분에, 모차르트는 겨우 여섯 살 때 바이에른 왕족 앞에서 연주를 했다.

모차르트는 짧은 생애를 살면서 600곡이 넘는 곡을 작곡했다. 그는 심포니와 오페라, 미사곡, 그리고 그 밖에도 여러 종류의 곡을 만들어 낸 음악 천재였다. 일생 동안 그는 모든 작곡가 중에서도 가장 위대한 작곡가로 널리 인정받았다. 그의 작품은 사실상 지금까지 아무도 필적하지 못하는 청명함과 조화로움을 보여주었다. 이러한 이유로 모차르트의 작품은 현재까지도 그 인기를 유지하고 있다.

Reading Skills

1 C, E 2 E, C

• Exercise 5 • ───────── p.86

[정답] Q1 Ⓑ Q2 Ⓐ Q3 Ⓓ

[해석]
그래미상

1950년대 들어, 음악은 미국인들의 의식 속에 중요한 일부분이 되고 있었다. 흥미로운 밴드들이 많이 결성되고 있었다. 그러한 밴드들의 음악을 라디오에서 듣고 TV에서 보는 것은 흔한 일이 되었다. 사람들은 가장 뛰어난 밴드들을 알아보고 상을 줌으로써 그들에게 보상해 주고 싶었다. 그래서 미국 음반 예술 과학 아카데미는 그라모폰상을 만들어냈다. 후에, 그들은 그 이름을 그래미상으로 바꾸었다.

아카데미에서는 이 시상식을 매년 개최한다. 그래미상은 여러 분야에서 음악가들을 수상 후보로 지명한다. 그래미상을 수상하면 명성이 높아지기 때문에, 음악가들은 상을 받기 위해 최선을 다한다. 그래미상을 탄 음악가는 수상 후 음반 판매량이 증가하는 것 또한 기대할 수 있다.

오늘날 그래미상은 전 세계로 중계되기 때문에 매년 수백만 명의 사람들이 그 시상식을 시청한다. 올해의 음반상, 올해의 노래상, 올해의 앨범상과 올해의 신인상이 가장 받고 싶어 하는 상이다. 그래서 이 상을 받기 위한 경쟁이 아주 치열하다. 매년, 새로운 수상자들은 수상에 따른 명성과 부를 얻는다.

Reading Skills

Ⓑ

• Exercise 6 • ───────── p.88

[정답] Q1 Ⓒ Q2 Ⓑ Q3 Ⓓ

[해석]
색소폰의 개발

여러 다양한 악기들이 있다. 그러나 사람들은 이 악기들의 발명가에 대해서는 거의 알지 못한다. 색소폰이 바로 그런 경우이다. 벨기에인인 아돌프 삭스는 1840년대에 색소폰을 발명했다. 삭스는 악기 설계자의 아들이었다. 이 때문에 그는 악기에 대해 자신만의 흥미를 발전시켰다.

1840년대에 삭스는 군악대와 오케스트라에서 연주할 새로운 악기를 원했다. 그래서 그는 색소폰을 설계하기 시작했다. 그는 클라리넷과 같은 목관 악기와 트럼펫과 같은 금관 악기를 결합하는 것을 목표로 삼고 있었다. 그가 한 작업의 결과물이 색소폰이었다.

삭스에게 악기 설계는 쉬운 일이었기 때문에 그는 여러 형태의 색소폰을 만들어냈다. 그러나 색소폰이 그 즉시 인기를 얻은 것은 아니었다. 처음에 그보다는 몇몇 소수의 밴드만이 색소폰을 사용했다. 그러나 나중에는 더 많은 사람들이 색소폰 제작을 시도하기 시작했다. 이 때문에 색소폰의 인기가 높아지게 되었다. 오늘날 색소폰은 굉장히 인기가 많아서 많은 음악 장르에서 색소폰이 사용되고 있다.

Reading Skills

Ⓑ

• Exercise 7 • p.90

정답 Q1 Ⓑ Q2 Ⓐ Q3 Ⓓ

해석 로큰롤

세계 각지의 사람들이 록 음악을 듣는다. 그러나 록 음악은 비교적 새로운 장르의 음악이다. 그것은 불과 1940년대와 1950년대에 미국에서 발전했다. 그 이전에 미국인들은 빅밴드(열 명 이상의 대규모로 편성한 앙상블 형태의 밴드)와 컨트리 음악, 재즈 같이 그와는 다른 종류의 음악을 들었다. 그러나 많은 사람들이 새로운 연주를 원했다. 그래서 사람들은 다양한 형태의 음악을 결합시키기 시작했다. 특히 재즈와 블루스 같은 음악들로 실험해 보는 것이 흔한 일이 되었다. 그 결과물이 로큰롤이었다.

1954년, 빌 헤일리 노래 *락 어라운드 더 클락*이 음악 순위에서 1위를 했다. 이 일은 록 음악의 인기를 폭발적으로 증가시켰다. 이로 인해 척 베리와 빅 조 터너와 같은 다른 초기 록 음악가들의 인기가 높아졌다. 마침내 엘비스 프레슬리가 인기를 얻기 시작했다. 이로 인해 미국에서뿐 아니라 전 세계적으로 록 음악이 가장 인기 있는 음악 장르 중 하나로 자리잡게 되었다.

Reading Skills
Ⓐ

• Exercise 8 • p.92

정답 Q1 Ⓐ Q2 Ⓐ Q3 Ⓑ

해석 고전 음악의 변화

고전 음악은 가장 오해를 많이 받는 음악 형태 중 하나이다. 많은 사람들이 고전 음악은 오랜 세월 동안 전혀 변하지 않았다고 생각한다. 그래서 사람들은 고전 음악을 한 번 들어보고, 싫으면 다시 듣기를 거부한다. 실제로 고전 음악은 700년 역사 동안 여러 차례 변화해 왔다.

고전 음악은 중세 시대 교회의 성가로 시작되었다. 그러나 르네상스의 도래로 고전 음악에 변화가 일어났다. 사회가 세속적으로 변화함에 따라 고전 음악도 그렇게 되었다. 또한, 성가는 상당히 단순한 반면, 바로크 음악은 훨씬 더 복잡해졌다. 이 시기에는 모든 악기를 조화롭게 연주하는 것이 중요해졌다.

바로크 시대를 지나면서, 고전 음악은 상당히 다채로워졌다. 수많은 개인이 자신만의 음악을 작곡하기 시작했다. 이로 인해 여러 고전 음악 양식이 형성되었다. 예를 들면, 바흐, 베토벤, 모차르트는 고전 음악의 3대 음악가이다. 그러나 이들의 음악을 들어보면, 이들이 서로 동시대에 살았음에도 불구하고 그들의 스타일이 얼마나 다른지 알게 될 것이다.

Reading Skills
Ⓒ

Grammar Point p.94

Grammar Check-Up

Ⓐ 1 Listening
    2 designing
    3 Receiving
    4 increasing
    5 traveling

Ⓑ 1 ⓐ 2 ⓒ 3 ⓒ

Ⓒ going, playing, putting, paying, watching, staying, doing

Vocabulary Review p.96

Ⓐ 1 inspiring
    2 combine
    3 categories
    4 illiterate
    5 prodigy

Ⓑ 1 Ⓓ 2 Ⓑ 3 Ⓐ 4 Ⓐ 5 Ⓒ

Ⓒ 1 Ⓒ 2 Ⓒ 3 Ⓐ 4 Ⓓ 5 Ⓑ

Ⓓ 1 televise
    2 result
    3 chivalry
    4 versions
    5 Countless

Practice Test p.98

1 Ⓑ 2 Ⓒ 3 Ⓐ 4 Ⓑ 5 Ⓓ
6 Ⓐ 7 ② 8 ①, ②, ⑥

해석 르네상스 시대의 음악

르네상스 시대는 약 1400년에 유럽에서 시작되었다. 그 시대는 약 200년 동안 지속되었다. 르네상스 시대는 중세 시대 이후에 등장했다. 이 두 시기는 서로 크게 달랐다. 그러한 차이 중 일부는 르네상스 시대의 음악에서 찾을 수 있었다.

중세 시대에는 대부분의 음악이 종교 음악이었다. 사람들은 주로 교회와 성당에서 음악을 들었다. (그들은 또한 다양한 종교 축제에서 음악을 듣고 연주했다.) 하지만 이것은 르네상스 시대 때 바뀌었다. 여전히 종교적인 음악들이 매우 많이 있었다. 하지만 세속적인 음악 또한 많아졌다. 실제로 음악은 사람들을 즐겁게 해주는 매우 중요한 방식이 되었다. 또한 사람들이 연주하는 음악의 종류도 많아졌다.

르네상스 시대에는 합창 음악이 인기를 얻었다. 합창단은 함께 노래를 부르는 여러 명의 사람들로 구성되었다. 마드리갈(성악 실내음악곡) 역시 인기 있는 음악 양식이었다. 보통 세 명에서 여섯 명의 가수들이 마드리갈을 불렀다. 가수들은 낭만적인 시와 같은 감성적인 노래를 불렀다.

르네상스 시대에는 새로운 악기들이 많이 등장했다. 그중 하나가 바이올린이었다. 바이올린은 1500년대에 만들어졌다. 바이올린은 시간이 지나면서 세계에서 가장 인기 있는 악기 중 하나가 되었다. 마침내, 이 시대에 사람들이 악보를 적기 시작했다. 이 때문에 음악이 널리 퍼져나갈 수 있었다.

CHAPTER 5 Anthropology

Understanding TOEFL Question Types & Reading Skills
p.102

1 Question Types ▶ Sample Question
Ⓑ

해석　　　　　　　민속
인류학자들은 과거 인류 문화의 양상에 대해 연구한다. 이런 연구를 하는 방법 중 하나는 어떤 문화의 민속에 대해 조사하는 것이다. 민속은 여러 가지 요인들이 결합될 수 있다. 민속에는 이야기, 전설, 문화, 신앙 등이 포함될 수 있다. 오늘날에도 여전히 현대의 많은 사람들이 자녀들에게 민속을 전승하고 있다. 이러한 전통과 관습들을 어느 정도 연구함으로써, 인류학자들은 과거에 대해 아주 많은 것을 알 수 있다.

2 Reading Skills ▶ Check-Up
Ⓐ

• Exercise 1 •
p.104

정답　Q1 Ⓐ　Q2 Ⓓ

해석　　　　　　　루시
인류학계의 한 학파는 인류가 영장류에서 진화했다고 말한다. 물론, 이렇게 진화하는 데는 틀림없이 수백만 년의 시간이 걸렸을 것이다. 안타깝게도 인류학자들은 이러한 주장을 뒷받침할 만한 증거를 전혀 찾아내지 못했다. 그러나 이런 상황은 1974년, 어느 연구팀이 루시를 발견하면서 바뀌었다.

루시는 원인(原人)이었다. 그녀는 완전한 사람이라고 보긴 어렵지만 비슷한 어떤 존재였다. 과학자들은 루시를 오스트랄로피테쿠스 속으로 분류했다. 루시의 키는 대략 1미터였고 이족 동물이었으므로 직립 보행을 할 수 있었다. 더욱 중요한 것은, 그녀가 350만 년 전에 살았다는 것이다. 인류학자들은, 그때 이후로 루시가 현생 인류의 고대 선조 중 하나라고 판단하고 있다. 어떤 이들은 그녀가 유인원과 인간 사이의 잃어버린 연결 고리라고 믿는다.

Reading Skills
Ⓒ

• Exercise 2 •
p.105

정답　Q1 Ⓑ　Q2 Ⓑ

해석　　　　　　　석기 시대
석기 시대는 굉장히 긴 시간을 장악했다. 이 시대는 대략 백만 년 전쯤 시작되어 기원전 3500년경에 끝났을 것이다. 이 기간 동안 인류의 문화에는 수많은 발전이 있었다.

사람들이 이루어 낸 가장 중요한 발전은 도구의 사용에 있었다. 그 이름이 말해 주듯, 석기 시대 동안 사람들은 돌로 만든 도구를 사용했다. 그러나 이것이 사람들이 이루어 낸 유일한 발전은 아니었다. 인류는 농업에 대해 학습했고, 그에 따라 토지를 경작하여 다양한 작물들을 재배하기 시작할 수 있었다. 또한 이 시기에는 동물, 특히 개를 길들였다. 그들은 또한 도기를 발명했고 수렵 채집 생활을 포기하면서 큰 집단을 이루어 정착하기 시작했다.

Reading Skills
Ⓒ

• Exercise 3 •
p.106

정답　Q1 Ⓐ　Q2 Ⓓ

해석　　　　　　　네안데르탈인
네안데르탈인은 현생 인류와 가까운 친척 관계였다. 그들은 약 40만 년 전에 살았다. 하지만 4만 년 전 쯤에 사라졌다. 그들은 주로 유럽, 소아시아, 그리고 중앙아시아의 일부 지역에 살았다.

네안데르탈인은 서 있는 경우 키가 168센티미터 정도였다. 그들은 현생 인류보다 훨씬 더 힘이 셌다. 뇌 또한 현생 인류의 뇌보다 더 컸다. 전문가들은 이들이 지능을 가지고 있었다고 생각한다. 그들은 또한 말도 할 수 있었다.

하지만 네안데르탈인이 현생 인류와 만나게 되자 그들은 경쟁하기 어려웠다. 현생 인류가 유럽에 도달한 지 약 5천 년이 지나자 모든 네안데르탈인이 사라졌다. 전쟁이 있었을지도 모른다. 기후 변화를 겪으면서 네안데르탈인이 영향을 받았을지도 모른다. 그들이 사라진 이유에 대해 정확히 아는 사람은 없다.

Reading Skills
Ⓐ

• Exercise 4 •
p.107

정답　Q1 Ⓒ　Q2 Ⓒ

해석　　　　　　　초기의 도구 제작
인류는 오랫동안 도구를 사용해 왔지만, 이러한 도구들의 성질은 수천 년을 거치면서 변화해 왔다. 인간이 최초로 도구를 만들기 시작했을 때, 그것은 동물의 뼈로 만들어졌고 그다지 효율적이지 않았다.

백만 년 전에 석기 시대가 시작되면서, 인류는 돌로 도구를 만들 수 있었다. 이러한 도구들은 비교적 단순했는데, 사람들이 돌을 단순히 자신이 원하는 모양으로 천천히 깎았기 때문이다. 가장 흔한 도구는 창이나 화살 같은 무기에 쓸 뾰족한 끝 부분 등의 무기였다.

동기 시대가 되어서야 사람들은 금속으로 된 도구를 만들기 시작했다. 이 시기는 기원전 4000년경에 시작되었다. 청동기 시대와 철기 시대는 인류가 더 새롭고, 더 훌륭하며, 더 효율적인 도구 제작 방식을 학습함에 따라 빠르게 등장했다.

Reading Skills
Ⓑ

• Exercise 5 •
p.108

정답　Q1 Ⓓ　Q2 Ⓐ　Q3 Ⓐ

해석　　　　　　　마거릿 미드
세월이 흐르는 동안 많은 유명한 인류학자들이 있었다. 가장 유명한 인류학자 중 한 사람은 마거릿 미드였다. 1901년에 태어나 1978년에 사망할 때까지, 미드는 인류학 연구가 주목을 받는 데 공헌했다. 그녀가 없었다면, 많은 인류학자들이 여전히 이름도 알려지지 않은 채 연구하고 있을 것이다.

미드는 수많은 책을 썼으나 가장 영향력이 있는 것은 *사모아의 청소년*이라는 제목의 첫 저서였다. 이 책은 사실 남태평양에 관한 세 권의 시리즈 중 첫 번째 책이었다. 이 책에서 그녀는 성별에 따른 역할에 대해 탐구했다. 그녀는 남성과 여성의 서로 다른 역할이 생물학적이 아니라 문화적으로 결정될 수 있다고 믿었다.

그녀의 일생 동안, 미드의 연구 결과는 매우 많은 논쟁을 불러 일으켰다. 많은 이들이 그녀의 연구를 강력히 지지한 반면, 어떤 이들은 그에 대해 맹렬하게 반대했다. 그녀가 사망한 후에도 그런 점은 변화하지 않았다. 그럼에도 불구하고 그녀는 여전히 현대 인류학에서 중요한 인물로 남아 있다.

Reading Skills

Ⓓ

• **Exercise 6** • ─────── p.109

정답 Q1 Ⓒ Q2 Ⓓ Q3 Ⓐ

해석 　　　　　　베링 해협의 육교

오랜 세월 동안, 인류학자들은 아메리카 대륙이 인류가 정착한 마지막 대륙이라고 인정해 왔다. 그들 대부분이 인류가 아프리카에서 시작되었다고 믿는다. 그곳에서 시작하여, 인류가 아시아와 유럽으로, 그리고 후에 아메리카 대륙으로 퍼졌을 거라고 생각한다. 그러나 그들은 어떻게 해서 이렇게 되었는지는 알지 못했다.

현재는 많은 이들이 어떻게 초기 인류가 아메리카 대륙에 정착했는지 알고 있다고 생각한다. 어떤 이들이 생각했던 것처럼, 이들 정착자들은 배를 타고 대서양이나 태평양을 건넌 것이 아니었다. 대신에, 베링 해협의 육교를 가로질렀다. 이것은 사람들이 건넜던 얼음으로 된 좁은 다리로 현재의 시베리아와 알래스카 사이에 있었다.

수천 년 전 여러 차례의 빙하기 동안, 이 다리는 아시아와 북아메리카를 연결하고 있었다. 그러나 기온이 따뜻해지면서 수위가 상승했다. 이로 인해 그 육교는 물에 잠겨 사라지게 되었다. 그러나 이 무렵, 인류는 이미 아메리카 대륙으로 건너간 상태였다. 그들은 그런 후 남아메리카까지 내려가 두 대륙의 많은 지역에 정착했을 것이다.

Reading Skills

Ⓑ

• **Exercise 7** • ─────── p.110

정답 Q1 Ⓐ Q2 Ⓑ Q3 Ⓑ

해석 　　　　　　호모 에렉투스

과학자들은 보통 동물을 속과 종으로 분류한다. 속이 더 큰 군이다. 종은 더 구체적인 분류이다. 과학자들은 원인(原人)의 한 종을 호모 에렉투스라 이름 붙였다. 호모 에렉투스는 현생 인류의 초기 조상 중 하나이다. 호모(Homo)는 라틴어로 '사람'을 의미하고, 에렉투스(erectus)는 '직립'을 의미한다. 간단히 말해, 호모 에렉투스는 직립 보행을 하는, 초기 원인이다.

호모 에렉투스는 사실 호모 사피엔스와 매우 흡사하게 생겼는데, 호모 사피엔스는 '지혜 있는 인간'이라는 뜻으로—호모 에렉투스보다 더 현대에 가까운 인류에 붙인 학명이다. 무엇보다도 그들의 외형은 상당히 유사하다. 얼굴 골격과 키, 흉부, 팔 길이 등이 그렇다. 호모 에렉투스는 또한 뇌강의 크기가 호모 사피엔스와 가깝다.

마지막으로, 과학자들은 아프리카와 유럽, 그리고 아시아 등 전 세계 각지에서 호모 에렉투스의 표본을 발견하고 있다. 확실히 호모 에렉투스는 호모 사피엔스처럼 떠돌아다니는 인류였다. 호모 에렉투스는 유목 생활을 했으며 그 덕분에 현생 인류와 유사한 생명체가 세상에 널리 퍼져 살게 되었다.

Reading Skills

Ⓐ

• **Exercise 8** • ─────── p.111

정답 Q1 Ⓑ Q2 Ⓓ Q3 Ⓐ

해석 　　　　　　수렵 채집민

초기 인류 사회에서 영구적인 정착 생활은 없었다. 그 대신 사람들은 대개 여기저기 떠돌아다녔다. 이러한 이유로 인류학자들은 그들에게 수렵 채집민이라는 별명을 붙여주었다.

수렵 채집민이라는 이름이 알려주듯, 그들은 두 가지 별개의 방식을 이용해 생존했다. 첫째로, 그들은 동물을 사냥하곤 했다. 이것은 그들의 주요 생존 방식이었다. 사실, 이것은 또한 그들의 방랑 생활을 설명해 준다. 초기 수렵 채집민들은 동물의 무리를 따라다녔기 때문에 여기저기로 자주 이동하곤 했다. 이 동물들을 사냥할 수 없었다면 그들은 생존할 수 없었을 것이다.

채집은 그들의 생존에 또 다른 필수 요소였다. 그들은 주로 과일과 견과류, 딸기류를 채집했다. 또한 야생에서 자라는 곡물은 무엇이든 모았다. 이러한 곡물에는 쌀, 옥수수, 밀 등이 있었다.

수렵 채집민의 생활 방식은 2백만 년 가량 지속되었다. 몇천 년 전이 되어서야 인류는 농사 짓는 법을 알게 되었고, 인류 사회는 영구적인 주거지에 정착하기 시작했다.

Reading Skills

Ⓓ

Grammar Point　　　　　　p.112

✅ Grammar Check-Up

A　1 Can
　　 2 would
　　 3 will
　　 4 did
　　 5 Have

B　1 ⓑ　　2 ⓒ　　3 ⓐ　　4 ⓓ　　5 ⓑ

C　1 May
　　 2 has
　　 3 did
　　 4 will
　　 5 could

Vocabulary Review
p.114

A
1 level
2 relatives
3 Biology
4 nomadic
5 limelight

B 1 Ⓑ 2 Ⓒ 3 Ⓒ 4 Ⓐ 5 Ⓓ

C 1 Ⓐ 2 Ⓑ 3 Ⓐ 4 Ⓑ 5 Ⓑ

D
1 continents
2 climate
3 gender
4 traverse
5 currently

Practice Test
p.116

1 Ⓑ 2 Ⓓ 3 Ⓑ 4 Ⓒ 5 Ⓒ
6 Ⓓ 7 ❷ 8 ❶, ❷, ❺

해석 고대 이집트의 미라 제작

고대 이집트의 날씨는 덥고 건조했다. 시체가 부패하는 경우가 있었기 때문에 사람을 매장하기가 어려웠다. 따라서 수천 년 전 이집트인들은 미라를 만드는 법을 알아냈다. 이 과정을 미라화라고 한다.

미라화로 인해 이집트인들은 시체를 보존할 수 있었다. 그것은 매우 긴 과정이었다. 먼저 시체의 장기 대부분이 제거되었다. 이 장기들은 항아리에 담겨졌다. 하지만 심장은 시체에 남겨졌다. 그 다음에는 시체를 나트론으로 덮었다. 이것은 소금의 일종이었다. 이것이 시체의 수분을 모두 제거했다. 약 70일이 지나면 나트론을 제거한 후, 시체를 닦았다. 그런 다음 기다란 아마포천으로 시체를 감쌌다. 부적 및 기타 보석들을 시체에 붙였다. 그런 다음 한 번 더 아마포천으로 시체를 감쌌다. 이로써 과정이 완성되었다.

그런 다음에 미라가 매장될 수 있었다. 파라오와 그 가족들의 미라는 주로 피라미드에 매장되었다. 부유한 사람들의 미라는 보통 무덤에 안치되었다. (안타깝게도 그러한 많은 무덤들이 이후에 귀중품들, 특히 금을 도굴 당하였다.) 대부분의 경우, 다양한 보물들이 미라와 함께 매장되었다. 여기에는 금, 보석, 무기, 악기, 식품과 음료 등이 포함되었다. 이집트인들은 사후 세계에서 고인들에게 이 물건들이 필요할 것이라고 믿었다.

CHAPTER 6 Weather

Understanding TOEFL Question Types & Reading Skills
p.120

1 Question Types ▶ Sample Question
Ⓑ

해석 기상 위성

사람들은 날씨를 예측하기 위해 여러 가지 방법을 사용한다. 가장 좋은 방법 중 하나는 기상 위성을 이용하는 것이다. 기상 위성은 지구 주위를 돌며 지상의 기상학자들에게 지구를 정밀하게 찍은 사진들을 전송한다. 이것은 일기 예보관들이 온도계나 기압계를 사용하는 것보다 더 정확하게 예측하도록 도와준다. 위성 덕분에 일기 예보가 과거보다 더 정확해졌다.

2 Reading Skills ▶ Check-Up
Ⓐ

• Exercise 1 • ─────── p.122

정답 Q1 Ⓑ Q2 Ⓐ

해석 기상 전선

날씨는 여러 지역에 걸쳐 끊임없이 변화한다. 서로 다른 기상 조건 사이에는 경계가 있다. 이런 것들을 일컬어 기상 전선이라고 한다. 전선에는 몇 가지 독특한 종류들이 있지만, 가장 흔한 두 가지는 온난 전선과 한랭 전선이다.

온난 전선에서는 따뜻한 공기가 찬 공기를 대체한다. 온난 전선은 천둥번개를 동반한 폭풍우로 시작되는 경우도 있지만, 보통 온화한 날씨를 동반한다. 그것은 또한 한랭 전선보다 더 천천히 이동한다. 마지막으로, 온난 전선에는 대체로 맑은 날씨가 뒤따른다.

반대로 한랭 전선은 대기 중의 따뜻한 공기를 찬 공기로 대체한다. 한랭 전선은 모든 기상 전선 중에서 가장 빠르게 이동한다. 한랭 전선은 또한 가장 사나운 날씨를 동반하며 항상 추운 날씨가 뒤따른다.

Reading Skills
Ⓒ

• Exercise 2 • ─────── p.123

정답 Q1 Ⓑ Q2 Ⓑ

해석 기후

지구상의 대부분 지역에서 날씨와 기온이 변화한다. 시간이 흐르면서, 사람들은 대개 이러한 변화들의 반복되는 패턴을 알아차린다. 과학자들은 이것을 기후라고 한다. 지구상에는 다양한 기후가 존재한다.

열대 기후는 보통 적도 근처에서 나타난다. 열대 기후는 거의 1년 내내 높은 기온을 유지한다. 열대 기후에서는 또한 지구상 어느 곳보다 더 많은 강수량을 경험한다. 이것은 생명체가 풍부한 지역을 생성하는 데 도움이 될 수 있다. 아프리카와 남아메리카의 정글과 열대 우림이 열대 기후로 존재한다.

열대 기후와는 달리 한대 기후는 굉장히 춥다. 보통 연중 대부분 영하의 기온이 지속된다. 또한 북극권 주변과 같은 곳에서는 강설량이 많을 수도 있다. 그렇지만 남극 대륙과 같은 어떤 한대 기후에서는 눈은 물론 비조차 거의 내리지 않는다.

Reading Skills
Ⓑ

• Exercise 3 • ─────── p.124

정답 Q1 Ⓒ Q2 Ⓑ

해석   **엘니뇨 현상**

몇 년마다 북아메리카와 남아메리카의 기상 조건은 급격하게 변화한다. 많은 과학자들이 이것을 엘니뇨 현상 때문이라고 본다. 안타까운 것은, 그들이 엘니뇨 현상과 그 원인에 대해 아는 것이 거의 없다는 점이다.

엘니뇨 현상은 태평양에서 발생하는 불가사의한 기상 현상이다. 이따금 열대 태평양 지역의 해수면 온도가 평년보다 더 따뜻해진다. 이것은 여러 요인들이 복합적으로 작용해서 생긴다. 그러면 온도의 상승이 날씨가 이상하게 작용하는 원인이 된다.

예를 들어, 엘니뇨 현상은 무역풍을 약하게 만든다. 이로 인해 따뜻한 해수가 태평양 전체로 퍼지게 된다. 그러면 특정 지역의 날씨가 평년보다 더 따뜻해지거나 추워진다. 그런 곳들은 엘니뇨 현상 때문에 홍수나 가뭄을 겪을 수도 있다. 한 마디로 말하면, 엘니뇨 현상은 여러 예측 불가능한 기상 조건들을 만들어낸다.

Reading Skills

Ⓓ

• **Exercise 4** • ——————————————— p.125

정답   Q1 Ⓐ   Q2 Ⓓ

해석   **열대 지방**

적도는 지구의 중앙을 가로지르는 가상의 선이다. 열대 지방은 적도의 북쪽과 남쪽에 인접해 있는 지역이다.

열대 지방은 다른 지구의 지역보다 보통 더 덥다. 많은 경우, 열대 지방에는 태양이 바로 내리쬔다. 이 때문에 열대 지방의 날씨는 일반적으로 1년 내내 따뜻하거나 덥다. 게다가 열대 지방에는 주로 많은 양의 비가 내린다. 많은 지역에서 폭우를 동반한 우기가 나타난다.

열대 지방의 많은 지역이 우림으로 덮여 있다. 우림은 아프리카, 아시아, 그리고 남아메리카에서 찾아볼 수 있다. 적도에서 멀리 떨어진 곳에는 열대 사막이 있다. 이러한 사막으로는 사하라 사막과 칼라하리 사막 등이 있다.

Reading Skills

Ⓐ

• **Exercise 5** • ——————————————— p.126

정답   Q1 Ⓑ   Q2 Ⓑ   Q3 Ⓐ

해석   **홍수와 가뭄**

물은 지구상의 생명체에게 가장 중요한 물질 중 하나이다. 물 덕분에 사람들은 생존할 수 있다. 그러나 물은 이따금 다양한 문제가 발생하는 원인이 될 수도 있다. 이러한 문제들 중 두 경우는 홍수와 가뭄이다.

때로는 물이 너무 많을 때가 있다. 전 세계 대부분의 지역에서 우기를 겪는다. 이 기간 동안에는 며칠 동안 비가 억수 같이 내릴 때가 많다. 이 때문에 수위가 평균보다 더 높아지게 된다. 이렇게 되면 홍수가 발생한다. 홍수는 그 지역에 막대한 피해를 입힐 수 있다. 홍수는 건물과 도로를 파괴하고, 농작물을 휩쓸어 가며, 때로는 사람은 물론 동물들까지 갈 곳이 없게 만들거나 심지어 사망에 이르게 한다.

반면, 어떤 지리적 위치에 있는 지역에서는 비가 충분히 오지 않는 경우가 있다. 비가 오지 않으면 가뭄이 발생할 수 있다. 가뭄의 시기에는 토지가 메마르게 된다. 호수와 연못은 보통 증발하여 마르거나 수위가 낮아진다. 농작물과 동물들은 대체로 죽는다. 가뭄은 몇 주나 몇 개월, 심지어 몇 년 동안 지속되기도 한다. 비가 충분히 내려야지만 마침내 가뭄이 끝나게 된다.

Reading Skills

Ⓐ

• **Exercise 6** • ——————————————— p.128

정답   Q1 Ⓒ   Q2 Ⓓ   Q3 Ⓐ

해석   **겨울 기상 조건**

많은 지역에서 겨울에는 악천후가 발생한다. 이러한 악천후는 추운 날씨와 다양한 형태의 강수를 동반할 수 있다. 강수는 그 습기 때문에 사람들에게 위험한 상황을 만들 수 있다.

눈은 겨울 강수의 가장 대표적인 형태이다. 눈은 단순히 물이 언 것이다. 눈은 육각형의 결정체로 땅에 떨어지지만, 기온이 영하일 때만 떨어질 수 있다.

진눈깨비는 눈과 유사하지만 얼음 형태로 땅에 떨어진다. 진눈깨비는 눈의 형태로 시작하지만, 땅에 떨어지면서 영상의 공기를 통과하게 된다. 이 때문에 눈이 녹아 비로 바뀌게 된다. 계속 떨어지다 보면, 비는 영하의 공기를 통과하면서 다시 언다.

눈과 진눈깨비 둘 다 몇 가지 이유로 위험하다. 그것들은 운전자들에게 미끄러운 환경을 만들어 많은 사고를 일으키는 원인이 된다. 이런 사고에 노출된 사람들은 심각한 부상을 입을 수도 있다. 또한 눈이나 진눈깨비가 너무 많이 내리면 재산상의 손해를 입을 수도 있다.

Reading Skills

Ⓒ

• **Exercise 7** • ——————————————— p.130

정답   Q1 Ⓐ   Q2 Ⓐ   Q3 Ⓑ

해석   **계절의 변화**

지구의 온대 지방들은 1년 내내 계절 변화를 겪는다. 이러한 온대 지방은 지구에서 가장 넓은 지역을 차지한다. 지구에는 사계절 즉 봄, 여름, 가을, 겨울이 있다. 각 계절은 날씨가 서로 뚜렷이 다르며, 매년 각각 4개월 정도 지속된다.

지구는 태양 주위를 공전하면서, 지축을 중심으로 자전한다. 그런데 그 지축은 한쪽으로 기울어져 있다. 이렇게 기울어져 있기 때문에 태양 광선은 다양한 각도로 지구에 도달한다. 태양 광선이 지구를 수직으로 비출 때 날씨는 더 더워진다. 이 때문에 여름 기온이 발생한다. 태양 광선이 지구를 비스듬히 비출 때 날씨는 더 추워지고, 겨울이 나타난다.

태양 주위를 도는 동안, 지구의 여러 부분들은 태양을 향해 기울어졌다가 반대쪽으로 기울어진다. 그래서 계절은 끊임없이 변화한다. 또한, 북반구와 남반구는 항상 반대의 기상 조건을 겪는다. 그러니까 북반구가 여름일 때 남반구는 겨울을 겪는 것이다.

Reading Skills

Ⓒ

• Exercise 8 • p.132

정답 Q1 Ⓑ Q2 Ⓑ Q3 Ⓒ

해석 멕시코 만류

모든 바다에는 해류가 있다. 이 해류들은 바닷속에서 강처럼 움직인다. 해류는 그것이 통과하는 지역의 기후에 커다란 영향을 끼친다. 멕시코 만류가 그러한 해류 중 하나이다.

멕시코 만류는 주로 대서양에 위치해 있다. 그것은 멕시코 만에서 시작된다. 하지만 멕시코 만류는 곧 그곳을 벗어나 대서양으로 유입되고, 미국의 동부 연안을 따라 캐나다의 뉴펀들랜드를 향해 북쪽으로 올라간다. 그런 다음, 대서양을 가로질러 북유럽과 서아프리카 양쪽을 향해 계속해서 이동한다.

멕시코 만류는 날씨에 많은 영향을 끼친다. 멕시코 만류 때문에 많은 곳들의 날씨가 평균 겨울의 기온보다 더 따뜻해진다. 멕시코 만류는 멕시코 만에서 따뜻한 해수를 운반하여 이런 현상을 일으킨다. 이 때문에 실제로 날씨가 영향을 받는다. 이러한 이유로, 미국 동부의 수많은 해안 지역이 20마일 떨어진 내륙 지방보다 더 따뜻하다. 마찬가지로, 버뮤다와 마서스 비니어드와 같은 멕시코 만류 인근 섬들도 비슷한 위도에 위치한 다른 지역들보다 기후가 더 온화하다.

Reading Skills
Ⓑ

Grammar Point p.134

🌀 Grammar Check-Up

Ⓐ **comparative forms:** more violent, milder, deadlier, more tremendous, bigger, colder, more important, nearer
superlative forms: most useful, swiftest, highest, warmest, most different, most severe, weakest, most unique

Ⓑ 1 a greater
2 more severe
3 the most important
4 more useful
5 fastest

Ⓒ 1 ✓ Winter weather such as snow and ice can cause the most severe driving conditions.
2 ☐ Weather satellites predict the weather best than people on the ground can.
3 ☐ Warm fronts create more milder weather than cold fronts do.
4 ✓ El Nino brings more unpredictable weather than other phenomena.
5 ✓ Tropical climates are warmer than the climates in other areas.

Ⓓ 1 ⓒ 2 ⓓ 3 ⓐ 4 ⓒ

Vocabulary Review p.136

Ⓐ 1 drought
2 unpredictable
3 exposed
4 precipitation
5 equator

Ⓑ 1 Ⓐ 2 Ⓐ 3 Ⓓ 4 Ⓑ 5 Ⓒ

Ⓒ 1 Ⓒ 2 Ⓐ 3 Ⓑ 4 Ⓓ 5 Ⓑ

Ⓓ 1 Hemisphere
2 currents
3 rainfall
4 slippery
5 thunderstorm

Practice Test p.138

1 Ⓐ 2 Ⓒ 3 Ⓒ 4 Ⓓ 5 Ⓑ 6 Ⓑ
7 ① 8 Characteristics: ⑤, ⑥ Effects: ①, ③, ⑦

해석 토네이도

지구의 날씨는 여러 가지 강력한 폭풍우를 만들어낸다. 이러한 폭풍우에는 눈보라, 허리케인, 태풍, 사이클론 등이 있다. 그러나 자연이 만들어내는 가장 파괴력이 큰 현상 중 한 가지로는 토네이도(회오리바람)가 있다. 토네이도는 지면에 닿은 채 원을 그리며 매우 빠르게 회전하는 공기이다. 토네이도는 기상 재해로서 토지와 건물, 인명에 막대한 피해를 끼칠 수 있다.

토네이도는 그다지 사납지 않은 날씨에서도 나타날 수 있지만, 천둥번개를 동반한 폭풍우가 칠 때 생성되는 경우가 많다. 그런 것들은 대체로 크기가 작고 풍속이 시속 130마일 이하 정도로 회전하는 경우가 많다. 이러한 토네이도는 1~2마일에 걸쳐 지상에서만 발생하다가 그냥 없어져버리기도 한다. 이러한 토네이도는 매년 수천 건이 발생한다. 사실, 큰 피해를 끼치지 못하거나 사람이 없는 지역에서 발생하기도 하기 때문에 발생하는 토네이도의 모든 경우를 기록하지는 못한다.

그러나 토네이도의 풍속이 시속 300마일 이상이고, 길이는 1마일에 이르면서, 50마일 내지 60마일 아니면 심지어 100마일에 걸쳐 지상에 발생하는 경우들이 있다. 이러한 초강력 토네이도들은 수백만 달러의 피해를 끼치고 수백 명의 목숨을 앗아갈 수 있다.

토네이도는 남극 대륙을 제외한 전 세계 모든 대륙에서 나타나고 있지만, 보통은 대부분 미국에서 나타난다. 토네이도는 특히 미국의 남동부와 중서부 지역에서 흔히 나타나는데, 봄철에 천둥번개를 동반한 폭풍우가 이들 지역을 강타할 때 주로 같이 발생하는 경우가 대부분이다. (사실 미국에는 토네이도 앨리라고 불리는 지역이 있는데, 토네이도가 그곳에서 너무 많이 발생하기 때문이다.) 토네이도는 초저주파를 생성해내기 때문에 레이더 센터에서는 토네이도에 대한 감시를 하고 있다가 토네이도가 나타나게 되면 지역 주민들에게 재빨리 알린다. 이를 통해 최근 몇 년 동안 인명 손실을 최소한으로 막아냈다. 그러나 토네이도는 여전히 상습적이면서도 치명적인 자연의 산물이다.

CHAPTER 7 Geology

Understanding TOEFL Question Types & Reading Skills
p.142

1 Question Types ▸ Sample Question
Ⓐ

해석
지진

지구의 땅속 깊은 곳에는 수많은 단층들이 있다. 이러한 틈들은 가끔씩 움직인다. 이런 현상이 발생하면 지진이 일어나고 땅이 이리저리 흔들리기 시작할 것이다. 지진은 그 크기와 규모가 다양하다. 어떤 때는 사람들이 그 영향을 거의 알아차리지 못하지만, 또 어떤 경우에는 지진 때문에 땅이 긴 시간 동안 흔들리는 동시에 인명과 재산 모두에 막대한 피해를 입는다.

2 Reading Skills ▸ Check-Up
When, and

• Exercise 1 •
p.144

정답 Q1 Ⓓ Q2 ③

해석
금의 특성

금은 지구상에서 가장 귀중하면서도 가장 희귀한 원소 중 하나이다. 이러한 가치 때문에 사람들은 역사적으로 금을 화폐 단위로써 사용해 왔다. 그러나 금은 여러 가지 다른 중대한 특성들을 가지고 있어서 사람들이 그것을 아주 많은 이유로 사용한다.

한 가지 이유로는, 금이 최상의 전도체라는 점이다. 구리와 은이 실제로 전도가 더 잘 되고 더 잘 가열된다. 그러나 금은 녹슬지 않아서 전자 산업에서 구리나 은보다 더 가치 있게 여겨진다.

금은 또한 매우 가단성이 있는 원소라서 그것을 두드려 비교적 쉽게 여러 다양한 형태로 만들 수 있다. 의사들은 의료용으로 금을 효과적으로 사용해 왔다. (사실, 금은 의료 업계에서 많이 사용된다.) 예를 들면, 많은 치과의사들이 금을 치아 충전재로 사용한다. 어떤 의사들은 사람의 귓속에 넣는 청각 임플란트로 금을 사용한다.

Reading Skills
Ⓑ

• Exercise 2 •
p.145

정답 Q1 ① Q2 Ⓒ

해석
알프레트 베게너와 대륙 이동설

사람들은 일곱 개의 각기 다른 대륙을 보여 주는 세계 지도에 익숙하다. 그러나 과거에는 오직 하나의 커다란 대륙만이 있었다. 현재 일곱 개의 대륙이 있는 이유는 대륙 이동 때문이다.

1915년, 지질학자인 알프레트 베게너는 *대륙과 대양의 기원에 관하여*라는 책을 펴냈다. (그의 책은 그가 몇 년에 걸쳐 수행한 모든 연구를 담았다.) 그는 과거에는 단 하나의 대륙만이 존재했다고 믿었다. 그는 그것을 판게아라고 명명했다. 그는 지구의 상판, 즉 지각이 끊임없이 이동한다는 학설을 세웠다. 그리고 이것이 판게아가 쪼개진 이유였다. 베게너는 대륙들이 이동해 떨어져 나가는 데 수백만 년이 걸렸다고 생각했다.

처음엔 많은 이들이 베게너의 연구 결과를 받아들이려 하지 않았다. 그러나 많은 지질학자들이 베게너의 연구를 이어 나갔다. 이제는 대부분의 사람들이 대륙의 이동이 실제로 일어났음을 인정하고 있다.

Reading Skills
1 However 2 So

• Exercise 3 •
p.146

정답 Q1 Ⓓ Q2 ②

해석
석탄

화석 연료의 한 가지 일반적인 형태는 석탄이다. 석탄은 토탄(생성되지 얼마되지 않은 탄화가 덜 된 석탄, 이탄)에서 만들어진 형성된 어두운 색의 암석이다. 석탄은 수백만 년의 시간을 거쳐 만들어진 퇴적암의 한 유형이다.

석탄에는 몇 가지 유형이 존재한다. 각 석탄은 서로 다른 조건에서 형성된다. 무연탄은 가장 어둡고 가장 단단한 석탄이다. 무연탄이 가장 오랫동안 탄다. (이는 그것이 가정 및 산업 난방에 주로 사용되는 이유이다.) 아탄(갈탄)은 갈색 빛깔의 석탄으로 이를 태워 전기를 생산한다. 역청탄도 종종 전기 생산에 사용되는 석탄의 일종이다. 오늘날 석탄은 전 세계적으로 널리 사용되고 있다. 사람들은 석탄을 이용해서 건물 난방과 전기 생산을 한다. 하지만 석탄을 태우면 오염 물질이 발생하기 때문에 사람들은 향후에 석탄의 사용량이 감소하기를 바라고 있다.

Reading Skills
Ⓐ

• Exercise 4 •
p.147

정답 Q1 ④ Q2 Ⓓ

해석
동굴

동굴이란 암석이나 토양이 빠져나가 지하에 생긴 공간이다. 동굴은 대체로 사람이 통과하고 탐험할 수 있을 정도로 크다. 어떤 동굴은 땅 밑에서 수백 마일에 걸쳐 있기도 하다.

동굴은 몇 가지 방식으로 형성된다. 한 가지 일반적인 방식은 지표면의 물이 지하로 침투해 토양을 용해시키거나 씻어내는 것이다. 이런 식으로 종종 빈 틈이 만들어져 그로 인해 동굴이 형성된다. (이러한 방식으로 형성된 동굴들은 매우 부드러운 종류의 암석인 석회암인 경우가 종종 발견된다.) 어떤 경우 동굴은 단순히 낙석 사이의 공간에 형성되기도 한다. 또 다른 일반적인 방식은 화산의 용암이 냉각하면서 암석 사이에 공간을 남기는 것이다. 전체적으로, 세계 각지에 수천 개의 동굴이 있다. 많은 동굴들이 탐험되었으나 아직 발견되지 않은 동굴들이 훨씬 더 많다.

Reading Skills
1 and 2 nevertheless

• Exercise 5 •
p.148

정답 Q1 Ⓓ Q2 ② Q3 Ⓑ

해석   노천 채굴

오랜 세월 동안, 광산업자들은 땅속에서 귀중한 광물과 광석을 캐내기 위해 여러 가지 방법을 사용해 왔다. 그러한 방법 중 하나가 노천 채굴이다.

노천 채굴은 채굴하고 있는 광물이 지표면 가까이에 있을 때 흔하게 쓰인다. 그런 광물 중 하나가 석탄이다. 먼저 광산업자는 토양의 최상층을 일단 제거한다. 광산업자는 이 작업을 위해 폭약을 사용하거나 단순하게는 지표면을 팔 것이다. (어떤 경우에는 중장비를 사용하여 매우 넓은 지역에 이르는 지면을 파야 한다.) 이렇게 하면 원하는 광물이 노출되므로 광산업자는 광물을 쉽게 입수할 수 있다. 그러나 채굴이 완료되면 대개는 토양이 완전히 노출되어 쓸모 없게 되어 버린다.

과거에는 광산업자들이 그러한 토양을 그대로 버려 두고 전혀 복원하지 않았다. 그러나 오늘날엔 정부의 규제 덕분에 광업 회사들이 그 땅을 복원해 쓸모 있게 만들어야 한다. 이렇게 해야 사람들이 미래에 그 땅을 사용할 수 있게 된다.

Reading Skills

Ⓒ

• **Exercise 6** ──────────────── p.150

정답   Q1   Ⓐ   Q2   ❷   Q3   ❹

해석   지구의 층

수십억 년 전 지구가 형성될 때, 지구는 세 가지 서로 다른 층으로 나눠졌다. 지질학자들은 그 층들을 지각, 맨틀, 핵이라고 부른다. 그러나 과학자들이 그 층들에 대해 알게 된 것은 불과 20세기에 들어서였다. 지난 백 년 동안, 그들은 각 층에 대해 수많은 사실들을 발견해 냈다.

지각은 가장 바깥에 있는 층으로, 어느 곳에나 있으며 두께가 5킬로미터에서 100킬로미터에 이른다. (그러나 그것은 보통 바다 밑에서는 두께가 더 얇고 지면 위에서는 더 두껍다.) 지구 표면의 모든 것들이 지각의 일부를 차지한다. 시간이 흐르면서 많은 원소와 광물이 결합하여 지각을 형성했다.

두 번째 층은 맨틀이다. 맨틀은 어떤 곳에서는 두께가 2,900킬로미터에 이르기도 한다. 철과 마그네슘 같이 무거운 편에 속하는 금속들이 맨틀의 많은 부분을 형성하고 있다. 맨틀은 몹시 뜨겁고 심지어 가끔은 이리저리 이동하기도 한다.

지구의 가장 내부에 있는 층은 핵이다. 사실, 핵에는 외핵과 내핵, 두 부분이 있다. 외핵은 액체인데 그 깊이에서 생기는 모든 열과 압력 때문이다. 그러나 철과 니켈로 이루어진 내핵은 고체이다. (당연히, 그곳의 압력으로 인해 사람은 즉사하기 때문에 지금까지 핵에 접근한 사람은 아무도 없다.)

Reading Skills

1   when   2   and

• **Exercise 7** ──────────────── p.152

정답   Q1   Ⓓ   Q2   ❶   Q3   Ⓑ

해석   환태평양 화산대

지구의 지각은 하나의 완전한 구조로 이루어져 있지 않다. 그보다는 여러 개의 판들이 결합하여 지각을 구성하고 있다. 이러한 판들은 단층이라고 하는 위치에서 서로 만난다. 단층은 대체로 지질학적으로 불안정하여 지리학적인 단층 구조 근처에서는 정말 많은 화산들이 형성되고 지진이 발생한다. 화산과 지진 둘 다 굉장히 많이 발생하는 지역 중 하나가 환태평양 화산대이다.

여러 단층이 환태평양 화산대를 구성하고 있다. 가장 잘 알려진 것이 캘리포니아의 산 안드리아스 단층이다. (그곳에서는 그 단층이 대지진을 그만큼 많이 일으키기 때문에 사람들은 산 안드리아스 단층에 대해 다른 어떤 단층보다 더 잘 알고 있다.) 그러나 환태평양 화산대가 미국에만 있는 것은 아니다. 실제로 그것은 뉴질랜드에서 시작하여 인도네시아를 향해 북쪽과 서쪽으로 이동하며, 그 다음 필리핀과 일본을 통과해 북쪽을 향해 움직인다. 그 단층은 계속해서 태평양을 건너 알래스카를 통과하고 이어서 북아메리카와 중앙아메리카, 남아메리카를 걸쳐 남쪽으로 이동한다.

환태평양 화산대에는 400개가 넘는 화산이 있다. 게다가 지구에서 일어나는 지진의 80% 이상이 그곳에서 발생한다. 환태평양 화산대에는 단층이 많기 때문에 그것이 걸쳐 있는 지역은 상당히 불안정하다.

Reading Skills

Ⓐ

• **Exercise 8** ──────────────── p.154

정답   Q1   ❶   Q2   ❸   Q3   Ⓐ

해석   빙하 작용

지구의 기온은 끊임없이 변화한다. 때로는 빙하기라고 하는 극도의 냉각 시기에 들어서기도 한다. (많은 동물 종이 극도로 추운 날씨를 견딜 수 없어 이 시기에 멸종되는 경우가 빈번하다.) 사실, 많은 이들이 현재 지구가 아직도 소빙하기에 있다고 생각한다. 빙하기의 한 가지 특징은 빙하들이다. 빙하는 육지 위에 거대하게 쌓인 얼음 덩어리들이다. 빙하는 길이가 수 마일에 이를 정도로 굉장히 길 수 있으며, 심지어 전방이나 후방으로 움직이며 이동하기도 한다.

기온이 떨어지면 빙하는 팽창한다. 이것이 빙하 작용이다. 빙하는 대체로 하루에 몇 인치씩만 팽창하지만, 심한 경우에는 하루에 100피트 이상 증가하기도 한다. 빙하는 굉장히 두꺼워서 얼음의 무게가 수천 톤에 달한다. 그에 따라 빙하 작용은 빙하가 덮고 있는 지역에 엄청난 영향을 끼칠 수 있다. 예를 들면, 빙하는 한때 미국 중서부 지방의 대부분을 덮고 있었다. 빙하가 물러나면서 땅이 평평해졌다. 또한 빙하가 땅을 깎아내 커다란 구덩이를 만들었다. (그 큰 구덩이들 중 일부는 미국과 캐나다 사이의 오대호가 되었다.) 빙하 때문에 현재 중서부 지방은 수없이 많은 호수들이 여기저기에 분포해 있는 반면 언덕이나 산은 거의 없어 평평하다.

Reading Skills

1   As   2   Therefore

Grammar Point   p.156

✓ Grammar Check-Up

Ⓐ   1   will be leaving
     2   used
     3   have accepted
     4   will expand
     5   continue

Ⓑ   1   ⓒ   2   ⓐ   3   ⓓ   4   ⓐ

Ⓒ   1   ⓑ   2   ⓐ   3   ⓓ   4   ⓐ

Vocabulary Review
p.158

A
1. published
2. dissolves
3. tarnish
4. liquid
5. incredibly

B 1 Ⓐ 2 Ⓒ 3 Ⓒ 4 Ⓑ 5 Ⓓ

C 1 Ⓐ 2 Ⓓ 3 Ⓑ 4 Ⓓ 5 Ⓓ

D
1. thick
2. property
3. electricity
4. regulations
5. drift

Practice Test
p.160

1 Ⓐ 2 Ⓒ 3 Ⓐ 4 Ⓓ 5 Ⓑ
6 Ⓒ 6 ❷ 6 ❸, ❺, ❻

해석 석유 채취 방식

인류는 석유에 대해 수천 년 전부터 알고 있었다. 현재 석유는 수없이 많은 곳에서 사용되고 있지만, 과거에 인류는 석유를 거의 사용하지 않았다. 그것은 사람들이 석유를 연료로 이용하는 기계를 발명하기 시작한 산업 혁명 시기와 수백만 명의 사람들이 자동차를 운전하기 시작한 20세기를 거치면서 바뀌었다. 그러자 사람들이 직면하게 된 문제는 땅속에서 어떻게 석유를 채취하는지에 대한 것이었다.

땅속에서 석유를 얻는 방법에는 세 가지 단계가 있다. 첫 단계는 사람들이 가장 흔하게 석유를 채취했던 방법이었다. 사람들이 그저 파이프를 땅에 묻으면 석유가 분출되어 나왔다. 그러나 이것은 너무 비효율적이었고 많은 양의 석유가 낭비되었다. 그래서 사람들은 석유에 뚜껑을 덮어 석유가 여기저기로 뿜어져 나오는 것을 방지하는 방법을 개발했다. 오늘날 석유 회사들은 첫 단계에서 유출되는 석유가 거의 없지만, 지하에 매장된 석유의 20% 정도만 회수한다.

두 번째 단계에서, 석유 회사는 석유가 지면으로 나오게 어떻게든 압력을 생성해 내야 한다. 이렇게 할 수 있는 방법은 다양하다. 가장 흔한 것은 유전에 펌프로 물을 주입하는 것이다. 이렇게 하면 석유가 솟아오르게 하는 데 필요한 압력을 생성해 낼 수 있다. 어떤 환경에서는 석유를 뽑아 올리기 위해 펌프로 가스를 주입할 수도 있다. 이 두 번째 단계의 결과, 보통 석유가 10% 더 지면으로 추출된다.

세 번째 단계는 석유를 가장 많이 지면으로 추출하지만, 가장 어렵고 가장 값비싼 방식이다. (이런 이유로 많은 회사들이 이 방식을 전혀 사용하지 않는다.) 보통, 회사는 어떻게든 지하에 있는 석유에 열을 가한다. 이렇게 하면 석유 회수가 더 쉬워진다. 이 방식으로 회사는 유전에서 50% 이상의 석유를 채취할 수 있어서, 이것은 가장 효율적인 방식이다.

석유 회사들은 석유 채취를 위한 새로운 방법들을 끊임없이 찾고 있다. 지구상에서 석유의 공급이 고갈됨에 따라 가능한 한 많은 석유를 채취하는 것이 그들에게 중요한 일이 되었다.

CHAPTER 8 Medicine

Understanding TOEFL Question Types & Reading Skills
p.164

1 Question Types ▶ Sample Question
Ⓐ, Ⓒ, Ⓓ

해석 히포크라테스

사람들은 히포크라테스를 '의학의 아버지'라고 부른다. 기원전 5세기에 살았던 그는 환자를 관찰하는 것이 매우 중요하다고 믿었다. 그는 관찰을 통해 환자의 건강상 문제를 진단하고자 했다. 히포크라테스는 그가 살았던 시대의 다른 많은 이들과는 달리 질병에는 초자연적인 원인이 아니라 자연적인 원인이 있다고 생각했다. 오늘날까지도 사람들은 의사가 되기 전 히포크라테스 선서를 암송함으로써 그를 기억한다.

2 Reading Skills ▶ Check-Up
observations, natural

Exercise 1
p.166

정답
Q1 Ⓒ, Ⓓ, Ⓔ
Q2 Discovery: Ⓑ, Ⓖ   Effects: Ⓐ, Ⓒ, Ⓕ

해석 페니실린

많은 경우에, 연구자들은 의도적으로 특정한 약을 발견해 내기 위해 노력한다. 그러나 그렇지 않은 경우도 있었는데, 모든 항생 물질 가운데 가장 중요한 것 중 하나로 꼽히는 것이 그랬다. 사실 페니실린의 발견은 완전히 우연이었다.

1928년, 알렉산더 플레밍 박사는 병원 내 자신의 실험실에서 연구를 하고 있었다. 그는 평판 배양 접시에 있는 어떤 세균에 주목했다. 그 세균은 곰팡이가 있는 특정 부분 주위에서 성장을 멈추고 있었다. 그는 좀 더 면밀히 조사하였고 그 곰팡이가 세균을 파괴하고 있었음을 알아냈다.

이것이 페니실린의 시작이었다. 그 후 몇 년 사이에 페니실린은 매우 널리 사용되는 약이 되었다. 특히, 그것은 제2차 세계 대전 때 엄청난 수의 인명을 구했다. 오늘날 의사들은 여러 다양한 감염병을 퇴치하는 데 페니실린을 사용한다.

Reading Skills

mold, WW II

Exercise 2
p.168

정답
Q1 Ⓑ, Ⓒ, Ⓓ
Q2 Medicine before its publication: Ⓑ, Ⓔ
     Medicine after its publication: Ⓒ, Ⓓ, Ⓕ

해석 그레이 해부학

수백 년 동안, 사람들은 대체로 의사를 신뢰하지 않았다. 의료 교육, 의학 지식과 능력이 부족했기 때문에 많은 의사들이 환자들에게 매우 열악한 의료 행위를 제공했다. 게다가 의사가 치료하는 중에 환자들이 죽는 경우도 많았다.

의사들에게 부족했던 것 중 하나는 전문 분야에 대한 기초 지식이었다. 헨리 그레이 박사는 그러한 지식을 사람들에게 전달하고자 노력했다. 1858년, 그는 사실적이고 정확한, 그레이 해부학이란 책을 출판했다. 오늘날 사람들은 그 책을 간단히 그레이 해부학이라고 부른다. 이 책은 의학 전문 분야에 대한 포괄적인 지식을 제공한다. 처음 출간된 이후로 여러 번 개정되면서, 오늘날 많은 이들이 이 책이 의료계에서 가지는 중요성을 인정하고 있다. 이 책 덕분에 많은 사람들이 의사를 더욱 신뢰하기 시작했다.

Reading Skills

Henry Gray, updated

• **Exercise 3** • ———————————————————— p.170

정답 Q1 Ⓐ, Ⓑ, Ⓓ
Q2 General anesthesia: Ⓐ, Ⓒ, Ⓕ
Local anesthesia: Ⓔ, Ⓖ

해석 　　　　　　　　　마취

의사는 마취제라는 약물을 사용하여 환자를 마취시킨다. 이로써 환자는 고통을 느끼지 않는다. 그로 인해 의사들은 온갖 종류의 수술을 할 수 있다.

마취의 한 가지 유형은 전신 마취이다. 그것은 신체 전체에 영향을 미친다. 의사는 정맥 주사 또는 가스를 이용하여 체내에 약물을 주입할 수 있다. 약물로 인해 환자는 움직이거나 고통을 느낄 수 없다. 이러한 유형의 마취 덕분에 의사는 대수술을 할 수 있다.

국부 마취는 신체 일부분에 대한 고통을 차단시킨다. 국부 마취로 환자가 의식을 잃지는 않는다. 하지만 신체의 어떤 부위에서 아무것도 느끼지 못한다. 치과 의사들이 국부 마취를 이용한다. 또한 눈 수술에도 국부 마취가 사용된다.

Reading Skills

unable to move, dentists

• **Exercise 4** • ———————————————————— p.172

정답 Q1 Ⓐ, Ⓑ, Ⓔ　　Q2 Life: Ⓑ, Ⓔ　　Work: Ⓐ, Ⓒ, Ⓖ

해석 　　　　　　　　　윌리엄 하비

의학 역사에는 중요한 발견들이 많이 있었다. 이러한 발견들은 히포크라테스와 갈레노스의 시대까지 거슬러 올라간다. 의학 역사상 중요한 인물 중 한 명으로는 윌리엄 하비가 있었다. 그는 영국인 의사로 1578년부터 1657년까지 살았다. 하비는 혈액의 순환에 대해 연구했다.

중요한 것은, 하비가 실험과 관찰이라는 과학적인 방법에 의존해 발견을 이루었다는 점이다. 첫째로, 그는 동물을 대상으로 실험을 했다. 또한 그는 심장이 하루에 얼마나 많은 혈액을 펌프질하는지 면밀하게 조사했다. 그는 연구를 통해 혈액이 인체를 순환하는 두 가지 방식을 알아냈다. 그는 또한 정맥에 대해, 그리고 정맥이 혈액 순환에 기여하는 일에 대해 중요한 발견을 했다.

Reading Skills

circulation, veins

• **Exercise 5** • ———————————————————— p.174

정답 Q1 Ⓑ, Ⓒ, Ⓔ

Q2 Unaffected by vaccines: Ⓑ, Ⓔ
Affected by vaccines: Ⓐ, Ⓒ, Ⓖ

해석 　　　　　　　　　백신

바이러스는 지구상에서 가장 치명적인 것들에 속한다. 바이러스는 DNA 또는 RNA 그리고 단백질 핵만으로 이루어진 미생물이지만, 매우 치명적이다. 바이러스는 소아마비와 말라리아, 수두, 홍역, 그리고 일반적인 감기와 같은 질병을 일으킨다. 이러한 질병들은 매년 수백만 명의 목숨을 앗아간다. 안타깝게도 의사들은 바이러스에 대한 치료법을 단 한 가지도 발견하지 못했다.

그러나 과학자들은 바이러스에 대한 백신을 만들어냈다. 백신은 바이러스로부터 인체를 보호하는 데 도움을 준다. 일반적으로 백신에는 죽거나 약화된 바이러스가 들어 있다. 그리고 의사는 그 백신을 사람의 몸에 주사로 주입한다. 인체는 약화된 바이러스를 탐지하고 그것을 공격해 죽인다. 그러면 인체는 바이러스가 다시 돌아오더라도 그 바이러스와 싸울 항체를 만들어낸다. 앞으로 인체에 그 바이러스가 들어오더라도 항체가 그것을 파괴할 것이다. 백신 덕분에 사람들은 많은 치명적인 바이러스로부터 안전하게 되었다.

Reading Skills

chicken pox, viruses, antibodies

• **Exercise 6** • ———————————————————— p.176

정답 Q1 Ⓐ, Ⓒ, Ⓔ
Q2 Positive effects: Ⓑ, Ⓔ, Ⓕ　　Negative effects: Ⓐ, Ⓖ

해석 　　　　　　　　　장기 이식

때때로 사람의 신체 장기는 약화되거나 질병에 걸리거나, 완전히 기능을 하지 못하게 된다. 새로운 장기가 없으면 이런 사람들은 대부분 죽게 될 가능성이 높다. 이러한 경우에 의사들은 이들에게 장기 이식을 실행한다.

최초로 장기 이식이 성공한 경우는 어느 의사가 쌍둥이 한 명의 신장을 다른 쌍둥이에게 이식했던 1954년이었다. 의사들은 초기에 여러 번 실패를 경험했는데, 특히 환자의 몸이 새로운 장기에 거부 반응을 일으키는 경우가 많았기 때문이었다. 그러나 근래에는 의사들이 장기 이식에 관해 많은 것을 알아내고 있다. 이제 그들은 심장과 폐, 신장, 간, 그리고 췌장을 성공적으로 이식할 수 있다. 이는 사람들의 삶을 여러 해 더 연장시키는 데 도움을 준다.

많은 경우, 이식되는 장기는 죽은 사람에게서 받게 된다. 그러나 항상 그런 것은 아닌데, 특히 신장 이식의 경우에 그렇다. 요즘에는 수천 명의 사람들이 장기 이식을 기다리고 있다. 안타까운 것은 장기 기증자가 충분치 않다는 것이다. 그에 따라, 모든 사람들이 필요한 이식을 받는 것은 아니기 때문에 많은 이들이 수술을 받기도 전에 죽는다. 그리고 어떤 신체는 이식 받은 장기에 대해 여전히 거부 반응을 일으킨다.

Reading Skills

hearts, dead people, reject

• **Exercise 7** • ———————————————————— p.178

정답 Q1 Ⓐ, Ⓓ, Ⓔ
Q2 Effects: Ⓑ, Ⓓ, Ⓕ　　Treatments: Ⓒ, Ⓔ

해석 　　　　　　　　　암

질병은 종종 인간의 몸을 공격한다. 그중 가장 치명적인 것으로 사람들이 암이라고 부르는 질환군이 있다. 암에는 여러 종류가 있으며, 암은 인체의 다양한 기관을 공격할 수 있다. 모든 암에는 보통 다음과 같은 특징이 있다. 암은 매우 공격적이며, 인체의 다양한 기관에 침투하고 처음에 공격하지 않았던 다른 신체 기관으로 전이될 수 있다.

의사들은 암에 대해 많은 것을 알아내고 있다. 그들은 유전 물질이 변형된 비정상적인 세포가 거의 모든 종류의 암을 일으킨다는 점을 알고 있다. 여러 종류의 암이 극도로 치명적이다. 사실, 암은 모든 사망 원인의 10% 이상을 차지한다.

다행인 것은, 연구자들이 암과 싸우기 위해 많은 연구를 하고 있다는 것이다. 그들은 이제 많은 종류의 암을 퇴치할 수 있다. 그들은 수술, 화학 요법과 방사선 요법 등 여러 가지 다양한 방법을 이용한다. 모든 종류의 암을 정복한 것은 아니지만, 미래에 획기적인 발전이 나타나 대다수 암에 대한 치료법을 찾는 것이 가능할 것으로 보인다.

Reading Skills
spread, abnormal, operations

• Exercise 8 • — p.180
정답 Q1 Ⓑ, Ⓓ, Ⓔ
Q2 CAT scan: Ⓐ, Ⓔ MRI machine: Ⓑ, Ⓒ, Ⓕ

해석 의료 영상

의사는 환자의 신체 내부 영상이 필요할 때가 많다. 한 가지 방법은 의료 영상을 이용하는 것이다. 의료 영상에는 몇 가지 종류가 있는데, 가장 중요한 두 가지로 CAT 스캔과 MRI가 있다.

CAT 스캔은 X선을 사용하는 방식이다. CAT 스캔은 인체의 2차원 X선 영상이나 3차원 영상을 생성해 낼 수 있다. 그것은 수많은 X선 영상들이 겹겹이 겹쳐지면서 만들어진다. 때로는 의사들이 좀 더 선명한 영상을 얻기 위해 인체에 염료를 투입하기도 한다. 의사들은 인체 기관의 내부 구조를 찍은 영상을 보기 위해 CAT 스캔을 이용한다.

MRI 기계는 자력을 이용하여 인체 내부를 들여다본다. MRI는 방사선을 이용하지 않기 때문에 CAT 스캔보다는 사실상 더 안전하다. MRI 또한 2차원이나 3차원 영상을 제공할 수 있다. MRI가 만들어내는 영상은 상당히 자세하다. 이것은 상당히 새로운 기술인데, 불과 1980년대 즈음부터 쓰이고 있다.

Reading Skills
X-rays, magnets, radiation

Grammar Point — p.182

✓ Grammar Check-Up

Ⓐ 1 is
2 Each
3 A number of
4 are
5 have

Ⓑ 1 ⓒ 2 ⓓ 3 ⓐ 4 ⓔ 5 ⓑ

Ⓒ wants, Every, A number, most of, asks, The number of

Vocabulary Review — p.184

Ⓐ 1 intentionally
2 antibodies
3 observe
4 skeptical
5 natural

Ⓑ 1 Ⓐ 2 Ⓒ 3 Ⓑ 4 Ⓐ 5 Ⓓ

Ⓒ 1 Ⓓ 2 Ⓐ 3 Ⓑ 4 Ⓐ 5 Ⓓ

Ⓓ 1 protein
2 investigate
3 unconscious
4 block
5 publication

Practice Test — p.186

1 Ⓓ 2 Ⓐ 3 Ⓑ 4 Ⓓ 5 Ⓐ 6 Ⓓ
7 Ⓑ 8 Herbalism: 2, 3 Acupuncture: 1, 5, 6

해석 대체 의학

전 세계 많은 사람들이 서양 의학에 의존하고 있지만, 어떤 이들은 그렇지 않다. 이러한 사람들은 병을 치료하기 위해 대체 의학으로 방향을 돌리는 경우가 많다. 대체 의학은 과학적인 근거가 없는 치료 방식이다. 아니면 어쩌면 과학자들이 그 효능을 아직 입증하지 못한 것일 수도 있다. 그러나 대체 의학을 이용하는 많은 사람들은 그것이 효과가 있다고 주장한다. 이 대체 의학에서 가장 대중적인 두 가지 유형으로는 약초 치료와 침술이 있다.

약초 치료는 현대 의학 이전에 사람들이 한때 사용했던 전통 의학에 의존한다. 이러한 경우 약초 치료를 시술하는 사람들은 질병에 대한 치료법을 찾는 데 민간 전승에 크게 의존한다. 이들은 수목과 초목, 꽃, 뿌리, 그리고 다른 천연 산물로 만들어진 약을 복용한다. 어떤 경우에는 동물이나 광물의 일부를 이용하여 치료하기도 한다. 인도, 중국, 그리스 등 많은 문화권에서 약초 치료를 실행하고 있다. 현대의 과학자들은 약초학자들의 여러 치료법에서 실제 효능을 찾아내고 있다. 그러나 그 방법으로 만든 많은 약에서는 과학적 가치를 입증하지 못하고 있다. 이러한 사실 때문에 약초 치료가 대체 의학의 범주에서 벗어나지 못하고 있다.

침술 또한 대체 의학의 한 종류이다. 최근 침술은 전 세계적으로 많은 추종자들을 얻고 있다. 이런 형태의 의학에서 침술가라고 불리는 의사는 고통을 경감시키기 위해 인체의 다양한 부위에 침을 꽂는다. 침술가는 인체의 구석구석에 많은 압점이 있다고 믿는다. 예를 들어, 사람의 귀 어느 한 지점에 침을 꽂으면 환자의 등, 무릎, 혹은 다른 신체 부위 일부의 통증을 완화하는 데 도움이 될 수 있다는 것이다. 많은 사람들이 침술이 도움이 된다고 굳게 믿는 반면, 아직까지 의사와 과학자들은 침술에 과학적인 근거가 거의 없다고 판단하고 있다. 그럼에도 불구하고 치료를 받은 즉시 상태가 좋아지는 사람들의 경우가 무수히 많이 있다.

약초 치료와 침술은 대체 의학의 여러 종류 중 두 가지일 뿐이다. 지금은 일반적이지 않지만, 과학자들이 그것에 대해 더 많이 알아내게 되면 미래에는 더 많은 의사와 환자들이 대체 의학을 인정하게 될 가능성이 높다.

Actual Test

Actual Test 1
p.190

1 ⓓ 2 ⓑ 3 ⓓ 4 ⓐ 5 ⓑ 6 ⓒ
7 ⓐ 8 ⓑ 9 ④ 10 Solution Caves: ③, ⑥, ⑧
Lava Caves: ①, ⑦ Sea Caves: ⑤, ⑨

해석 동굴

동굴은 커다랗고 자연 발생적으로 지면에 생기는 구덩이로 사람이 안에 들어갈 수 있을 정도로 크기가 크다. 동굴은 산에서 많이 발견된다. 지면의 다른 곳들에서 발견되기도 한다. 어떤 동굴들은 크기가 작을 수 있다. 미국의 매머드 동굴처럼 수백 킬로미터에 이르는 동굴들도 있을 수 있다. 동굴에는 몇 가지 유형이 있다. 동굴은 각각 다른 방식으로 형성된다. 흔히 볼 수 있는 세 가지 유형으로는 용해 동굴, 용암 동굴, 해식 동굴이 있다.

용해 동굴은 지하수의 영향으로 형성된다. 토양의 틈으로 물이 침투한다. 시간이 지나면 물이 암석을 침식하여 암석이 쓸려 나간다. 많은 용해 동굴들은 석회암 지대에서 발견되는데, 그 이유는 석회암이 쉽게 침식되기 때문이다. 하지만 때때로 대리석, 백운석, 석고 등 다른 암석들도 물에 의해 침식될 수 있다. 이러한 동굴들은 형성되기까지 오랜 시간이 걸린다. 어떤 경우는 수백만 년에 걸쳐 형성되지만, 크기가 상당히 클 수도 있다.

용암 동굴은 과거에 화산 활동이 있었거나 또는 현재 화산 활동이 있는 지역에 존재한다. 이 동굴은 화산 분출 후에 형성된다. 용암이 분출되면, 용암은 보통 물줄기를 따라 흐른다. 이러한 물줄기에서 물이 빠질 수 있는데, 그러면 지하에 길고 속이 빈 관이 남는다. 과거에 사람들은 이곳을 매장지로 사용했다. 어떤 사람들은 그 안에서 살기도 했다. 하와이, 일본, 이탈리아, 그리고 케냐에 많은 용암 동굴들이 있다.

해식 동굴은 바다의 조석력에 의해 형성된다. 파도가 해안가 절벽에 부딪치면 지형이 침식된다. 시간이 지나면서 틈이 생긴다. 서서히 틈이 더 커지면 동굴이 형성된다. 대부분의 해식 동굴은, 특히 만조 때 물로 채워져 있다. 이곳은 사람들이 보고 싶어 하는 인기 장소지만, 또한 매우 위험한 곳이기도 하다. 많은 수영객과 스쿠버 다이버들이 이 안에서 길을 잃고 사망했다. (그들은 출구를 찾지 못하면서 산소가 부족해져 익사한다.) 뉴질랜드, 그리스, 그리고 영국에 모두 해식 동굴이 있다.

Actual Test 2
p.194

1 ⓒ 2 ⓐ 3 ⓓ 4 ⓑ 5 ⓑ 6 ⓒ
7 ⓒ 8 ⓐ 9 ① 10 ②, ③, ⑥

해석 의수와 의족

때때로 사람들은 팔이나 손, 다리, 혹은 발과 같은 신체 기관을 잃을 수 있다. 사고, 전쟁, 혹은 질병 때문에 이러한 일이 발생할 수 있다. (예를 들어 의사들은 사람들이 다치면 신체의 일부를 잘라야 할 수도 있다.) 과거에는 잃어버린 팔다리를 대체하기 위해 그렇게 된 개인이 할 수 있는 일이 없었다. 오늘날에는 의사들이 의수와 의족을 인체에 장착할 수 있다. 그중 일부는 정상적인 신체 일부와 거의 같게 기능할 수 있다.

의수와 의족은 새로운 것이 아니다. 그것은 적어도 3,000년 동안 존재해 왔다. 고고학자들은 나무로 된 발가락을 가진 고대 이집트의 미라를 발굴했다. 고대 그리스인들과 로마인들도 나무를 이용하여 원시적인 의수와 의족을 만들었다. 해적들 또한 나무로 만든 의족을 착용하는 것으로 악명 높았다. 손을 잃은 어떤 해적들은 신체에 갈고리를 장착해 손을 대체했다. 이러한 수족들은 모두 쓸모는 있었지만, 잃어버린 많은 기능까지 사용자에게 되찾아 준 것은 아니었다.

1400년대에서 1800년대까지 유럽에서 발전이 이루어졌다. 기술자들은 나무, 가죽, 금속을 이용해서 다양한 유형의 의수와 의족을 제작했다. 의수의 손가락은 물건을 집어서 붙잡고 있을 수 있었다. 여러 방향으로 구부러지고 움직일 수 있는 의수와 의족들도 있었다. 1900년대에는 제1차 세계 대전과 제2차 세계 대전과 같은 전쟁이 많이 일어났고, 수백만 명의 군인들이 전쟁 중에 부상을 입어 고통 받았다. 다수의 군인들이 팔다리를 잃었다. 이 때문에 과학자들은 의수와 의족 기술을 발전시키려고 노력했다.

오늘날 의수와 의족은 첨단 소재들로 제작된다. 이들은 종종 실제 잃어버린 팔다리처럼 보이기도 한다. 많은 경우 사용자들은 팔다리를 잃기 전에 했던 것처럼 똑같이 기능할 수 있다. 일부 수족들은 심지어 생각으로도 조종이 가능하다. 이러한 수족은 값이 비싸지만, 기술이 발전함에 따라 미래에는 비용이 감소할 것으로 보인다.

Actual Test 3
p.198

1 ⓒ 2 ⓐ 3 ⓓ 4 ⓐ 5 ⓓ 6 ⓒ
7 ⓐ 8 ⓒ 9 ② 10 ①, ④, ⑥

해석 우림

우림은 나무와 그 외 다른 초목들이 무성한 곳으로, 비가 많이 내리는 지역에 조성된다. 열대 우림이 가장 유명하다. (게다가 그곳은 다른 종류의 우림보다 더 넓은 면적을 차지한다.) 하지만 다른 유형의 우림들도 존재한다. 각 우림은 그곳만의 고유한 특성을 가지고 있다.

온대 우림은 기온이 서늘한 지역에 조성된다. 이러한 우림에서는 매년 각기 다른 사계절을 볼 수도 있다. 일부 온대 우림은 오스트레일리아의 남부와 미국의 남서부 지역에서 발견된다. 동남아시아에는 몬순 우림이 존재한다. 이러한 숲은 매년 건기를 겪는다. 이곳의 나무들은 또한 해마다 잎을 떨군다. 마지막으로 산악 우림이 있다. 이들은 산이 있는 지역에 조성되며, 거의 항상 구름으로 덮여 있다. 이 우림은 남아메리카와 아프리카 등지의 많은 지역에 위치해 있다.

열대 우림의 경우, 이들은 열대 지방에 위치해 있다. 열대 지방은 적도의 남쪽과 북쪽에 인접해 있는 지역이다. 동남아시아, 아프리카, 오스트레일리아와 남아메리카, 그리고 중앙아메리카에 열대 우림이 존재한다. 남아메리카의 아마존 우림은 세계에서 가장 큰 우림이다. 열대 우림은 4개의 부분으로 구분된다. 돌출층, 임관층, 하목층, 그리고 임상층이 그것이다.

돌출층은 최상층이다. 그곳은 높이가 50미터 이상일 수도 있다. 이곳은 가장 많은 햇빛을 받는다. 새, 원숭이, 곤충들이 이곳에서 산다. 그 다음은 가장 높은 나무가 있는 임관층이다. 하목층은 세 번째 층이다. 여기에는 키가 작은 나무는 물론 관목, 덩굴, 그리고 기타 종류의 초목들이 있다. 뱀, 도마뱀, 작은 포유 동물과 새들이 그곳에서 산다. 그곳은 햇빛을 덜 받는데, 임관층의 나뭇잎들이 상당량의 햇빛을 차단하기 때문이다. 임상층은 햇빛을 거의 받지 못하여 어둡다. 이 때문에 여기에서는 식물들이 거의 자라지 않는다. 호랑이, 재규어, 개미핥기와 같은 커다란 포유 동물들이 이곳에서 산다. 수많은 도마뱀, 양서류, 그리고 곤충들도 이곳에서 산다.